From Island to Continent

By

Marie-Josée Maujean

© 1998 Marie-Josée Maujean

This book is copyright. Apart from any fair dealing for the purpose of study, research, criticism, review, or as otherwise permitted under the Copyright Act, no part may be reproduced by any process without written permission. Inquiries should be made to the author.

Typeset by
Dennis Hillen

Front cover design by
Ivan Nozaïc

1st Edition printed by
Llenlees Press
6 Clarice Road, Box Hill 3128 VIC.

2nd Edition Published by Gecko Tales Publishing - 2022

For the author
Marie-Josée Maujean
14 Zamia Street, Holloways Beach 4870 QLD

Cover printed on 300 gsm 1/Sided Gloss
Interior printed on 115 gsm Matt Stock

Body text set in 11pt Times on a 12pt body. Genealogy text set in 7pt Times on a 7pt body.

ISBN-13: 978-0-6454893-0-9

CONTENTS

ACKNOWLEDGEMENTS vi

INTRODUCTION vii

R.I.P. x

PART 1 1

CHAPTER 1
MAURITIUS, THE STAR OF THE INDIAN OCEAN
CRADLE OF MY YOUTH 3

CHAPTER 2
KALEIDOSCOPE . . . CULTURE AND RELIGION 9

CHAPTER 3
NENENNES, SEGA AND SIRANDANES 17

CHAPTER 4
THE LIFEBLOOD OF THE ISLAND . . . THE SUGAR INDUSTRY 27

CHAPTER 5
A TRIP DOWN MEMORY LANE 41

CHAPTER 6
THOSE GREAT PEOPLE OF THE PAST . . .
MONNIER, ARNULPHY, CHAROUX AND NOZAIC 55

CHAPTER 7
THOSE GREAT PEOPLE OF THE PAST . . . BERENGER AND CANTON FAMILIES 77

CHAPTER 8
THOSE GREAT PEOPLE OF THE PAST . . . MAUJEAN FAMILY 97

CHAPTER 9
THE TENDER YEARS . . . CHRISTMAS, MAIDEN CYCLONE 107

CHAPTER 10
CUPID STRIKES 121

CHAPTER 11
THE DEEP BLUE SEA! 127

CHAPTER 12
POINTS OF INTEREST . . . JARDIN OF PAMPLEMOUSSEESS, PAUL AND VIRGINIE
PIRATES AND CORSAIRS 139

CHAPTER 13
POT-POURRI AND FAREWELL! 143

PART 2 151

CHAPTER 14
AUSTRALIA! HERE WE COME! 153

CHAPTER 15
EARLIER DAYS ... THE ADVENTURE BEGINS 161

CHAPTER 16
WEDDING BELLS! ... HAPPY TIMES AND TRAGEDY! 169

CHAPTER 17
BEGINNINGS 179

CHAPTER 18
A NEW START ... MOVING TO SUNNY QUEENSLAND 187

CHAPTER 19
THE SEVENTIES AND EIGHTIES 199

CHAPTER 20
AN INSIGHT INTO CAIRNS HISTORY 205

CHAPTER 21
EXTRACTS FROM MY JOURNAL 217

CHAPTER 22
BACK TO MAURITIUS ... THE TRIP OF A LIFETIME 229

GENEALOGY 253

BIBLIOGRAPHY 276

This book is dedicated to
the memory of my father —
France Nozaïc

To my children —
Patrick and Roselyne,
my granddaughter Krysten

Forever and ever ...

ACKNOWLEDGEMENTS

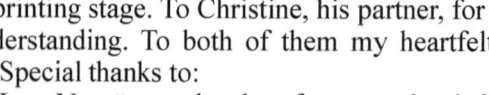

I will forever be grateful to Dennis Hillen, a member of the Maujean family, for all the hard work and long hours spent on his computer helping me to get this book to printing stage. To Christine, his partner, for being so understanding. To both of them my heartfelt thanks.

Special thanks to:

Ivan Nozaïc, my brother, for procuring information and documents relating to the Nozaïc family. For proofreading my manuscript and for designing the cover of this book from my passport.

My Mum, Myriam Hogan, for all information relating to the Arnulphy family.

My brother-in-law, Jean-Claude Maujean for proof-reading my manuscript.

My parents-in-law, Philippe and Violette Maujean, for their patience in being "interviewed" regarding the Maujean family.

Yolande Berenger (Tante Yol), now deceased, for information regarding the Berenger family and procuring photographs.

Special thanks to relatives living in Mauritius:

Joëlle Nozaïc in regards to providing information and documents obtained from the Mauritian archives.

Sylvie Mayer for procuring documents from the Mauritian archives in regards to both Nozaïc and Maujean families.

Rivaltz Mayer for the loan of his books connected to the Arnulphy and Charoux families.

Claude Nozaïc, my aunt, for providing photographs and information regarding Nozaïc genealogy.

Cyril Arnulphy, my uncle, for providing the Arnulphy genealogy.

Daisy Lionnet, my aunt, for letting me print her poems in my book.

Last, but not least, my husband Philippe, for his understanding, support and encouragement.

INTRODUCTION

"If in the twilight of memory we should meet once more,
We shall speak again together and you shall sing to me a deeper song."

KAHILL GILBRAN — The Prophet

This is the day! Saturday the Seventeenth of February, 1990. It is exactly eight o'clock in the morning and the weather forecast is for a fine hot day with an expected temperature of thirty-four degrees celsius. I have finally put pen to paper as they say, and started on my project, dreamed of many years ago.

This book is not written with the idea for it to be a novel, but just a simple, truthful account of my life and that of those around me. I have now at forty-one years of age lived most of my life in Australia and feel part of this land where I have given birth to two children, Patrick and Roselyne. My husband Philippe (Popy), feels the same way.

Our status as this book is written is as such: We are both of the same age and were born on Mauritius island in 1948. We have been married for twenty-one years last August and have been living in the same house at number fourteen, Zamia Street in Holloways Beach for the last fifteen years. In fact we moved in just three weeks before Roselyne, our daughter, was born. I will not forget to mention Sooky, our family pet, a mongrel who is very much part of our household.

We both came to Melbourne, Australia with our respective parents and family in 1965. Philippe with his parents Philippe and Violette Maujean, his sister Monique and younger brother Cyril on the ship "Northern Star" after spending a few weeks in Durban, South Africa at Violette's sister's place whose name was Jeanne D'Unienville.

They were accompanied by Philippe and Violette's brother and sister, Roger and Paule Maujean with their two daughters Chantal and Christine and their third son, Paul. Their eldest son Marcel, was living in South Africa while their second son, Jean-Claude was with the merchant navy at the time.

I came to Australia with my parents France and Myriam Nozaïc and my five sisters, Marielle, Micheline, Sylvianne, Marie-France and Rose-Marie. My elder brother Ivan arrived two months before in August 1965 at the same time as the Maujean family.

From Island to Continent *Marie-Josée Maujean*

We travelled by Qantas Britannia turbo prop airliner and the flight lasted twenty-two hours.

We landed twice in-between, once at Cocos Island and then again at Perth airport. I was nearly seventeen. Also travelling with the two Maujean families were my maternal uncle and aunt, Leon and Monique Arnulphy and their son, Leon Jnr. After living in Melbourne, Victoria for nearly nine years, we moved up north to Cairns in 1974. We were followed by many.

As it stands today, the Mauritian families in Cairns are such: Philippe's parents living at 32 Oak Street in Holloways Beach. Their brother and sister Roger and Paule Maujean, their now married children Marcel, Jean- Claude, Paul, Christine and Chantal, with their respective families.

Yolande and Nemour Berenger.

My brother Ivan Nozaïc and his wife Françoise and children Francois, Joelle and Laita.

My sister Marielle married to Yves Fayd'herbe and children Michael, Caroline and Sandra.

My sister Micheline, married to Popy's cousin Jean-Claude, with children Pauline (deceased 1986), Miriam, Dominic and Daniel.

My brother-in-law Gilles Mackie lives with two of his sons, Gilles and Denis.

Living in Kuranda my first-cousin Daniel de Speville and wife Charlotte. Popy's sister, Monique, married to John Harris and their children, Scott, Kristian and Michael, live in Magnolia Street, Holloways Beach.

Cyril Maujean and his wife Chantal, live in Brisbane with their children Michael, Christopher and Belinda.

Also living in Brisbane are my three sisters. Sylvianne married to Jean-Raymond Mallac with children Veronique, Corinne, Sophie and Tristan.

Marie-France Mackie and son Nicholas.

Rose-Marie and husband François Audibert with children Geraldine, Eric and Catherine.

My father, France, passed away suddenly in 1971.

My mother has remarried to Arthur Hogan. They presently live in Rosebud, Victoria and plan to move to Bribie Island, Queensland as soon as their house is sold.

Philippe works for Wreckair Hire as a sales representative and I do casual work at Woolworths of Smithfield.

Patrick, our son, is currently doing C.T.C. (Career Training Course) at St Augustine's College in Cairns. He hopes to be able to start an apprenticeship as a diesel fitter next year.

Roselyne, our daughter, is in grade 9 at St Monica's College. She does not know yet what she wants to do in the future. But who knows, she might turn out to be a writer as she has a fertile imagination. God knows it would

Introduction

be justified, as Clement Charoux and Fernande Berenger were writers from both sides of her family.

The reason why so many Mauritian families decided to emigrate in the sixties, was because of political and racial unrest at a time when the Indian majority government wanted its independence from Great Britain.

The turning point for my family came when Robert Brousse, a first-cousin of my mother, was murdered on the way back to his home on Savannah Sugar Estate, after visiting his parents in Quatre Bornes. Barricades had been erected on the road to block his way. He did not stand a chance! The reason is believed to be because he was in possession of a list of dissidents.

Robert left behind a wife, Genevieve, and two children, Jean-Robert and Marcus (who now live in Australia). What a tragedy!

So it was that after living in Mauritius for nearly two centuries, since 1773 when the first generation of Nozaïc arrived on the island on the ship "Les Deux Amies" (The Two Friends) from their native Britanny, the seventh generation had to leave their homeland.

I have always wanted to write about the kind of life we led in Mauritius, so different as compared to that of Australians.

I felt it would be a waste if those childhood memories were to be left untold, and the future generations of children of Mauritian ancestry were ignorant of their family background, of all those customs and beliefs so unique to the Mauritian way of life.

It is also a kind of tribute to our courageous parents who sacrificed so much to ensure our future.

So to you all, my future grandchildren and great grandchildren, I have this to say: "Be proud of your ancestry, and when you find yourself facing some hardship in your life, may the courage and determination of your fore-fathers be a reminder to you of human faith and endurance. This book I am writing for you, is a labour of love . . . my gift to you!

Marie-Josée Maujean

R.I.P.

A special mention of our dear niece, Pauline Maujean, daughter of Jean-Claude and Micheline, who passed away on the twenty-second of July 1986, aged sixteen. Her death affected us very deeply. Pauline was born on the fourteenth of January, 1970, in Victoria. She went to school at Mother of Good Counsel school during her primary years and at the time of her death was doing grade 12, her last year at St Monica's College. Her best friends were Christine Armstrong and Anne-Marie O'Brien.

Pauline was a sweet, gentle girl who was popular as denotes her role as president of the Catholic Youth Movement. She did her "debut" three weeks prior to her death and it was her night. She looked beautiful. We have a video cassette of that special event. Sister Denise, the then principal of St Monica's College, made sure that it was a memorable funeral, a testimony to her short young life which touched so many people. A requiem mass was held at the cathedral and it was packed with school children and relatives. One of the teachers sang the song "The Rose" that she particularly loved. Her memory lives in our heart.

"I say, love it is a flower, And you its only seeds."

R.I.P.

Glenn Cowans passed away in September, 1987. He was only 38 years old. He left a wife, Christine (nee Maujean) and a son Shannon. Glenn was another of those "special" people that touched our lives. He had a sunny personality that did not falter, even when enduring a battle with cancer some time before his death. Glenn played the drums in a band as part-time work and was going to teach our son, Patrick. Unfortunately it was not to be, as Glenn was killed in a car accident.

We lost three members of the family in three consecutive years from 1986 to 1989. The third one was Auntie "Helena" (as we called her). Eleanor Berenger, wife of Nemour Berenger, only brother of Paule, Violette and Yolande. Eleanor came to live in Cairns in 1975. She received the two

Maujean families at her place in Melbourne in 1965. She met her husband John, during the last world war when she was a nurse in England. Eleanor Riley was born in Scotland. Her death of leukemia in October, 1988, has left her husband John devastated, especially as they lived for each other, having no children. Aunty Eleanor gave me a photo, presumed to be that of our Lady, that has been appearing to three young people in Yugoslavia.

They all live in our hearts until we meet again.

Part 1

Mauritius – Island in the Sun

From Island to Continent

Marie-Josée Maujean

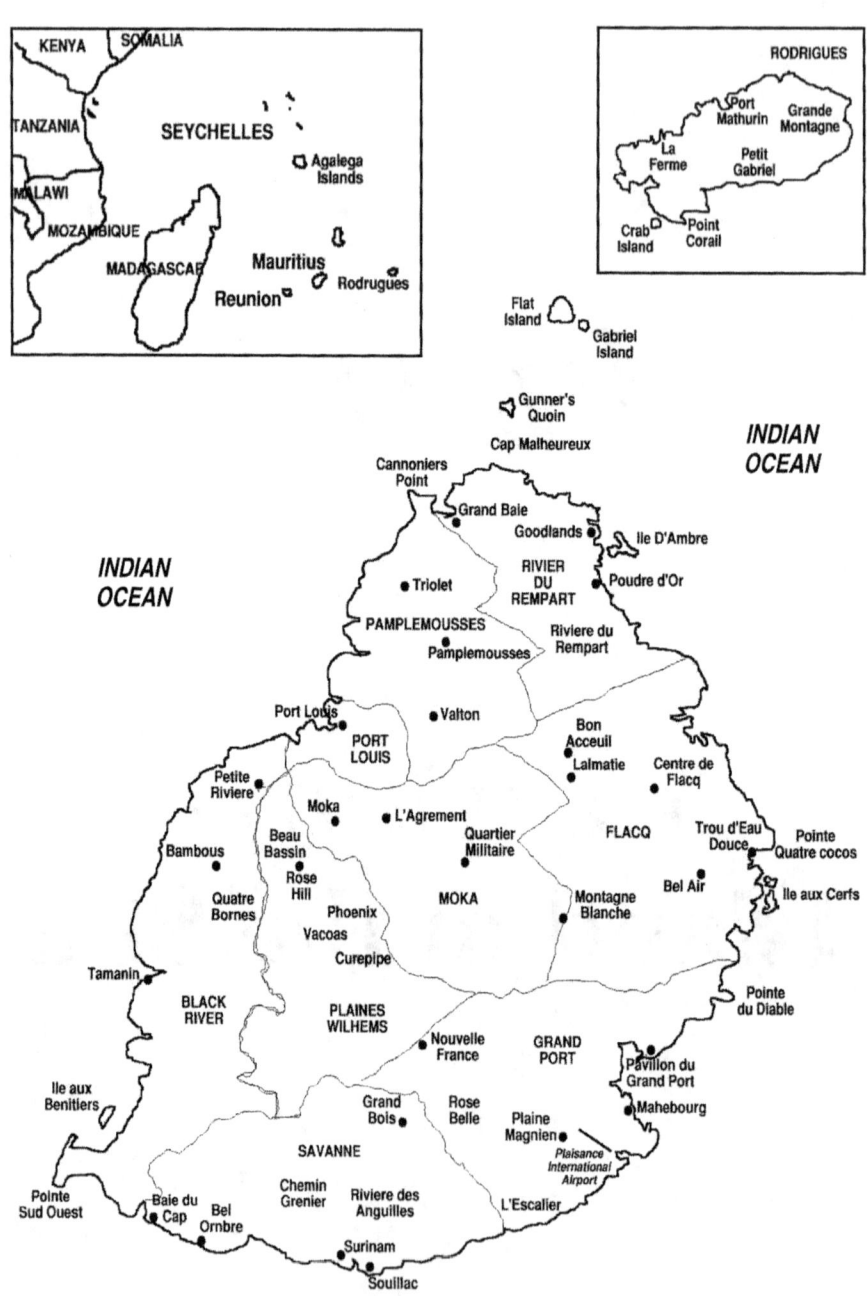

CHAPTER 1

Mauritius, the Star of the Indian Ocean . . . Cradle of my youth . . .

I came into the world in the early hours of a November morning, the third daughter and fourth child to France and Myriam Nozaïc at the Clinique dubon Pasteur.

I was told that one of the nuns present at the birth remarked "elle sera d'une blancheur eclatante!". It is very hard to translate literally, but it goes something like this: "She will be of a dazzling whiteness!". We have always joked about it and taken it as meaning a very white complexion. Without sounding conceited, I like to personally take it as a kind of omen, meaning a purity of heart.

Ivan, the oldest in the family is my only brother. It goes without saying that with so many sisters (five of them) he was treated as a kind of "pasha". Not that I felt jealous for it. Women's lib did not exist in those days, machovinism ruled! He was followed by Marielle and Micheline.

Marielle, being the eldest of the girls was in a sense expected to look after us, especially when the nénenne (nanny) was unable to do so. She became a bit bossy for it. I can imagine her reaction when she reads this, for you see the two of us always manage to come to words whenever we meet. That does not mean that we do not care for each other, just siblings differences.

Micheline was and still is the saint of the family. She first earned this reputation at three years of age when the family doctor, Dr Remy (he used to call us "mon p'tit chouchou" meaning "my little pet", and yes, they made house calls in those days), was about to lance an abcess that had formed on her foot. Micheline asked him to "Please wait!" as she went to fetch some rosary beads that she held during the entire operation. From then on she was nicknamed "Soubirou" after St Bernadette Soubirou.

I love all my sisters but Micheline and I get on the best. I suppose it stems

Page 3

from the fact that I came straight after her in a line of seven children, smack in the middle, followed by three more sisters Sylvianne, Marie-France and Rose-Marie. Because of this I went through some lonely times during my early teenage years when I was too young to be invited to the surprise par- ties the three eldest were invited to and too old to go to the petites (little ones) birthday parties. As a result I took a passion for reading. Many were the days during school vacations when I spent most of the time with my head buried in a book, stopping only when my Mum called me for a meal.

I also used to keep a diary and did so for about three years. But would you believe the two volumes that I brought to Australia disappeared. I have a suspicion that they fell victim to my Dad's hands, who at one stage before starting to work again used to burn some rubbish in the backyard in the newly acquired incinerator.

I will not elaborate more on my childhood memories as I think that first of all I should give you an insight into the cultures and setting of that island of mine.

The island was created by volcanic eruptions. It is about thirty-six miles long and twenty-four miles wide (I have not been able to find a book that agrees on its measurements yet, but these measurements are what we were told at school, so I think they will have to do).

Mauritius covers a varied expanse of seven hundred and twenty square miles. It is situated in the Indian Ocean, five hundred miles from Madagascar, one thousand two hundred and fifty miles from the east coast of Africa and ten thousand miles from Europe. It is the terminal for several air routes.

On the map of the world it is nothing but a speck. Some islets in its vicinity are Amber Island, Round Island, Gunner's Coin, Flat Island and the Benitiers. Rodrigues, at three hundred miles from the east coast, is one of Mauritius' main dependencies.

The island has beautiful beaches whose sand is of a powdery texture, the coral reefs being so close to the shore. In fact, less that a mile away.

I used to love looking out to sea, to the white band of foam that it formed around the island. Its whiteness standing out against the topaz colour of the sea.

Mauritius is at about the same latitude as Mackay on the Queensland coast. There are no snakes, noxious insects or marine stingers there. Many Mauritian families had their own personal campement (a bungalow at the beach that was so special with its thatched roof) for use during school holidays.

Mauritius enjoys a sunny, tropical climate with temperatures at sea- level ranging from twenty-four degrees celsius in August (mid- winter) to twenty-eight degrees in January and February (mid- summer). The only dark side to its climate is the formation of cyclones that affects the island every year.

The island was first recorded in the files of history in the sixteenth century. Malay and Arab sailors are thought to have visited it as it is located on a chart drafted in 1502.

The Portuguese, Domingos Fernandez, is usually considered to be the first European to have landed on this small island. Pedro Mascarenhas, another Portuguese, discovered Reunion Island, one hundred miles from Mauritius. As a tribute to his memory, the two above islands as well as Rodrigues, were known as the Mascarenhas group of islands.

In its history, Mauritius experienced a Dutch childhood followed by a remarkable French adolescence and attained its majority with the British. (Quote from a tourist book on Mauritius).

The Dutch named it Mauritius after Prince Maurice van Nassau when it was under their rule from 1598 to 1710. Legend has it that it was abandoned by them and left to its own fate, owing to a plague of rats. In 1715, Captain Guillaume Dufresne took possession of the island for the king of France as commander of "Le Chasseur" (The Hunter) and named it Isle de France, thus starting the French period.

From 1715 to 1767 when the French assumed direct control, Isle de France was governed by the French East India Company.

The regime introduced that year (1767) divided the administration between a governor, primarily charged with military matters and an intendant. To one of the intendants, Pierre Poivre, was due the introduction of clove, nutmeg and other spices.

It is interesting to mention that Mathew Flinders, the British navigator and explorer who was first to circumnavigate Australia, landed at Baie du Cap estuary in Mauritius (Isle de France) in 1803. He was kept in captivity there until 1810 when he was released with the promise never to fight against France. While in captivity, Mathew Flinders, who was given a house with servants, befriended some Mauritian families such as the De Chazal and Labauve d'Arrifat.

The first French governor, François Mahé de Labourdonnais, a Breton, was considered a genius and left his mark on the island. He was Governor General of both Isle de France and Bourbon (Reunion). This is a brief account of his life: Bertrand François Mahé de Labourdonnais (1699-1753) was born in St Malo on the eleventh day of February, 1699. He started as deckhand in the merchant navy when he was only ten years old.

In 1733 he married Anne Marie Lebrun de la Franquerie and arrived in the colony on the fourth of June, 1735. The Government Hotel, his project, was completed in 1736 in Port- Louis. The family lived at Mon Plaisir in the Pamplemousses district where Labourdonnais had orchards and established farming to help the needs of the population as well as crews on ships on call in the harbour.

In 1744 the first factories of sugar were started as well as the production of coffee, cereals, indigo and cotton. In the port, construction of ships began. (This must be what brought the first Nozaïc, Louis to the colony, for he was a marine carpenter). Labourdonnais suffered his fair share of tragedies, for in 1738 he lost his son, and a few months later his wife, whom he adored.

He went back to France in 1740 and came back the following year after he was captured and set free by the British who had much respect for him.

Later on, the governor was accused of embezzlement and of being a spy to the enemy (British). He was imprisoned in the Bastille and after a trial where two to three hundred witnesses were called, he was acquitted. François Mahé de Labourdonnais was greatly affected by this and had to rehabilitate. He died a few years after at the age of fifty-four. A college bears his name in Mauritius, as well as the township of Mahebourg.

In 1810 Isle de France was taken from the French by the British during the famous battle in the bay of Grand-Port, where the Dutch had landed one hundred and twelve years previously. This naval battle lasted from 24th to 26th of August and resulted in the fleet of Capitaine Duperre falling prey to the British whose leader was Captain Pym.

This famous battle is engraved on a wall of the Arc de Triomphe in Paris. One interesting anecdote is about Capitaine Duperre and a British captain, Willoughby, being nursed side by side in a room of a house at La Rivière La Chaud and being on amicable terms. That house was later turned
into a museum that still stands today.

The British renamed the island Mauritius. England gave a pledge to respect the religions, languages and customs of its inhabitants.
So it is that although it was officially a British colony, French is still the main language spoken there. Up to this day, the island has retained much of the old France.

Mauritius is also known throughout the world as the place where the now extinct dodo bird once lived during the Dutch period. It was said that the bird was too clumsy to survive. Heard of the expression "as dead as a dodo"? Scientists named it Raphulus Cucullatus. Marja, a Dutch friend of mine recalls seeing a picture of the dodo in a museum in Holland.

The first British governor to the island was Sir Robert Townsend Farquhar.

Another governor, still remembered in connection with the famous blue penny stamp that is worth a fortune, envied throughout the world of philatelists, was Sir William Gomm.

It all started in 1846 when Lady Gomm sent invitations to dignitaries in Europe for a most important ball that was to take place the following year at the Government Hotel on the 30th September, 1847.

The stamps for the occasion (Mauritius was then the fourth country after England to use postal stamps) included five hundred stamps of one penny and five hundred of two pence, in two colours, red vermilion and indigo. Those stamps bore the effigy of Queen Victoria and the inscription "Post Office" instead of "Post Paid". This was rectified in the second edition which had "Post Paid" stamped on them.

Why? Whose mistake? As it turned out that first edition used by Lady Gomm was the only one ever used in Mauritius with "Post Office". Had the guests been aware at the time how famous those stamps were to become, they would have all been millionaires.

The British era came to a close at a time in history when the people of Mauritius felt they were ready to take charge of their own destiny. After much turmoil so many left their native land to start anew, as they felt they should for their future and that of their families.

The new state of Mauritius was born on the twelfth of March, 1968. The Union Jack was lowered and the first Mauritian flag hoisted. Sir Seewoosagur Ramgoolam was the Prime Minister. At the time, the population of Mauritius stood at eight hundred and fifty thousand.

There were descendants of Breton sailors and others with ancestry from Africa, India, China and Madagascar. Since independence, the government has retained the opening of parliament ceremonies with the wearing of wigs, plumed hat and mace, which also with a speech in the name of Queen Elizabeth II by the Governor General, shows allegiance to the monarchy.

Points of interest:

Quoting Robert Willox in the book "Mauritius, Reunion and Seychelles, A Travel Survival Kit" (a book that I found very interesting and would recommend to anyone).

The Labour Party was founded in 1936 to fight for the labourers, and did so on the streets the following year.

After the war when a new constitution gave the vote to anyone over 21 years of age who could write their name, the Labour Party gained support.

Under the leadership of Dr Seewoosagur Ramgoolam, who was later knighted, the Labour Party grew in strength during the '50s.

Direct opposition came from the Parti Mauricien Social Democrate (PMSD) which represented the white and Creole populations. Mauritius was granted independence on 12 March 1968.

Sir Seewoosagur was elected Prime Minister and remained in office for the next 13 years.

Eventually in coalition with the PMSD in 1982 the leftist Movement Militant Mauricien (MMM) led by Franco-Mauritian Paul Berenger, and the Parti Socialiste Mauricien (PSM) led by Anerood Jugnauth, gained power.

Jugnauth became Prime Minister. The MMMs policy to nationalise the sugar industry and end trading links with South Africa sent the country into a disastrous economic dive.

Jugnauth split with Berenger's MMM and teamed up with the Labour Party. The PMSD under the former mayor of Curepipe and Port Louis, Sir Gaëtan Duval and two other parties.

Berenger was back in contention and his MMM forced Jugnauth to go to the polls on 30 August 1987.

Jugnauth won capturing 39 of the 62 contested seats.

The grand leader Sir Seewoosagur Ramgoolam died in 1986 aged 86.

In 1986 the population of Mauritius was 1,034,255. Ethnolinguistic composition in 1983: Creole 55.5%; Indian 39.6%; European 3.8%; Chinese 0.6%; other 0.5%.

Cholera caused the death of 17,000 persons in 1854.

30,000 died of malaria in 1866-1867.

In 1893 a great part of Port Louis was destroyed by fire.

Emigration reduced the annual rate of population growth between 1972 and 1982 to 1.4%.

Legislative power is vested in a legislation assembly elected every five years.

Executive power is exercised by a council of ministers headed by the Prime Minister. The Supreme Court is the highest judicial authority.

The industrial sector accounts for approximately one quarter of the GNP and employs a comparable fraction of the workforce. Although construction activity is decreasing, there has been a steady increase in manufacturing.

The Mauritius export processing zones which concentrate on labour intensive processing of imported raw materials or semi finished goods for the export market have successfully attracted foreign investment. Major manufacturers include textiles, electronics, plastic and leather goods and synthetic gemstones.

CHAPTER 2

Kaleidoscope... Culture and Religion, Père Laval

After mentioning the different races that formed the Mauritian community over the years, you can imagine how it resulted into such a mixture of cultures that adds its own spice to the way of life there. Every race is proud of its religion. Especially when they can practice it in peace, respected by others. The Hindus, Moslems, Chinese, Creole and Europeans all doing their own thing side by side on this small island of mine.

The Hindus came to Mauritius during the British era. They were brought in to work in the sugar cane fields in place of those poor African slaves who stopped work when slavery was finally abolished. It was the same kind of colonial life as in India, New Orleans and other colonies where there were sugar plantations.

The Chinese came to Mauritius for commerce, as it was a very important port of call on the way to India before the opening of the Suez Canal. That is why it is known as the "star and key of the Indian Ocean".

In Port Louis, the capital, you can find the Dravidian temple of the Hindus, the White Mosque of Moslems, the Silent Pagoda of the Chinese and the Roman Catholic Cathedral, St Louis. Oriental religions have bizarre rites to Europeans. One example is the Hindu feast of "Maha Shivatree", celebrated in the month of February where pilgrims from all over the island will meet at Grand-Bassin (a sacred lake situated at the centre of the island). There they pray, wearing their traditional langhoutee, a white cloth wrapped around their loins. You would have seen some members of the Hari Krishna faith wearing one. To quote Robert Willcox in his book "Mauritius, Reunion and Seychelles, A Travel Survival Kit":

"Many pilgrims dressed in white, start walking in groups from their village a day or two beforehand, depending on how far they have to travel.

They carry a "kanvar", a light wooden frame or arch decorated with paper flowers, in the manner of a trade union banner.

The majority of pilgrims however arrive in buses for a day trip. At the lake, some pilgrims perform "poojah" by making food sacrifices in the water or at various shrines; others bathe and many take sacred water home. Events are much the same as those on the banks of the Ganges in India.

On the return journey from the lake, the pilgrims are given fruit and drinks by people in the villages they pass through."

This pilgrimage is in honour of the god, Shiva.

There is also the feast of Cavadee, a most spectacular Indian feast. Men and women form a procession, ladies wearing their colourful saris and the men bare chested who have needles poked through different parts of their anatomy, their tongue, chest and arms while they carry domes of flowers decorated with mirrors. Spectacular to watch, especially the effect of the mirrors as they reflect the sun.

Pots of milk (sambos) are suspended from each end of the "cavadee" that the pilgrims carry from the bank of a river to a temple in order to fulfil a vow in honour of "Subramanya", the second son of the god Shiva, to pay penance and cleanse their soul. The milk in the sambos must not have curdled by the time they reach the temple." — Robert Willcox.

The main cavadee throughout the year takes place in January or February and is called the Majo Thaipoosam cavadee.

The Hindus also have the festival "Divali" at the end of the year to celebrate the victory of Rama over the evil deity Ravana. At this time candles and lamps are lit around homes. It is no wonder that it holds great attraction for tourists.

There is also the Hindu fire-walking ceremony, comparable to the Easter of the Europeans in the sense that it is the culmination of a very strict period of mortification and sacrifice. Depending on how much they had followed their Lent as they should, they would then be able to take part in the ceremony of fire-walking, "believing that they would feel no pain as the merciful saint Draupadee would protect them by spreading her veil over the purifying and sanctifying fire, a pit of glowing embers." — Robert Willcox.

Popy, my husband, as a teenager had poked needles through the flesh of his arm to show off in front of his friends. I would not advise you to do the same, even though he did not feel any pain. He was lucky he did not get a nasty infection as can happen if the needle is slightly corroded.

He must have been a bit of a dare-devil for he tells me (it was witnessed by my sister Micheline) that he and my cousin Sylvain (they had their family bungalow next to each other) walked on embers. They would do it amongst their friends on the beach at night while the parents were asleep.

Culture and Religion, Père Laval

Popy tells me that there is a special way you can do so without getting burnt by only having the heel and ball of the feet touching, with the toes curled up.

Now all over the world there are Europeans that do so. I saw it on television once. They do it with the belief that it would benefit them by conquering any fear they might have. Rubbish, if you ask me!

Our "Bibi", Sabite, a domestic of Indian origin, used to tell us how so and so really felt the embers and got burnt because they were not pure enough for not following their period of Lent as they should.

Sabite worked for years in our employ. She was a very gentle woman whose duty included that of dressing us, would you believe. She would comb the hair of the petites, and quite shamefully now I remember her putting socks on my feet to go to school. I was about thirteen at the time.

Noellie was another domestic, a Creole who lived on the premises with her two children, Brigitte and Alain in the dependance of the house we lived in at Quatre-Bornes.

My sister, Marielle, when she was a teenager once sewed a dress for Brigitte to go to a dance. When she was married we were all invited. We even danced with some of the Creole men.

I must mention that there was a strict social structure adhered to by the different races, where they never mixed as a rule as there was a class system.

For my part, I am glad that my children do not live in this kind of social structure. This is a part of the Mauritian way of life of the time that I am not very proud of. To me it was petty, but I suppose it had to be for it had been so for centuries.

Coming back to the different cultures, the Chinese community of the island, the Cino Mauriciens as they were called, had their special feast of Chinese New Year that they would celebrate in great pomp on one of the main roads of Rose-Hill, near the Plaza, the town's main building which served as Town Hall, theatre and cinema. It also contained a municipal library and administrative offices.

At night they would have a dragon dance, enhanced by deafening crackers in the middle of the main road of various towns. That dance would be to the accompaniment of a mono-syllabic gong. I remember being a spectator to one of those events and I must have been very young for I was wearing pyjamas and was being held in my Dad's arms. I remember feeling excited by the whole thing.

On the eve of Chinese New Year (at the end of January or beginning of February) homes are spring-cleaned and decorated in red (a colour of happiness). Firecrackers are let off to get rid of evil spirits. On New Years Day rice-flour and honey cakes are given to family and friends. No knives or scissors are to be used.

The Moslems had their mosque called Jummah (meaning Friday), their special day for prayer, where they would meditate and worship in a beautiful room that is a fine example of Moslem art, with its chiselled doors, crystal chandeliers and ingenious woodwork. It is a place of silence, disturbed every now and then by the call of the Muezzin, a call for prayer.

They celebrate Id el Fitr to mark the end of the fasting month of Ramadan, which is the ninth month of the lunar year.

The Créoles call the Muslims "Lascars" and the non-Tamil Hindu "Malabar". The Tamils are known as "Madras". The Chinese are "Chinois".

I was interested to learn that Mahatma Gandhi visited Mauritius in 1901 to push for civil rights.

Most Europeans and Créoles are Roman Catholics, and one of the highlights of such religious celebration was the mass, celebrated at Marie Reine de la Paix every year.

That mass would take place during a working day, and every Catholic school child of the island would attend through their school. Buses were hired to take us there and during the travel we would sing religious songs directed by the nuns and teachers.

Marie Reine de la Paix is situated in Port Louis, the capital. It is a monument to our Lady - a statue of Mary holding the globe in her hands, erected on the top of a hill so this white statue of our Lady can be seen from a great distance.

I must mention that Marie Reine de la Paix means "Mary, Queen of Peace". The shrine was erected to thank Mary for having spared Mauritius from the horrors of war. The statue stands on top of an opened shelter where mass is celebrated in view of all participants, who sit in the open on the grassy slopes. We would hear the voice of the priest through loud speakers. Unfortunately, due to the heat, there were a few faintings taking place every year.

Another important religious event on the island that unfortunately I never took part in, being too young I suppose, was the pilgramage to the tomb of Père Laval, a priest who was considered the saint of the island.

Marie Reine de La Paix Monument

Culture and Religion, Père Laval

My elder sisters, Marielle and Micheline accompanied by my parents took part in the procession to Sainte Croix (Holy Cross) parish where Father Jacques Desiré Laval was buried in the chapel in 1864. An effigy made of plaster, bearing a great likeness to the man was placed on a sarcophagus carved out of solid rock containing the remains of the priest in a wooden and lead coffin.

Even though I never took part in those processions, I went with my parents a few times to pray by his grave. For you see, every Mauritian has a great devotion for that priest who did so much good for the population of the island, and many are the people who claim to have been miraculously cured by him. At present he is Blessed Father Laval, there is only one more step for him to be declared a Saint of the Catholic Church.

Tante Jacqueline Brousse, my mother's sister, is considered to have been miraculously cured by him in 1969 after her sister, Marcienne, laid a handkerchief she had previously put on Père Laval tomb onto her stomach. The doctor had given up hope of saving her life after suffering the formation of abscesses from having a hysterectomy, thus causing serious infections that could not be brought under control. Apparently Aunt Jacqueline had already received the last rites of the church, thus the seriousness of the situation. Soon after the laying-on of the handkerchief however, the last abscess rup- tured and the doctors were then able to operate and clean the abdominal cavity, resulting in her recovery. So I think it is worth giving you more insight into the life of that priest and tell you about one of his miracles that was witnessed by many people and acknowledged by the Catholic Church.

Jacques Desiré Laval came to Mauritius as a missionary priest from France in 1841. Though still French speaking, the island had become a British colony since 1810 when it had been taken from the French by the British during the Napoleonic wars because it sheltered French pirates who harassed British ships trading with India. The government thus did not want any French men on the island.

The nine Catholic priests present in 1841 were English, Irish, Belgian or Savoyard. Bishop Collier had to choose his clergy from these categories. Père Laval was tolerated as an exception. The then governor, Sir W. M. Gromm, declared that he did more to keep order than 2 constables.

Slavery was abolished on the island on the 15th April, 1839. 60,000 slaves were freed. Those who had been working as domestics continued their work, as did the artisans. These were happy in their situation, contrary to the ones that used to work the sugar cane fields. They were the vast majority who once liberated, refused to go back to work. (Legend has it that quite a few of them that lived in the Rivière-Noire district, misunderstood the abolition of slavery for what it was and believing they would be sent back in exile, threw themselves off the cliffs of the Morne out of desperation).

Thousands of them came to settle around Port Louis, the capital, and once their freedom money was finished they lived by stealing, begging, fighting and lying as well as other crimes which brought hundreds of them to prison or the scaffold. These were the people for whom Père Laval worked for his dear blacks.

Since the French Revolution in 1789, many Catholics did not practise their faith anymore because of political persecution or from social pressures. The slaves had followed the example of their masters. Apparently when Father Laval arrived in the country, the Catholic faith was hardly more than three ceremonies of baptism, marriage and burial.

Father Laval obtained permission from the bishop to look after the black population of the capital exclusively.

He lived as a poor man in a 2 room hut near the cathedral. A coconut mat on a few planks was his bed. Little by Little he won the confidence of the people, especially that of the Indians who were despised by everyone, the whites, Créoles and free-born blacks.

A few months after his arrival, Father Laval wrote to his superior. "This colony is in a pitiful state. There are some 80,000 blacks on the island and

Jacques Desiré Laval

I am alone looking after them. Half of them have not been baptised and those who are Christians, live like idolaters. Very few have been married in church. They rarely call a priest to the dying. Most of them know nothing of their religion. They can't even make the sign of the cross!"

Father Laval had all the odds against him. He was even beaten by some of the youths. This did not deter him, for in the end he succeeded and was much loved and respected by the whole population of Mauritius.

He died in 1864 after suffering several strokes that gradually altered his health. Even so, he still managed to help and comfort families when there was an epidemic of cholera in Mauritius in 1861.

Apparently before dying, Father Laval said: "What a joy to have worked for our Lord's poor friends . . . what a good idea I had to come and work for the poor. Thank you Lord for that." The crowd was estimated to be around 40,000 at his funeral.

A graceful monument, an underground chapel surmounted by a hillock of cut stones was erected. On top of it, a fine teak cross with a cast-iron figure of Christ, and at the foot of the cross, cast-iron statues of the four evangelists. Brother Vidal C.S.Sp., Arts Master in College St Louis, Port Louis, made the effigy that I mentioned earlier. It was laid there on the 9th of September, 1870.

In 1965 a new church was built after the original one had been destroyed by two cyclones in 1960. Father Laval's remains were transferred to a more spacious but less beautiful modern vault.

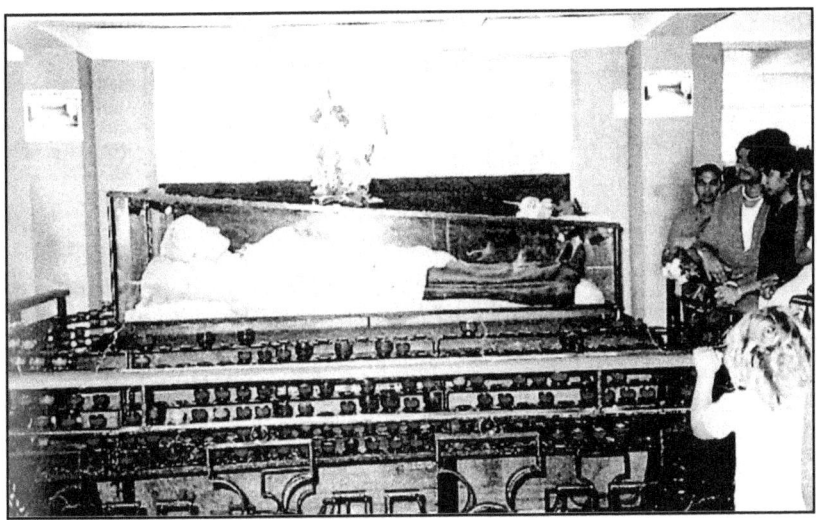

The vault of Jacques Desiré Laval

On the 13th of December, 1975 the medical commission of the congregation for the causes of Saints, accepted the cure of Mr Edgar Beaubois after examining all the evidence, as a first class miracle.

Mr Beaubois was a sixty-four years old accountant of the Rose-Belle sugar estate, who in 1923, had a bad exema at the back of the neck that became purulent and spread over his head and forehead. He got worse and was in terrible pain. On the 17th of July, Mr Bazerque, Henri Beaubois (his son) and Mr Francis Bigara took the sick man in his car to Port Louis, 22 miles away. They went once more to consult the doctor, Dr Rouget, head of the civil hospital who then considered the case as hopeless.

Leaving the hospital, Mr Bazerque suggested they go to Father Laval's tomb while the chemist prepared a new prescription that was just to alleviate the itchiness. Arriving at the tomb, they went down to the vault, knelt down, and Mr Beaubois removed the towel he wore to cover his sores.

"Father Laval", he prayed. "I am a protestant, but if you wish it, you can cure me. Grant me this favour, and I promise to become a Catholic." He then remained silent as he prayed.

Thinking he heard a stranger coming down the step, he put the cloth back on his head and felt that the supuration had completely gone. "I am cured!" he exclaimed. His companions fearing an illusion, tried to calm him and told him to continue his prayer.

After a few minutes he could barely restrain himself. He removed the cloth and carefully felt over his head and forehead. Then, almost speechless with emotion, he murmured, "I am cured! I assure you!".

The three men went out in the daylight and to their astonishment, the terrible sores had all disappeared, leaving no trace. One witness said that no- one could have suspected that he had been ill. After a fervent prayer of thanksgiving in the church, they drove back to Rose-Belle where the whole village was able to see that he was completely cured.

Mr Beaubois never suffered a relapse and his cure was permanent. He kept his promise and became a fervent Catholic.

I obtained all this information from a book written by Father Gerald Bowe. I believe that failing to mention Père Laval in this book would be to leave out a very important part of our growing years, as whenever someone dear was suffering a life threatening disease, one member of the family would always have recourse to this priest as either a rosary or handkerchief placed upon Father Laval's vault and then laid upon the patient for the miracle to take place.

So is the faith of the Mauritian people for a great man of the past. To this day, no matter of what race or religion, the whole community of Mauritius joins together for the procession to his grave, and they all call him "our Saint".

CHAPTER 3

Nénennes, Sega and Sirandanes

Our parents were lucky! No dirty nappies to wash (for there were no washing machines in the days I was growing up). In fact a woman's duty consisted of giving orders to the numerous domestics — a cook, grande-nénenne (nanny in charge), second nanny (who would perform the cleaning and washing chores), gardener and quite often a couturiere (dressmaker).

Nowadays I believe the life style is different, as most young mothers work outside their home and the younger generation of domestics find it more worthwhile to work in various industries where they are protected by the union.

But in those days, they were quite happy working as domestics. Generations stayed with the same family, for in most cases they were well looked after as they lived on the premises in a dependance, as it was called.

Three room godons that consisted of living room, kitchen and bedroom with an outside latrine. The godons were always very clean. The Créoles loved to plaster their walls with newspaper and magazines. It looked quite attractive to our eyes.

Many a day were spent visiting the nenennes when they were off duty. I especially remember talking to André, Agnes's husband who had been a soldier during the Second World War and so had learnt some English.

At one stage he was giving me English lessons. He mentioned the word "buttocks" which started me giggling, as young ladies were not supposed to utter such words. This has stuck to my mind ever since.

Those Créoles and sometimes the Indian domestics were very superstitious. When our parents would go out in the evenings - usually to play cards at some relatives place - they would be begged without much reluctance on their parts, to tell us about "names" (ghost) stories. We would listen starry-eyed to those stories of "d'aienes" (banshee, witch), "loupgarou" (human turning into animal), enjoying to be frightened in the security of our home.

So it was that we were told about this woman, who walking on her own down the street saw a baby by the side of the road, crying and obviously abandoned (and of course it was night!). As she hurriedly carried it to her home, the baby gradually felt heavier and heavier, until it was nearly a grown man. How terrifying! I wonder how come we did not suffer from nightmares.

The "d'aienes" were women who stole children from their homes and took them under a bridge where they lived, and then they would do some p'tit albert (voodoo rites).

The nenennes also told us never to drink a full glass of water if we awoke thirsty during the night, because we could drown our heart. (Now I realise it was to stop us from wetting our bed. What a scare tactic). Another one was not to play with matches (fire) because it would also cause us to wet our bed.

The domestics would issue "maledictions" (curses) at the drop of a hat. They did not really mean it, I think it was merely an automatic reaction.

For instance, once while my parents were holidaying in Europe and Grandmère, who lived a couple of houses away (my grandparents owned the whole block of about six houses) came to visit us and unfortunately walked unaware on the freshly polished floor. She was then cursed by Marie, the domestic, who said "ou vie lipied pou pourri" — (your old feet will decay grand-madame). They would call an elderly lady grand-madame, and the lady of the house madame. We were addressed to as mamzelle (mademoiselle, meaning miss). The same for the males, grand-missie (mon- sieur, sir) and missie (sir, Mr).

They spoke the Creole language, a dialect derived from French with some English words thrown in. It is the same as spoken in Martinique. There is no grammar to it. It is easy to pick up, and tourists to Mauritius would pick it up before being able to speak French. One example was when one night Roselyne, not wanting to go to sleep, was begging me to tell her another story. I thought I'd put an end to it by telling it to her in Creole! Well, I was the loser, for she understood exactly what I was talking about.

It is a colourful "lingo", very expressive and dramatic. If you were to go to Mauritius and hear a Creole say "ayo maman", you would know exactly what I mean, for by those two words his face would tell you the full extent of his misfortune.

I remember nénenne Marie taking me for a walk every afternoon. I was about three at the time. This was part of the routine: Every afternoon after the tiffin (afternoon tea), she would give me a bath and dress me prettily with ribbons in my hair and wearing patent black shoes with socks. Then nénenne would don her starched white apron bordered by "broderie anglaise" and take us for a stroll around the neighbourhood.

I was not allowed to jump puddles, nénenne was formal on that! Another superstition to stop us from getting dirty was "maman pou mort" (your Mum will die). The same fate would affect my poor mother I was told if I walked back- wards. If we counted the stars at night we would get warts.

Those Créoles were Catholic, but they still kept some beliefs and rites inherited from their African ancestors.

For instance, when someone of their family dies, for seven days they believe that the spirit is still around the house and needs food and drink that they would come and get during the night. I think some of them still practised voodoo, as they plucked a chook and used this mixture of feathers and blood for a type of ceremony.

There were odd families that were poisoned by the blacks as revenge. One source of slow, gradual poisoning was that of crushed glass mixed with food. This would cause symptoms of bleeding of the intestines that undetected would lead slowly to the death of the victim.

My Mum told me of such a case once when years later the culprit, suffering remorse, confessed on his death bed to the victim's father. He was mistreated by the man of the house, so he poisoned one of his children over a period of months that resulted in death.

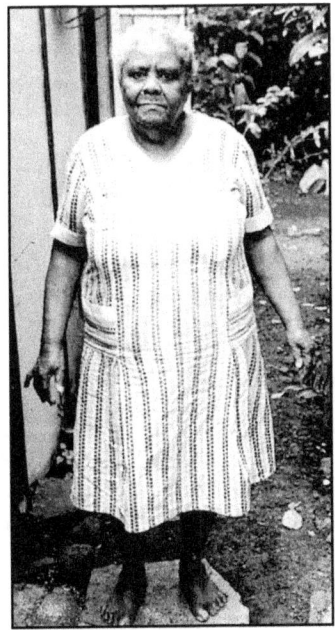

The Maujean family's nénenne, Eliane.

As a rule they were very devoted people. Sabite and Noellie wanted to come to Australia with us. We all cried when we parted.

Before I go on, I must tell you of a story that my Mum heard from my grandfather when she was a child. Mum says that my grandfather witnessed it, but still I find it hard to believe.

It's the case of a white man working on a sugar estate who after dismissing an Indian employee and using some abusive racial comments, was cursed. He was given a malediction. Apparently soon after, call it coincidence or whatever, he started to get sick. His health deteriorated and all the doctors consulted could not make a diagnosis. The poor man suffered terrible pain, and his skin was affected with ulcers all over his body. The poor man eventually died of this mystery illness.

When he was laid on a "canape" as was customary in Mauritius, having his head bandaged turban style and the complexion of his skin having turned a darker colour from his ailment, everybody there was stricken of how much he resembled an Indian. So they all came to the conclusion that it was due to the curse. Mum swears to me that Grand-Père saw it with his own eyes.

Those nénennes in most cases were like a mother to us. They had a knack to cure and soothe a child's little miseries by rocking you gently against their huge bosoms, while they would sing a song such as "La Rivière Tanier", a sure guarantee to send any unwilling child to a peaceful sleep.

It went like this:

Mo passé la riviere tanié.
Mo zoine ène vié grand-maman.
Mo dire li qui li faire là?
Li dire moi, li lapesse cabot!
Why, why mes enfants!
Il faut travailler pou gagner son pain!

Translated means:

I go pass the Latanier River.
I meet an old woman.
I ask her, what is she doing there?
She answers me, I am fishing cabots!
Oh well, children!
One must work hard to earn his bread!

Nénennes, Sega and Sirandanes

I remember my Mum singing to me as I lay cradled in her arms, as she wanted me to go for my afternoon nap. I was probably three or four at the time, perhaps younger. She would sing:
Dodo Mignonne,
Dodo pouponne!
Il y a dans la grange,de jolis petits poussins,
De jolis petits poussins,
Pour l'enfant qui fera dodo!

Translated:

Go to sleep sweetie, go to sleep little doll!
There are some cute little chicks in the barn,
Some cute little chicks,
For the child who goes to sleep!

I will now tell you about the séga, a dance that has its origin from the African slaves who, probably feeling nostalgic of their native land, expressed their feelings in the rhythms and songs accompanied by primitive instruments like the tam-tam or drum.

The tam-tam changed into the ravane, an instrument made of tanned animal skin stretched rigidly over a wooden circle surrounded by tiny bells. The skin is warmed by fire so that it can easily be stretched. Another instrument used is a metal triangle struck by metal.

Then there is also the maravane, an oblong container filled with pea pods or gravel, that is shaken to give the appropriate sound.

The séga (pronounced say-ga) is dance and song that express a state of mind, an event, sad or funny.

The séga often denotes a sense of humour and keen observation.

The dance is as follows: Men and women dance in front of each other without touching. They do little side steps by moving the hips to the cadence at the same time. Every now and then the man moves around the woman.

I believe the modern version of séga is very erotic for the benefit of tourists.

There are some ségas that are classics. A couple worth mentioning are "Mon P'tit Sir Zille" (My Little Sir Jules) and "Madame Ezene" (Mrs Eugène).

Mon Petit Sir Zille goes like this:
Roulé, roulé, roulé mon p'tit Sir Zille.
Courant là trop fort!
Ramène moi dans port!
Roulé, roulé, roulé mon p'tit Sir Zille,
Courant là trop fort
Ramène moi dans port.

Sega dancers

It is about a man travelling on board the boat "Sir Jules" who feeling the pull of his homeland, wants to go back to the safety of his port. (A figurative version). Serge Lebrasse and his band, accompanied by another singer, Marie-Josée Rochecoust, were very popular and much in demand during my teenage years.

One of their songs was "Madame Ezène", about a lady who wants to marry off her three daughters and resorts to voodoo practises to succeed, being warned about modern young men who do not marry without great considerations. It goes like this:

Ah! Madame Ezène oulé marié so trois zène filles
Li brille la bouzie rouze

Tous les minuit dans cimitière!
Pas bizain faire ça Madame Ezène
Pas bizain faire ça Madame Ezène
Pas bizain faire ça sinon ou a gagne désagrément.
Zene Zens zordi na pas bète
Zene zens zordi na pas bète
Zene zens zordi na pas marié bonavini.

Translation:

Ah, Mrs Eugène wants to marry her three daughters.
She burns red candles in the cemetery every midnight!
Don't do that Mrs Eugène
Don't do that Mrs Eugène
Don't do that or you will get into trouble.
Besides, young men nowadays are not stupid
Besides, young men nowadays are not stupid
Besides, young men nowadays do not marry just like that!

Another one worth mentioning is "Maman Zordi Mo Allé". It is about a son who leaves home and thanks his Mum for all her devotions and sacrifices.

Chorus:
Maman Zordi mo allé
Oui, mo quitte toi, mo allé
Si mone faire toi mizère
Pas bizain garde moi dans to leker. Quand mo ti éna dé zours
Qui sene na donne moi tete?
...Maman
Quand mo ti éna dé mois
Qui oquippe moi quand mo crié?
...Maman
Toi mo zoli maman
Zamé mo pas pou blié!

Translation:

Mum, today I am going!
Yes, I am leaving you and I am going away!
If I have caused you any misery,

Don't keep me in your heart, then.
When I was two days old,
Who gave me the breast?
...Mummy
When I was two months old,
Who took care of me when I cried?
...Mummy.
You my beautiful mother
I will never forget.

Sirandanes are riddles or guessing games with answers. They are of Creole origin and I have memories of a few fun evenings when the whole family took part in them after dinner. Some examples go like this:

Dileau diboute? Canne.
A pillar of water? Sugar cane.
Dileau pendant? Coco. Suspended water? Coconut.
Baionette par derriere? Mousse zonne.
Has got a bayonette at the back? A wasp.
P'tit bonhomme, grand capeau? Sampignon.
A little one with a big hat? Mushroom.
Ene missié qui amène so lacase lors so le dos? Courpa.
A man that carries his house on his back? A snail.
Mo éna ène barique ecque deux quantités di leau?
Di zef. I have a barrel containing two types of fluid? An egg.
Acotte mo allé, li suive moi? Mo lombre.
Wherever I go, he follows me? My shadow.
Mo zette la ligne, mo lève ene gros poisson et mo même manze li? Mo femme.
I throw a line in the water, I catch a big fish and I am the only one to eat it? My wife.

Some proverbs go like this: Lizié na pas éna balizaze.

Eyes have no frontier, they can look everywhere.
Zamé boeuf senti so corne trop lourd.
A bullock never feels the weight of its horns.
Quand ène femme lève so robe, diable guette so lazambe.
When a woman lifts up her skirt, the devil looks on.
Li fine marié ène bouteille vide. She has married an empty bottle (a poor man without money).

There was also this funny riddle that my father learnt from his parents. I think it is quite a few generations old. It goes like this:

Qui cahier? Cahier Devoir.
Qui devoir? Devoir Anglais.
Qui Anglais? Anglais potish.
Qui potish? Potish z'achard.
Qui achard? Achard mangue.
Qui mangue? Mangue la corde.
Qui la corde? La corde coco.
Qui coco? Coco dans arbre.
Qui arbre? Arbre dibois.
Qui dibois? Dibois colophane.

Translation:

What sort of book? A book for homework.
What sort of homework? Homework in English.
What sort of English? An English postich.
What sort of postich? A postich full of pickles.
What sort of pickle? Pickle made of mangoes.
What sort of mangoes? Mangoes that come from the tree.
What sort of tree? A tree that gives wood.
What sort of wood? Colophane wood.

Boeuf dormi, la corde marché. — Giromon.
While the calf sleeps, the rope walks. — Pumpkin.

On a personal level, there are two devoted domestics that are worth mentioning for they served my parents household as they were growing up.

Marguerite Babylone was a very tall and solid woman of African origins, who knew my father as a baby, hence the way she would still speak to him - to our great amusement - as if he was a little boy. Every month Marguerite would visit us. She was too old to work and was given a small pension from all the grown-ups that she used to look after. As there were still five of them living in Mauritius, I suppose it was not so small after all. She used to call Dad "Monsieur France". She would try to speak French to us kids and it sounded very funny.

We would always ask her to tell us about the story of the burglar, and quite flattered she would oblige willingly, and it went like this:

One night someone tried to break into her dependance and she could see from her bed this finger moving through a hole in the door next to the latch that it was trying to move up very slowly so as not to disturb anybody. Marguerite kept her cool. She got a cane knife and waited patiently near the door. The next time that the finger came through again, wham! She chopped it off and went back to bed. To make the story more gory, she told us that the next day she picked up the finger covered with red ants and wrapped it up in some newspaper and took it to the police station. How much was true I do not know, but it had its effect on us children. Marguerite had all our attention!

The other domestic was a woman named "Menne" who worked in my mother's household. She also would visit us quite regularly and would make no bones in letting us know that she would miss primarily all the goodies we gave her when we told her we were about to leave Mauritius. Menne also was retired and she would bring along her daughter Brigitte on those visits. The poor women were filthy! Brigitte was a teenager who even though did not have "looks", by the sound of it did not lack in admirers, for she always told us about her love life, especially when she was in love with a certain policeman.

One day she told us "Mo content Missie Ivan!" (I like Mr Ivan). Our poor brother made sure to disappear each time he could hear their loud voices approaching our house. He was not very happy when we teased him about it.

When Mum with a sad face told Menne that we were leaving, she replied "Mo pied dourri alle!" (My rice supply will stop!).

As you would have gathered, when you had about five small children and found yourself in the circumstance of no domestic to wash the clothes of all those sick children, it is something close to a catastrophe! So was the case for my poor mother. Desperate! One morning this Indian woman knocked at her door asking for employment. With something close to veneration Mum asked her to start straight away, which the woman agreed to by nodding. Apparently she washed the clothes in no time and had them hanging on the line. Mum asked her to please uncover her head (she wore a sahree) as she worked inside. Mum said that she pretended she did not hear. Mum asked her to polish the floor which she did with gusto. In the end, Mum said to her - a bit annoyed and louder this time - "Please remove that veil!". Apparently she looked at Mum, not blinking, and slowly removed her veil.

Mum was shocked. She became speechless. A man with shaven head was standing in front of her.

Mum quickly told "her" to go, and gave the man his dues. As soon as he got the money he took off, leaving my mother stunned.

She found out later that he was an escaped prisoner who was recaptured by the police a few days later. She read about it in the local newspaper.

CHAPTER 4

The lifeblood of the island . . .
The sugar industry

It was the Dutch who introduced sugar cane to Mauritius in 1639 from the East Indies (now Indonesia).
Europeans and Africans originally colonised Mauritius as I mentioned previously and later on were dominated in numbers by the arrival of Indians to work on sugar estates, and so with their descendants nowadays represent 70% of the island's population.
The Dutch built two factories. One at Grand-Port and the other one at Flacq. Sugar cane was then crushed in machines to extract a thick syrup that was fermented to produce a spirit called l' arack. Sugar was produced for the first time in 1696.
Mahé de Labourdonnais was the first governor (Mauritius then being called Isle de France) to be responsible for the first two proper sugar mills, more advanced of course than those built by the Dutch. They were both built in the same year, 1745. One was built at Fernay near Grand-Port and the other at Villebague in the district of Pamplemousses where the Governor General lived.
Apparently at first, the mills that were due to arrive to improve its operation were lost with the sinking of the St Géran off the coast of Mauritius.
In 1755, Mauritius was producing enough sugar for consumption by both Mauritius and Reunion islands (Isle de France and Bourbon Island).
At the end of French occupation, 10,000 acres of cane fields under the jurisdiction of a dozen sugar mills produced about 3000 tons of sugar.
In 1825, fifteen years after English occupation, 147 mills were producing about 11,000 tons of sugar and the abolition of right of entry taxes on Mauritian sugar on export to England, where it used to be disadvantaged as compared to the Antilles, promoted sugar production. At this time only seven sugar mills were steam activated. Eighty-eight operated by hydraulic force and sixty-one operated by mules power.

Page 27

In 1851 there were still two sugar mills operating with air pressure. In 1858 the industry consisted of 259 sugar mills, 11,000 acres producing 133,000 tons of sugar.

Unfortunately, when the first migrants from India arrived on the island they started the epidemics of malaria that rocked the social and economic structures of the island. This caused the Colons to move to higher grounds to live, bringing with this change a first centralisation, more functional than technical. The latter quickly followed.

A new sugar boom after the First World War brought the production of sugar to 260,000 tons in 1920. In 1950 production reached 450,000 tons. However, 1923 was a record year when 718,000 tons of sugar were produced on 207,000 acres of land and there were only 21 sugar mills. In 1973 production stood at 8890 kg at the exception of tons of white sugar and refined sugar, the bulk of the production of raw sugar exported to European refineries.

Part of it is used locally for distillation of rum and industrial alcohol, while the remnants of dried out cane (bagasse) serve the fabrication of wall panels.

The foundation of the Agricultural Chamber of Commerce took place in 1853, while research started with an agronomical station in 1893 that resulted in the creation of an Institue of Research (M.I.S.R.I.). Mauritius stands first in the world industry for sugar production.

Beau-Plan Sugar Estate factory during the 1960's.

The Sugar Industry

This Mauritian sugar industry has now an office in London that makes sure, in collaboration with the Mauritian Government, that the producers benefit the most in the competitive market.

Since 1975, Mauritius Island has been a member of the Lome Convention, after signing the regulative paper of the ACP/CEE between sugar producing countries of Africa, Caraibes, Pacific and the European Economic Community.

That also guarantees a market of 500,000 tons at a price equal to that paid to European producers, while the sale of production is sold at world prices.

Today, the sugar industry is still an essential element of the economy of the island. It is also the one that generates the most employment.

An heir to secular traditions acquired through long and arduous labour, the Mauritian sugar technician bears a reputation that is very much in demand in various sugar producing countries. There are Mauritians employed in Reunion, Madagascar, Africa (where he has often been the pioneer to the development of plantations and mills), India, Antilles, Australia and South America. — Ile Maurice Ancienne Isle de France.

After suffering for so many years, setbacks like epidemics that decreased the population or diseases of the sugar cane, cyclones, droughts and floods (against which they were not insured), often subject to the fall of the economy through political or governmental influences, the Mauritian planter succeeded in the role of man of action and technician.

Turbines at Beau-Plan Sugar Estate.

He holds the pride of his peasant ancestors, long ago leaving Britanny or Normandy, to often work with their own hands this rough, tropical soil.

Today, a master of research and sophisticated technology, he can be proud of his labour, and with the help and collaboration of co-workers working in the fields and factories, he can produce 700,000 tons of sugar to this little island in the Indian Ocean where the most illustrious governor, Mahé de Labourdonnais started the foundation to this industry. Of course many were my ancestors and present relatives on both sides of the Maujean, Arnulphy and Nozaïc families who earned their living from this industry.

Philippe's grandfather, Marcel Maujean, worked on a sugar estate in South Africa for part of his life (more details later), and a great-grandfather of his, Amédée Maujean, in 1864 was an engineer that worked on the first railway system of the north, from Port Louis to Beau-Plan sugar estate.

There were Nozaïc, Arnulphy and Maujean planters (from family genealogy).

My grandfather, Eugène Arnulphy, owned the sugar estate Saint Hubert in partnership with a Frenchman, Monsieur Merondo and a Mr Wiehe. He managed the estate for them.

I have memories of Grand-Père dressed in khaki shirt and shorts, wearing the colonial casque, and to protect his legs when walking in the cane fields some guetres (leather leggins).

Sugar cane brought from the fields were loaded by crane onto conveyor belts.

It was the standard colonial uniform that was universal, typical to all colonies producing sugar.

Popy and all his cousins lived on the sugar estate Beau-Plan where his father Philippe, and his brother Roger Maujean and Roger's son Marcel worked for many years prior to leaving Mauritius. A Nozaïc was involved with a D'Epinay in the establishment of the first steam driven sugar mill on the island.

My brother Ivan Nozaïc also worked there, so I think it is fitting that I give you an account about the history of Beau- Plan, a sugar estate in the north of the island situated in the district of Pamplemousses. All the information I will give you is genuine as I got it after reading a book written in French many years ago by Mr Auguste Toussaint. I did my best concerning the translation and it goes like this:

BEAU-PLAN SUGAR ESTATE
(History of) 1745-1963

Beau-Plan sugar estate has to date (1963) gone through six major stages since its early beginning in 1745. It was then called Les Forges de mon Desir.

This iron-work industry was one of the first enterprises on the island then called Isle de France when it was a French colony. In 1745 at the start of French colonisation, two officers who had served under the government of Mahé de Labourdonnais, Thomas Gilles Hermans and the count, Philippe de Rostaing, formed in partnership a metal work business that also included a refinery of salpetre (salpeter) and the making of gunpowder in the district of Pamplemousses. They started these enterprises after the discovery made by Rostaing of an iron mine.

Samples were sent to the director of the Indian Company in Paris for analysis which confirmed that there were sufficient amounts of iron to justify exploitation, and it is the company itself that encouraged Rostaing in going along with this venture.

The establishment was accorded some concessions by the council and in the span of 10 years, it developed into an estate of 4000 acres of land. It was then one of the most important of the time.

At first everything went well. It could supply enough iron and cast iron to the engineer Cossigny to build various fortifications, and in 1760, the establishment helped the Count D'Ache to repair its fleet that had been damaged during a cyclone.

In 1755, the British explorer, Dalrymple, considered that the industry would not survive for very long because of lack of timber caused when a vast part of the property had been logged to supply only a small amount of iron.

His prediction did not eventuate straight away, for in 1768 Mon Desir was still prosperous. It had produced three million pounds of various products in fourteen years. The annual production of iron at the time was one million pounds.

Later on, when Bougainville, another explorer, called on the island, he observed that the iron produced by the estate was one of the best quality, and the forge one of the best looking compared to European ones. The estate had at the time 900 negroes working for it.

Soon after, however, the enterprise started to go down and after trying to put it back to its original state and failing, it was sold on the 21st January 1774, for the sum of 1,100,000 pounds to Jean-Baptiste Michel Launay, for Jean-Baptiste Chevalier and the Count Jean Law de Lauriston.

Lauriston disowned the acquisition, and Launay being on his own could not afford the lot. The estate was subdivided after obtaining authorisation from the creditors of Mon Plaisir on November 14, 1774.

For his part, Jean-Baptiste Michel Launay kept 740 acres, less than a sixth of the original estate. It was then that it obtained the name of Beau-Plan (beautiful plan).

Jean-Baptiste Launay was born in Vannes, Britanny. He came to Mauritius in 1769 and was married in 1770 to Miss Julie Liesse. She passed away not long after and he followed her in 1779.

In his will he mentioned his brother, a colonel, and an elder sister married to a Mr Kerverho. It was his nephew, François Pierre Pehan who took care of his inheritance, his mother still living in Britanny. (It is interesting to note that the mother of one of my ancestors, Suzanne Peltier, married to Etienne Nozaïc in 1820, was the divorced wife of a Jean-Baptiste de Launay before marrying Louis Peltier in 1795. I wonder if perhaps he was a nephew of the above Jean-Baptiste Launay?).

The nephew decided to sell the estate and it was bought by Marin François Desveaux of Marigny, ex infantry officer, living in Pamplemousses, for the sum of 185,000 pounds, payable in five years from January 1, 1785.

At the time the property consisted of six pavilions, including one as main habitation and a large stone building that served as workshop. It had 89 slaves, 150 poultry, 41 goats and 12 ducks. There was also an orchard on the property that was considered to be in bad condition.

Some sugar cane had been planted on a piece of land leased to a Mrs Pigeot. It was then considered to be a good buy, and was estimated to be worth only 40,000 pounds soon after by the botanist Nicolas de Céré, manager of the botanical garden of Pamplemousses, after he considered the soil not suitable for cultivation.

The Sugar Industry

So it was that soon after the acquisition of the property, François Desveaux sold it again to the same François Pehan de Kerverho for the same price. On October 26, 1784, a society was formed to manage Beau- Plan and adjoining land of 156 acres that he privately owned.

Soon after Pehan bought more adjacent land, thus making the whole estate to consist of 907 acres.

Ten years later, on the death of its owner, the estate was sold for Mrs Pehan, his mother still living in Britanny, to Mr Jacques Saulnier and Co. for the sum of 1,500,000 pounds, 655,000 pounds payable a month after acquisition and 845,000 pounds in four years.

The estate of Beau-Plan then consisted of 163 slaves, different kinds of buildings, shops, furniture, animals, tools, different sorts of plantations and even indigo.

At that time indigo was the main production, but somehow it could not compete with other markets such as the one in Bengale that was of better quality.

As a result, sugar cane became the main industry of Isle de France, as at this time was the revolution of St Domaingue (West Indies) and the sugar industry of the Antilles was disrupted, causing a shortage in production of sugar on the French market. So it is not surprising that the new owners of Beau-Plan then replaced the indigo industry with that of sugar cane.

Sugar and arack were in great demand then, because the revolution wars did not facilitate the importation of wine and spirits that were very much appreciated from France.

This lack of supply turned the inhabitants of the island towards the consumption of arack or rum, an inferior alcohol.

The adjoining island of Reunion (then Isle Bourbon) got its supply from Isle de France.

When Jacques Saulnier & Co. took possession of the estate of 910 acres, 186 were cultivated in sugar cane, 14 of which recently harvested, 30 acres of manioc (cassava), 3 acres of barley, 45 acres of yard, vegetable gardens and orchards, 180 acres of woods, 435 acres in process of being cleared plus a fish pond on 17 acres.

The number of buildings consisted of 23, plus 2 sheds, 2 shacks being used as barn, a bullock enclosure surrounded by dry slabs, and finally a lime furnace and brick oven.

This is the description of the buildings used in the making of sugar and arack on the bill of sale. It reads like this:

No. 16 - A stone building whose roof is slanted and covered with tiles, 40 ft long by 30 ft wide, used as a sugar mill that contains a large wheel, a lantern, a huge spinning wheel, three iron cylinders, the mills table and a canal that supplies water to the mill. The said building in good condition.

No. 17 - Another stone building with a slanted tiled roof, 168 ft long by 30 ft wide, separated into 3 parts, one of sugar mill, one of distillery and one of cleansing room. In the sugar mill: An edifice of brick in which are five iron boilers with spoons and different utensils, a tub, wooden tables to receive the cooked products, a wooden rake.

In the distillery: A Scottish alambic with drums, fermentation tubs. The said building in good condition.

So the first mill was activated by water. There were 134 slaves and animals consisted of 38 bullocks and 3 mules.

On October 13, 1823 Beau-Plan was purchased by Mr Jean-Baptiste Germain who died two years later. His widow had the property for sale. An advertisement was placed in the Gazette de Maurice in 1825.

While belonging to Mr Germain the estate deteriorated. The report after his death consisted of no less than eight items, listed "in bad condition". On September 26, 1827 the contract of sale was signed by the new owner, Thomas Joseph Couve.

Even though it remained in his hands for a long time and knew a period of stability, Beau-Plan did not prosper very much. There was even a reduction in the area that occurred.

Thomas Couve was the son of a merchant from Montpellier who came to live in Isle de France in 1775. He was a very rich man who in 1800 inherited the properties of the late Mr St Aubin, one of the richest proprietors of the time.

Obviously his son Joseph acquired enough money of his own for in 1827 at the time of the purchase of Beau-Plan, he possessed enough money to be counted amongst the notorious and famous proprietors of the island.

Mr Joseph Couve figures as a representative of the Pamplemousses district Colonial Comity formed by Adrien d' Epinay in 1827.

Joseph Couve is also the man that demanded that Mauritian sugar exported to England be placed on the same scale as British Antilles sugar, that at the time obtained more value. This request was granted by the British Government in 1823. Beau-Plan remained the property of Mr Couves for a period of 27 years. It was a very exciting time (as mentioned earlier) in the history of the sugar cane industry.

Not long before his death, Jospeh Couve leased Beau-Plan to his son George (Contract: 30/10/1852 with Mr Jollivet, solicitor. Mr Jollivet was my great-grandmother's father).

After the death of his father he passed the lease on to Mr Gustave Martin for a period extending to February 1, 1869. From documents dated 1852, Beau-Plan consisted of 48 acres of new sugar cane. For the harvest of 1853 there were 65 acres of 1st ratoons (re-growth), 60 acres of 2nd ratoons and 10 acres of 5th ratoons, totalling 183 acres under cultivation.

In 1860 the property was sold to Mr Jean Edouard Piat for the sum of 84,000 rupees. In 1865 it was sold to Mr Gustave Martin (tenant of the land since 1860). He in turn sold it to a Mrs Aristide Meistre who became sole owner. She bought it for 86,000 rupees and sold it to Mr Barthelemy Meistre for the sum of 160,000 rupees.

In 1868 Mr Meistre went bankrupt and the property was sold at the request of Mr Jean Cesar of Port Louis, and the new owner Mr Edouard Martin bought it for 60,000 rupees. But he was not sole owner, as there was some money due to the children of Gustave Martin and Aristide Meistre. So it was that a society was formed for the exploitation of Beau-Plan for a period of seven years. It was under contract as follows: one-third for Edouard Martin, one-third for children of Gustave Martin and one-third for children of Aristide Meistre.

In April, 1882 Mr Ivanoff Autard de Bragard bought Beau-Plan for the sum of 290,000 rupees.
In the years 1866-68 there had been an epidemic of malaria that caused the population of Pamplemousses district to decline.
In 1864 the estate counted 200 male workers of Indian origin. In 1870, the total number was 345.

The island suffered a severe drought in the years 1869-71. Beau-Plan survived these disasters while many properties of the north closed down.
On May 21, 1864 the first railway system of the north (that I mentioned earlier) was started.

On April 25, 1882 Mr Autard of Bragard formed an association with other capitalists who remained anonymous. The association was called The Beau-Plan Sugar Estates Company Ltd.

The total capital of 300,000 rupees was divided into 1500 shares of 200 each. It received government approval by proclamation dated May 15, 1882. The first 570 shares (about one-third) were subscribed to Mr De Bragard, the rest to 18 other people listed below:

1. Jules Salamon Bloch (Director of Franco/Egyptian Bank).
2. William Newton (Lawyer).
3. Louis Aukille Victoire Delafaye (Lawyer).
4. Leonce Manes (Proprietor).
5. Emile Sauzier (Attorney).
6. Alphonse Barbe (Proprietor).
7. John Jacobs (Proprietor).
8. Frederic Feuilherade (Broker).
9. Casimir Nerac (Proprietor).
10. Adolphe Larcher (Proprietor).
11. Edouard Ellias (Merchant).
12. Alfred Mallac (Merchant).

13. Rodolphe De Chazal (Merchant).
14. Tristan Mallac (Merchant).
15. George Guibert (Lawyer).
16. Jules Rondeaux (Broker).
17. Maurice Maingard (Proprietor).
18. Thomas Paris (Broker).

The members of the first administration comity were: Jules Salomon Bloch, Emile Sauzier, Rodolphe de Chazal and Jules Rondeaux, the latter was also the secretary and manager.

On the 21st of June 1882, Mr Autard de Bragard sold the domain of Beau-Plan and its annexes to the association mentioned above. The same as purchased from Mm Martin on the 6th of April 1882. The whole property for the sum of 300,000 rupees. (The deed passed by Mr Gimel). - Mauritius archives NA 118/49.

Before the ten years of expiry date the association was renewed for another fifteen years dating from the 1st of April 1882 by an act received by Mr Maurice Maingard on the 7th and 30th of September 1891. (Mauritius archives. NA 109/24).

The social fund and the number of actions remained the same. On the 9th of October 1906 the association was again renewed for another 15 years dating from the 1st of April 1907.

In 1912 a new legislation was passed concerning commercial associations.

In Ordinance 35 of that year, every one of them had to register at the Government Registry Office and submit a report of their financial status every year to the director of that department. In 1921 at the fifteen years date of expiry, the regulations of the Beau-Plan association were modified to give it unlimited duration.

Office block at Beau-Plan Sugar Estate

Those arrangements contained in a deed dated the 20th and 21st of December 1921 by Mr Eugène Rousset and figuring now amongst the minutes of Mr Philippe Rousset (1963) are the last important regulations concerning the settlement of the Beau-Plan Sugar Estates Company Limited. From 1882 to 1921 the domain was considerably enlarged by several acquisitions. The most important being the estate of "Souvenir", a property of some 175 acres, bought by Mr Pierre Aristide Régnard on the 22nd of April 1920.

In 1912, the area of Beau-Plan (excluding the annexes) was 710 acres. 650 were cultivated. The average production for the years 1909-12 were estimated to be 3175 to 3940 tons respectively, and the annual production of about 4865 was an estimated average. There were 59 mills operating in 1912, including Beau-Plan.

In 1908, Dr Ronald Ross, sent to Mauritius to help stamp out malaria, advised the drying out of the Beau-Plan "pond", which he considered to be a factor in the epidemic. His report was as follows: "The factory and camps of this estate situated in the flat, low-lying part of the district (Pamplemousses) have in their immediate vicinity a large marsh, resulting from the daming of the discharge canal of all the ponds in the botanical gardens.
"The land all round this marsh is boggy over a considerable area and contains numerous pools and puddles overgrown with aquatic plants and weeds. "The malaria committee have under consideration a scheme for the suppression of this dangerous nuisance."

In that same report he recommended the drying out of the Beau-Plan "pond" as one of the first steps to irradicate the disease-causing mosquitoes. He estimated that it would cost 50,000 rupees for such a project (a large sum of money in those days).

The drying out was not finalised until 1914. Here is a report forwarded after completion of the task by the Medical and Health Department in their annual report for the year 1914: "The extensive marsh at Beau-Plan of 20 acres area which has caused so many deaths during the last quarter of a century, has been entirely drained. "A masonry channel, 4 ft wide and 18 inches deep, 3000 ft long and an earth channel 1200 ft long were made to deviate the waters of the powder mills and villebague canal which caused the marsh. The dyke which formed the marsh has been removed."

However, despite these measures, malaria was not totally eradicated in Beau-Plan until after the Second World War.

Since 1921, the Beau-Plan sugar estate acquired other annexes such as Fair Fund in 1922, Souvenir and Vallombreuse in 1941, Maison Blanche in 1946 (this is where my husband, Philippe Maujean jnr was born in 1948) and L'Esperance and Mon Gout in 1961.

To date (1963) the property of Beau-Plan since 1882 had purchased 2992 acres including the main estate. This made it three times the size it originally was when bought by Jean- Baptiste Launay in 1775 when it only consisted of 740 acres. In 1929, Beau-Plan had a distillery for the production of rum and alcohol. It lasted two years before being closed down.

The use of D.D.T. put a stop to the spreading of malaria in Mauritius in 1948.

My mother suffered the disease while growing up. She often told me of how the whole family had bouts of very high fever (a sympton of the disease), and they had to swallow quinine powder wrapped up in paper. Her father later on, injected it himself.

My father also suffered from it from going to the sugar estate where she lived, while they were engaged.

At one stage when she was thirteen, my mother suffered a very bad attack that kept her bed-ridden for so long that when in convalescence she could only walk with the aid of a cane, her legs being so weak!

COMITY OF DIRECTORS
1964
President: Mr Yves Rouillard, Mr André Raffray Q.C.
MM: Michel Harel, Henri Harel, Jean A. Harel, Maxime Rougier Lagane, Miss Georgina Souchon.
STAFF 1964
Manager: Mr Philippe Marrier d'Unienville.
Accountant: Mr Jean Chasteau de Balyon (now a priest, he made the toast to my in-law's wedding).
Assistants: Philippe Maujean (my father-in-law).
MM: Jean Whornitz (a friend that figures in family photo), Jacques d'Hotman de Villiers, Claude Wieh, François Chasteau de Balyon, Ivan Nozaïc (my brother).
Factory Manager: Mr Marc Labat. Technical Councillor: Mr Adrien Wiehe.
Assistants: Robert Wörhnitz, John Piat, Sylvio Dupuis. Chief Chemist: Mr Christian Desjardins.
Assistant: Mr Claude de Villecourt. Chief Mechanic: Mr Gabriel Lebon.
Chief Electrician: Mr Gervais Tourmentin.
Chief Director of Cultivation: Mr André Mamet.
Directors of Annexes: Maison Blanche and Esperance - Mr Louis Langlois.
Souvenir - Mr Christian de Speville.
Beau-Plan - Mr Maxime d' Unienville. Fair-Fund - Mr Frederic Staub.

The Sugar Industry

Philippe Maujean – Assistand Accountant of Beau-Plan

Assistants: Roger Jauffret (married to a cousin of mine and features in family photo), Antoine Coutet, Henri Fleurant, Nicholson Raffaut. Irrigation: Mr Robert Martin.
Weigh-Bridge Manager: Mr Alain Bechard. Assistants: Noel Morel, Benjamin Veron. Transport: Mr Roger Maujean (Uncle Roger).
Social Assistants: Dr V. Pierre Goupille (delivered my husband) and Dr Maxime Rousset.
Infirmary: Mr Serge Ferriere (lives in Melbourne) and Mrs Denise L'Hoste.
Liason: Mr Michel Cayeux.

There were many advantages for people working on sugar estates. A house was provided free of charge. The estate provided a car and chauffeur that was used by wives to go shopping in town. There was a school bus for the children. Most houses had a vegetable garden tended by a gardener.
Work started very early but there was time allowed for lunch at home. I remember Grand-Père even having a little nap after.
I have spent many a day at some relatives place during school holidays and used to enjoy it a lot (a big change for us town kids), and especially remember the dishes of venison served at almost every meal. A civet of hare was quite appreciated as well. I have even eaten flying fox stew. If your reaction is "yuck!", what about some fried wasp larvae?...Delicious! Not to mention curried monkey!

Adrien D'Epinay was one of Mauritius illustrious sons, especially where the sugar industry was concerned.

He was born at Bagatelle, Moka on the sixth of January, 1794. When D'Epinay was sixteen years old, Isle de France was taken possession by the British.

At the age of twenty-two, on the 28th of December 1816, he became a lawyer. Throughout his career D'Epinay was much involved in the politics of the day.

He was granted authorisation from the British Government to form a Governmental Council in Mauritius, with colonials as representatives.

D'Epinay is also the one who obtained liberty of press on the island and is the founder of the newspaper "Le Cerneen" in 1832 (the second oldest French language newspaper in the world) whose motto was Libertas Sine Licentia (Liberty Without License). It is interesting to note that this newspaper was still running in the seventies.

As a sugar estate proprietor, D'Epinay was the first to own a steam activated mill. He also defended the cause of Mauritian planters against the British anti-slavery council that threatened to abolish slavery without any financial assistance to planters, risking to destroy the island's economy.

D'Epinay won his case after many years of negotiations and through organising a strike by all professional and commercial businesses of the island when a British envoy, Mr Jeremy was in Mauritius, a strike that lasted four days.

D'Epinay also played a figure role in obtaining the abolition of a right of entry levy placed on Mauritian sugar exported to England at the time which resulted in it being placed on the same scale as that of the West Indies that was more advantaged to the detriment of Mauritius.

A statue of Adrien D'Epinay standing on "the place of arms' in Mauritius is the work of his son, Prosper, who was a world-known sculptor.

It is sad to note that D'Epinay left Mauritius in February 1839 to live in Paris with his family due to the fact that there was no love lost between him and the then Governor of Mauritius, Sir William Nicolay, who in 1834, dissolved the colonial comity that he founded.

Adrien D'Epinay passed away on the ninth of December 1839. He was forty-five years old. — Information from the Historical Society of Mauritius.

CHAPTER 5

A trip down memory lane

Growing up as a member of such a huge family (my mother had seven brothers and sisters, and my father six) with so many uncles, aunts, cousins, grandparents, great uncles and great aunts has given me a wonderful sense of belonging.

As a result I generally relate well to people and am fairly tolerant of lifes little bumps along the way. Not only due to the fact that my immediate family was large, but my earliest memories are that of people (family, relatives) visiting, nearly on a daily basis.

Mind you, it also had a disadvantage in the sense that you were not allowed any privacy, for I had never had a room of my own. We had to share rooms, the two eldest had one, I was with the petites and where Ivan was concerned it depended on the house we rented at the time. For you see, even though papa had a good position as Registrar General, with so many of us to feed and clothe, my parents never owned a house in Mauritius.

We were not poor, but there was a lot that we had to do without. For instance, we never had a refrigerator at home until the last years before we left Mauritius. I don't think we were any poorer for it, for fresh vegetables were bought almost daily and the "marchand de lait" (milkman) would deliver milk every morning. The milk did not come in bottles or cartons, but from a metal container attached to the milkman's bicycle, with a tap to pour into whatever size container the domestic would present to him. It was supposed to be 100% cows milk, but many a time we caught him at an adjoining tap trying to increase his supply.

We did not have to worry about storing ice cream because it was a luxury that was allowed for special occasions like Christmas, Easter and New Year or when we had visitors from overseas. We drank plenty of milk, had eggs regularly but only had cheese once a week on Sunday, when I remember papa cutting out a large block and sharing it amongst the nine of us.

Bread was delivered daily by the "marchand de pain" (bread man). He supplied us with crusty rolls and "moules" and the traditional "pain maison" that we used to take to school for lunch. The "pain maison" was inferior. It was not as crisp but a round bun with a line in the middle that would make it easy to break in half. Many were the times when we would find nasty surprises like a little piece of string encrusted in the bun, and one of my sisters even found a coin once.

We did not lack in fruit supply. Every house in Mauritius had lots of fruit trees (we had gardeners to look after the garden). There was a regular supply of mangoes, pawpaws, peaches, bananas and guavas, not to mention the delicious lychees and longanes.

To us apples and oranges were a delicacy. Every month the fruit merchant would call to our place. It was the only time we would each be allowed to choose a fruit. Orange, apple or pear, looking so special wrapped up in green tissue paper. These were imported fruits from Australia.

Once we were given a letter by the fruit merchant, one that he had found in a crate on opening. It was from a young Australian male living in Tasmania who wanted a pen pal. Unfortunately we never answered back. I think we were too self conscious of our English at the time.

We never had a water heater in the bathroom. Believe me, even though it does not get very cold during the winter months, it was not very pleasant. Don't think that most houses were like that. People who owned their house had those appliances, it is just the houses for renting that were not fitted with one.

As you can imagine, we made up for it when we stayed at our cousin's place, blissfully unaware of the cost. We used to have a cooked breakfast before going to school, some sandwiches coming back and dinner would be fairly late. (Popy, my husband, still cannot eat early in the evening).

There were mainly timber houses in Mauritius. As I was growing up, the modern ones were made of concrete. The yards were generally of a fair size with a bamboo enclosure. They were special in the sense that they consisted of a thick line of bamboo growing very close to each other. These were trimmed quite regularly by the gardener and separated the house from the road. These bamboo edges often served as a buffer, as was the case once when riding my cousin's bicycle (I never owned one). I panicked when I saw a car approaching and I just let go of the handle bars and went straight in the bamboo. Needless to say I ended up with a few scratches.

Inside, most houses had timber polished floors or some type of tiles that had to be polished as well. I remember the nénennes polishing it using a special "brosse coco", a circular polisher made of coconut fibre that would be used with the foot to polish the floor in a circular manner.

The floor would usually be of a dark red or green colour and would look beautiful and shiny afterwards. For fun (and to the relief of the nénennes I am sure) we used to have a go at it every now and then.

To sweep the floor, there were the usual "ballier coco". There again, used on the patio outside, it was made of a bundle of long layers of fibres removed from the middle of a coconut frond. These were tied together at different lengths. The broom used inside was not as coarse and was made by assembling together some "fatac" fibres obtained from a common weed.

There were huge colonial houses in Mauritius that could be called mansions. They were old houses that were strong enough for enduring the force of cyclones as proven by the fact that they had belonged to generations of the same family.

The Brousse family on my mother's side, my grandmother's sister, Tante Edith and Tonton André owned such a huge house. There was a verandah at the front and sides where it was good to sit on those hot tropical nights and listen to the sound of crickets.

Inside was a masterpiece of antique furniture, oriental rugs and vases, and walls beautifully chiselled. I attended a few of their children's weddings held there. The verandahs were furnished with cane furniture and quite often the wall would be adorned with the stuffed head of a stag or wild boar, proud testimony of a keen hunter, mounted on a wooden plaque. We never had one at our place, my father having lived in town most of his life.

A typical colonial house in Curepipe

(Just last week I saw the skull and horn of one that Ivan told me was killed by Papa on a hunting party while engaged). But it was a different matter for those used to life on a sugar estate, where only the odd ones did not participate in hunting parties. There was wild boar or deer hunting. (The deer were introduced to the island by the Dutch).

The Brousse's place of course had a huge garden where our energy would know no bounds as we children played on the meticulously clipped lawn. There was proof of English influence in the garden settings, with their trimmed lawns bordered by secular trees.

On a smaller scale, the houses I lived in while growing up were mostly timber ones, quite different in style to those of Australia of course. Usually each room would adjoin each other and were given access to by timber doors half glassed for light (French windows). At one stage, I was about seven then, we lived in a house on the same estate that my grandparents, Zelie and Eugène Arnulphy, owned and lived on

Mum and Tante Arlette Brousse with myself, Micheline and Marielle, standing in Tante Arlette's garden at Rose-Hill.

A Trip down memory lane

At first my grandparents had one of those huge colonial houses that I mentioned before. I remember how there was a cotton tree in the yard that fascinated us. It was in Rose-Hill, one of the towns. As a small child we used to have some fun in the orchard they had on the property.

Later on they demolished part of the house, leaving them with a much smaller one. They sub-divided the land (keeping the orchard) and had two more houses built, one for them to live in and one that they rented to us (this house was the third we lived in since I was born). They rented out the smaller original one.

I have vague recollections of the one I was born in. I know that it was supposed to be haunted. My parents experienced some weird happenings there. That did not stop them from living in the place for seven years though. Apparently my father met the previous tenant who when finding out during the course of the conversation that he was living in the same house, was astonished that he had done so for so long, as his family could not cope with the strain and they had to leave.

My parents told me they would hear doors open and shut, people walking etc, that when checked revealed no one there. They would hear noises in the kitchen at night as if someone was making a cuppa, for they would both distinctly hear the sound of a spoon being stirred in a porcelain cup. There again, when checked, no one was there. My father used to wake up early to study, as he was following a course as chartered accountant. One time the light bulb that was suspended from the ceiling by an electrical cord, supposed to be clamped inside the ceiling, moved up and down like a yoyo. At first Papa thought it might be a rat, and threw a tin of talcum powder to the ceiling to disturb it. It did not stop and went on for a while.

They never saw anybody (or ghost), but a cousin of Mum, visiting from South Africa, who had not been told of the situation as she slept there on the way back from the pictures one night, was frightened out of her wits and told Mum she would not spend another night in that house as she was awoken during the night by a black woman staring at her through the mosquito net. At first she thought it might be a night nénenne, but when she awoke her cousin (my Aunt Annie) and asked her if Mum employed a night domestic and was answered in the negative, she realised that it was abnormal.

My Mum was really frightened once when having a nap in her bedroom with her new born baby (me) asleep in the cot beside her. She heard sighs, the sound coming from a certain part of the room, and when going to investigate she came close to her wardrobe and heard heavy breathing straight into her ear. Apparently, in panic, she ran out of the house to the domestic quarters where she was told that it was probably the spirit of a young man who had previously died in this house. The domestics reckoned he probably was pining after her.

Mum told me in the end, all those happenings did not bother them. They got used to it.

The next house we occupied was in the same district. Next door lived the Duvivier family. We were on very good terms with them and I even called Mr Duvivier "Papa" once, to the amusement of my nanny.

I remember being at their place, when I had to go back home to say goodbye to Mum who was getting ready to go to the clinique as the birth of Sylvianne was imminent. I must have been two and a half years old. The next day, Dad came to our bedroom where all the girls slept (the three of us) and gave us the news that we had a new sister. I distinctly remember how once Mum was sitting at the sewing machine (not electric in those days, it was activated by the hand). She used to make magic things to my eyes, little booties of cardboard covered with cellophane paper, filled with candy. Pillow cases with pretty satin bows, things that she donated for the local Fancy Fair. So it was one of those days and as she worked, I had climbed onto a chair and was looking outside through the window pane. All of a sud- den I heard somebody yelling "lamino" a few times, and Mum would hold me in her arms. I would feel the house shake and rattle as a loud boom was heard. Each time I would hear this "lamino" I would look for cover as I hated this anticipated boom. I found out later that "lamino" meant "la mine" (mine), a warning before dynamite was used in connection to house building.

This was also the house I lived in when I started school. No pre-school in those days. I remember looking at myself in the mirror, dressed in my new uniform that consisted of a tie as well and thinking "I am really grown up now, I am going to school".

I attended school in Beau Bassin at a convent of "Bon Perpetuel Secour". I was so proud of my "valise", a suitcase much too big for my size.

We used to travel to school by steam train. I was impressed by the inside of the wagons with walls of polished wood and the netting at the top where our ports were stored. The station where we stopped was huge.

I had to make sure that I would not lose Ivan, Marielle or Micheline from sight, for I would not know my way. I remember once being frightened of this lady that was dressed like a lady of the last century, with this bonnet and long dress. She had lots of make-up on, specially where the rouge was concerned. I suppose I could sense that something was odd. Later on I found out that she was a poor lady who was not very sane and used to walk for miles. She was known all over the island.

In those days we used a slate and slate pencil to write on. I was very proud of my first text book called "Titi et Toto", about a little boy and girl and their dog called "Medor".

A Trip down memory lane

Dolls brought from Europe by my parents for the six daughters they left behind.

I loved those early days of school, when the friends of Marielle and Micheline would fuss over me.

During lunch breaks we would play school would you believe? We had our turns at being teachers and throwing our authority to those pupils who would use leaves in place of paper and thorns as pencils as we would perforate in mock writing.

Sometimes we would play games like "La Ronde du Muguet" where boys and girls form a circle holding hands and first sing this song as we move around that went like this: "C'est la ronde du muguet, sans rire et sans parler! La premiere qui rira, sortira dehors! (It is the ring of muguets (flowers), without a laugh or speech. The first one to do either is out). It would go on until the last one to stay was the winner. There was also the game of "Colin Magnard", where again we formed a circle around a chosen person who was blind-folded, and had by touching to identify one of the group. As we got older I am sure a lot of advantage was gained as far as the boys were concerned. Our "hide and seek" was called "Cook!". Those were the main games that we enjoyed during school holidays or at birthday parties.

Our hop-scotch, that consisted of a drawing traced with a stick on the ground, or with chalk on a slab, was called "La Marelle".
When all the cousins would get together, we would play "Cowboys and Indians" (I was given a costume of a cowgirl one Christmas), and with our cap guns we would have the time of our life as the prisoners would be locked in the chook houses that served as prisons, on my grandfather's property.

We invented all sorts of games. I was even Joan of Arc once and got tied to a tree. Mum called us for lunch and they all forgot about me as they rushed inside. Judging by the loudness of my screams to alert them, you would have sworn that I was really being burnt alive!

Then there would be the times when we would have concerts for the parents after dinner. We would have chairs in a row, so as to look like the real thing. We even had "no smoking" signs and charged them fifty cents each.

We have been soldiers, flowers, queens, Bluebeard, and I was even Saint Bernadette imploring the virgin (Micheline with a towel on the head) to "please, tell me your name", that she would solemnly answer "I am the immaculate conception". I have been a ballerina and a prima dona when I used to sing "Toreador" of Carmen at the top of my voice). Poor neighbours, probably thought I was being strangled!

My sister Micheline's first communion in 1953. From left – Ivan, Dad, myself, Sylvianne, Micheline, Mariel and Marie France in my mother's arms.

It was good clean fun. Micheline and I used to climb trees and sitting on a branch, pretended that it was a plane taking us overseas with our daughters (our dolls).

I was about six when my parents went to Europe for six months and took Ivan, the eldest with them. It was the only time that they took advantage of the fact that my father was allowed a trip overseas every year for his wife and one child, being an employee of the government.

So this once, after having to borrow some money for the expenses over there (the fares were paid by the government), they made the most of it. Later on I was told that my poor father really needed this break or he would have suffered a nervous break-down.

We were left to the care of my grandparents and their daughters, Annie, Marcienne and Jacqueline, our aunts who were not married at the time.

On the day of their departure we were given some money with the suggestion that we use it on a dolls christening (to console us). It really worked, for we gave it our full attention as to make it as close to the real thing as we could.

My first communion day. Back row from left – Roseline Doger de Speville, Christiane Nozaic, Marielle Nozaïc, Danielle Mamet and Ivan Nozaic. 2nd back row from left– Sylvain Doger de Speville, Micheline Nozaïc, Joel Nozaïc, and Roger Doger de Speville. Middle row from left – Daniel Doger de Speville, Françoise Nozaïc, and Marylee Duvivier. 2nd row from left – Marc-Henri Mamet, Marie-Josée Nozaïc, Marie-Anne Mamet and Pascaline Nozaïc. Front row from left – Marianne Doger de Speville, Michel Duvivier, Marie-France Nozaïc, Sylvianne Nozaïc, and Rose-Marie Nozaïc.

We even had the traditional packets of "dragés" (some type of coloured, sugar-coated seeds, individually wrapped in cellophane paper and tied by a satin ribbon, very much like pralines, served at weddings here).

We also dressed the doll in a proper christening gown (usually one that is used for generations and is hand embroidered). As was the custom, we donned our baby with the crocheted burnoo (a cape of lace design with a hood).

I think it is worth mentioning that in Mauritius a baby's christening usually took place a few days after the birth. In most cases, if it was not a "home birth" as it was for ladies living on sugar estates, the mother would still be in hospital. My mother had us all at the clinique and as she was in a private room, the small intimate party would take place there.

My parents and Ivan were away for six months. They went to France and England and numerous are the photos, in fact about three albums full are a reminder of all the places they visited.

I believe that poor Maman missed us all terribly all the time she was away from us. Imagine, Rose-Marie was only a six- months old baby! During this time I was being prepared through the school for that special day when I would make my first communion. For numerous Saturdays I would go to the Beau Bassin church for catechism classes and somehow the smell of egg rolls that Grand-Mère prepared for my lunch has stuck on my mind.

That special event took place a few weeks after my parents return. The night before I went to bed with "papillottes" in my hair so that I would look my best. Boy! Was I proud of those ringlets, quite a dramatic change from my straight hair. In those days, I was seven, and it was 1955, there were no hair rollers, so the only way to curl the hair was to have wet strands of hair tied at the tip with strips of material that was then twisted and tied around the top.

I wore the family white organdy dress that was hand-embroidered by Maman. The effect was quite good, with the also white embroidered type of vest that stopped at the waist, plus the "aumoniere" which is a silk pocket bordered by lace and embroidered worn at the waist, tied to a sash. Its purpose is to contain a rosary, handkerchief and a few coins for collection.

It was with much fervour that I received the host that day. I must mention that in those days there were lots of silly warnings that I think originated from some nénenne's stories. For instance, I was told to make sure that I did not bite on the host, or blood would come out of it, for it would be like a sacrilege. It was also mentioned that if one host fell off the priest's hand, he would only be able to pick it up with his tongue. It was all those kind of scare tactics that were part of religion in those days. At the time, we were not allowed to eat from midnight before receiving the host in the morning. We were not allowed to drink during the previous hour.

In those days Mass was in Latin and the altar was very elaborate and was separated from the congregation by a carved wood railing where we would kneel to receive communion.

I vividly remember the priest saying in Latin "Dominus vobiscum" and all of us to answer "Et cum spiritu tuo", which translated is "God be with you", answer "And also with you".

For my part, I much prefer the modern way for I feel it consists more of a feeling of love of God instead of a kind of remoteness. Thus the congregation can participate more.

In those days, young girls and ladies had to cover their head while in a church. So we wore hats or "mantille" (a triangular piece of material made of lace). I believe that the custom stems from the fact that people considered that as a woman's hair was supposed to be her most prized asset, it would distract the male congregation.

Nuns wore the habit at all times. I especially felt for those poor Irish nuns dressed in their long sleeved dresses and wearing the stuffy head piece that only left their faces exposed. How terrible to bear in that hot tropical climate so alien to their native land.

I was about fourteen years old when changes started to take place in the church. It started with the conversion from Latin to the native language. I was living in Australia and married when we were first allowed to have the host placed in the hand for communion. Until then it was placed on the tongue by the priest only.

As we are on the subject of religion, I will proceed to tell you about those other special events such as those of marriage and burial, but first, going back to my first communion it is worth mentioning the reception that took place at the family home after church.

As a rule the whole family, grandparents, uncles, aunts and cousins would be invited. Coffee and "brioches" (crossed buns) were served. As these had previously been blessed, we would make the sign of the cross before consumption.

After the party we would take a tray-full to share with the neighbours. I have no mementos such as presents left of this special day, as they were destroyed during a violent cyclone that hit the island five years later.

One special gift that I was very fond of was a portrait of St Maria Goretti holding a bunch of lilies. I was especially touched by the fact that she was considered a martyr that lost here life when she was only thirteen, murdered when she would not give in to sexual advances of a neighbour. Apparently before dying, he repented and made his peace with God.

I also treasured a fluorescent ornament of our Lady that shone in the dark and after winding, would play the tune of "Ave Maria". Mum and Dad bought me this from Lourdes.

Weddings were a grand affair, planned about a year before. Everybody, including the children, would dress formal.

Usually it took place during the week, around five o'clock in the evening. Prior to the church ceremony there would be a civil one, a few days before. This was the legal side of it where only the immediate family would be present and it took place at the town hall. (My father performed such marriages, being Registrar General). It would be followed by a small gathering at home where champagne and savouries would be served.

The church ceremony was very elaborate. There would be a red carpet laid out and all the pews would be decorated with flowers and ribbons. There would be a singer, male or female and songs such as "Ave Maria" of Gounault or "Panis Angelicus" sung while the witnesses and wedding partners signed the registry.

As the bride walked down the aisle on her father's arm, Mendelssohn's "Wedding March" would be played. The bride and groom would leave the church to the sound of bells. (This is the one thing that I miss. The bells that you hear every day, that sound for morning Mass, the Angelus weddings and baptisms when they are merry, and so sad at funerals, when the "glas" rings its monosyllabic sound).

The reception usually took place in a hall where at first the bride and groom stood with their parents on both sides as all the guests would kiss and congratulate them.

Afterwards those delicious "glaces" (sorbet) served in Coquilles Saint Jacques would be passed around to the delight of the children. They were of a light green colour, mint flavoured with almonds. Champagne would be served for the toast to the new couple after a speech was made by the groom's family friend.

When the formality was over it would then be time for the bridal waltz under the beaming eyes of parents and friends. there was no sitting meal, trays of savouries like caviar and petit four would be served by waiters dressed in white costume adorned with brass buttons.

I believe children probably enjoyed it most, as there would be no nénennes to restrain them and they would have the time of their life running free under the scrutinising eyes of the older generation. They would even take part in the dancing. The party would usually last until eleven after the newly-weds had departed for their honeymoon around nine or so amidst great fuss and cheers.

The honeymoon was usually spent at a private campement where complete privacy was enjoyed by the newly-weds at the start of their married life. Of course, no domestic chores for the bride as there usually are domestics consisting of an elderly couple who take care of the bungalow. The honeymoon (lune de miel) lasts about a month.

A Trip down memory lane

Funerals are a very morbid affair on the island, or should I say were, as I am sure there would now be funeral parlours there.

I must point out that being a child, I never attended a "veileé mortuaire" which consisted of the cadavre being layed on a "canape" (a sort of divan) with candles burning at the sides, while some close members of the family sit around praying and whispering to each other all night until the time of the funeral. Then the "croques morts" (literally 'corpse munchers'), usually creoles dressed all in black, would solder closed the casket.

While the body is being watched by the ladies, the men would be talking outside. Black coffee would be served to keep everyone awake during the night. I was told that the men would tell jokes and seemed to have a good time. Typical way of males to shut off an awkward situation I would say!

I heard of macabre stories when the corpse had to have a scarf tied around the jaws to keep the mouth shut by some people who seem to derive a certain pleasure in telling all the sordid details.

There is even a story that would be funny, albeit the circumstances, when a rather simple gentleman after showing the usual signs of compassion for the widow said to her, "Next time, please make sure that we don't have to travel so far!". And the one who was told "Thank you for coming" answered "It was a pleasure".

People that could not afford a hearse had the "croque morts" (pall bearers) carry the coffin to the cemetery all the way from church, followed by all the relatives. It used to frighten me when we would pass one such funeral, especially the "croque morts" wearing a black cape. They looked so macabre, and would deepen my fear of death!

The Indians used to burn their dead. The "bibi" (woman domestic) would tell us all the gory details.

Even the Créoles who were Catholic had their rituals. They believed that the spirit of the deceased was earth-bound for several days, so there should be no noise around the family home, as a sign of respect.

Even for our class you wore only black at a funeral, and depending on the relation to the deceased, you had to observe a period of grieving, usually twelve months, when you would only wear black and would abstain from any form of entertainment.

Children would wear black and white for six months, and if you did not adhere to these rules, you would be judged insensitive, I was told.

Every year on the feast of All Souls Day in November, the whole family used to go to the cemetery to pray on our paternal grandfather's grave, where we laid a bunch of flowers.

While walking amongst the tombstones we would read the inscriptions and be quite moved when coming upon a young person or baby's grave. As children, we felt as if their spirit was right there. I think it was due to all the ghost stories we had been told by the nénennes.

As you can judge, it was a very colourful childhood and we were never bored, being influenced by all those old wives tales and superstitions. Is it surprising that we can be quite dramatic?

Ready and eager to go to school – back row from left – Micheline, myself, Marielle. Front row from left – Sylvianne, Marie-France and Rose-Marie.

CHAPTER 6

Those great people of the past . . .
Monnier, Arnulphy, Charoux and Nozaïc

My maternal grandfather, Eugène Arnulphy, was also my Godfather and like me, he was born in November.

"Grand-Père" was the only offspring of his father's marriage to Clemence Rougier. Previously he was married to Augusta Toussaint and two daughters were born of that union, Cecile and Leonie Arnulphy. He was a widower when he met Grand-Mère and she had her son at the age of forty-three while living in Madagascar.

Grand-Père was only two years old when his father passed away. With his mother and sisters accompanied by their great aunt Mimi Raffray, they went to Mauritius to live.

When Grand-Père (Eugène) married, she moved in with them where she lived until her death.

Leon Arnulphy   Clemence Arnulphy

My Aunt Marcienne, one of Maman's younger sisters who never knew her as she was born a few years after her death, apparently saw her ghost. The story goes like this.

"Marcienne was getting ready to go to bed one night, when all of a sudden she started to scream (I believe she was about four years old). When asked what was the matter, sobbing, she told them how she had seen this old lady dressed in white with her hair done in a plat hanging down her back walking along the corridor. She had followed her and when they came to a door, the lady just disappeared. That's when she got frightened and screamed."

Apparently she had just described how Grand-Mère Clemence used to look before going to bed. I have photos of her and her husband. I can see a resemblance with my sister Rose-Marie.

It is amusing how Grand-Pere's (Eugène) and Grand-Mère's (Zelie) romance came about.

Apparently Eugène had confided to a mutual female friend that he liked Zelie Monnier and wanted to know her better. The friend, loving him herself, tried to discourage him by lying and saying "The poor girl, she's got horrible fat legs!".

Grand-Père did not leave matters to rest. He organised a picnic and invited Grand-Mère. He made sure they had to cross a little creek and stayed close to her when she had to lift up the hem of her long dress. He then discovered the lie, for in fact she had thin ankles, and from what he could see, nice legs.

Later on, when the fashion changed to shorter dresses, Grand-Mère and her sisters were noted for their nice legs.

Their union produced eight children. Leon, Roger, Lise, Myriam (Mum), Annie, Marcienne, Jacqueline and Cyril.

Zellie Arnulphy   Eugène Arnulphy

Grand-Père had two sisters, Cecile (married J. Baptiste Adam) and Leonie (my Mum's Godmother, married Maxime Griffiths).

Maman lived most of her life at St Hubert sugar estate that her parents owned in partnership with two other families as I mentioned earlier.

They had quite a good life. They had their own tennis court and numerous domestics to take care of them and look after the huge house they lived in. Grand-Père was quite strict raising his family, and beware to whoever stepped out of bounds.

Children had to reach a certain age to be allowed to sit at the dinner table, even then there were rules not to be broken, like never to speak without being addressed, otherwise you were sent to your room.

Grand-Père and his sons were keen hunters and had their dogs for such hunting parties. Maman told me that she went with them a few times and was especially impressed by a certain wild boar (cochon marron) chase. There were many of their prized shots whose head was stuffed and mounted on a wooden plaque to adorn a wall of the living room or verandah. I remember as a child being frightened of a wild boar that looked so fierce with its glassed eyes. To me it looked as if it was going to pounce on me at any minute.

Maman tells me that Grand-Père could cure a sprain or wasp sting by making some sweeping movement with a needle, something learnt from the blacks. Apparently it really worked. Who knows? Perhaps it is the metal that emanates some type of energy.

As a child I used to go to my grandparent's place quite often during school holidays. I used to have a ball! My cousin Marc-Henri (Marco) and I used to go for long walks on the estate and Marco would show me hare tracks. I remember when Grand-Père used to come home for a couple of hours during the day to have a cooked lunch and then a siesta. That's when he would doze off on his maurice (cane reclining chair) and to our amusement, made so much noise snoring. The sound would be interrupted every now and then by the buzzing of flies and that's when Grand-Père would leap out with his flyswat that would swish the air in search of the offenders. It went on until it was time for Grand-Mère to wake him up to go back to work.

When all their children were grown up, they moved to a town as Grand-Père was reaching retiring age.

He worked then as some sort of supervisor on building sites. I can still see him with his grey felt hat driving a little Morris.

Grand-Père gave me the nickname of "Bajo" (short for Baba Jojo - Baby Jojo) that some members of the family still call me.

Speaking of nicknames, a cousin of my mother whom we called Tonton Allen, used to call me "La Varicelle" (chicken pox), after I suffered of the disease pretty badly and had numerous scabs to prove it.

I was in Australia and expecting my son Patrick when he visited from New Caledonia. He still called me by that name when he greeted me.

Grand-Père and Grand-Mère from what I could judge, cared very much for each other, and us children thought it quite cute when once we witnessed Grand-Mère showing signs of jealousy when Grand-Père talked of a certain young lady with whom he had a conversation while shopping. He was around sixty.

Grand-Père enjoyed playing cards. I can still see him sitting at the table at my place with the rest of them, my parents, aunts and uncles and a family friend, Mr Dailhaut during a party of Belotte. I remember all the colourful expressions they used when totally carried away by the game, like "Viens dans mon avion" (Come into my plane, join me) and "Fait pipi" ("Have a wee!" Which means follow suit). Those games of cards were a ritual. They played cards every night of the week, except Sunday afternoons. Every night they would meet at whoever's place had their turn. It used to be Monday's at our place.

Usually there would be two tables going and the ones that had to wait for their turn would converse. I used to love it. Aunt Arlette (Allen's wife) was always knitting.

When you think of it, there was no television in those days, so this was their relaxation after a day's work. At least people got to really know each other and became very close. Those card games went on until we left Mauritius.

Poor Grand-Père was not feeling the best at the time. In fact, he suspected that it was serious, for he waited until after our departure to see a doctor who diagnosed cancer of the throat. He had been a heavy smoker all his life.

We left Mauritius in October and he passed away five months after, on March 4, 1966, the date of Marielle's twenty-first birthday. Grand-Père was seventy-five years old.

Grand-Mère was born Zelie Monnier. She is still alive. She turned 94 last August.

She has been a lady all her life and still takes care of her appearance. I have always seen Grand-Mère wearing high heel shoes whatever the time of day.

Initially her parents were quite comfortable financially. At first her Dad, Louis, owned a shop in Port Louis. Things went wrong and he lost the lot. As a result they became poor. Imagine, with twelve children. Grand-Mère suffered lots of tragedies in the loss of brothers and sisters. Roger was only about seven when he came home thirsty after school and drank rusty water out of a tap. As a result he suffered dysentry and died. He was about to make his Holy Communion and the clothes for the occasion were already made.

Grand-Mère tells me that before dying he said "Je peux voir Roger ecrit en lumiere dans le ciel" (I can see the word Roger lit up in heaven). Her father also died quite young, he was in his forties (she was 14 at the time). Louis Monnier passed away on New Years Eve 1909 after suffering a heart attack.

At his funeral was a first cousin of Grand-Mère, Frank Hobbs, who was born in England after his mother Emma, nee Pasque, had left Mauritius on her marriage to an Englishman.

He was on holidays in Mauritius at the time and was a sailor.

He was to die himself a couple of years later being an officer on the doomed Titanic's maiden voyage in April 1912.

There is some strange story that some member of the family had a psychic vision on his death bed of the sinking of the Titanic, shortly before it happened.

It is Stella Mackie (nee Bouchet) a descendant of Louis Monnier junior who told me about this. She got the story from her grandfather (he has passed away since).

Unfortunately, when I asked Grand-Mère she was not sure of the details. Anyway, someone did have a premonition or whatever for shortly after the Titanic did sink and a close member of the family was on board.

A freaky twist of fate is that France Monnier's wife, Ruth of South African origin, also lost a great uncle on the Titanic. He was violonist and pianist on board. As Lisa their daughter says, it is most probable that the two met.

So the eldest sister, Suzanne had to go to work, something that young ladies were not supposed to do in those days. It was while at work that she met her future husband, an Englishman, Andrew Watson.

Apparently Suzanne dreamt of the event after being encouraged by friends, for fun, to have a mirror and pair of scissors tied together, and having the full moon reflect off it she had to say "Belle lune! Beau Croissant! Fait moi voir, ce soir! En m'endormant celui que je dois epouser!" (Beautiful disc of full moon, while asleep tonight, make me see the face of the one I will marry!).

The blacks believed in those sort of things. Anyway, apparently it really worked for her, for the next day she told her excited friends that she had dreamt of a man walking into the shop where she worked and addressing her in English, wanting to buy a pair of spectacles. Apparently it really happened this way, and she married her Englishman and they moved to England where they lived happily ever after.

Maman tells me that she had always known her Mum with her hair tied back and never wearing sleeveless dresses, for past thirty a woman was considered old in those days.

Page 59

Also you could not talk to your Mum about such things as the birds and the bees, for it would be considered bad to think of such things.

Mum tells me that once she happened to mention that some lady they knew was "in the family way" and before she had finished the sentence she received a slap in the face and was asked where did she hear such a word. You can't really blame Grand-Mère. This was what it was like in those days, and she was herself brought up like that.

Actually nowadays, Grand-Mère has "rolled with the tide of change". I don't think she is aware of everything though. Not that I mean she is senile, but just innocent. If it is possible at 90!

Grand-Mère lost another brother, Edgar Monnier, who died of peritonitis when he was thirty.

Three brothers in fact, for the youngest one, Noel, drowned at Tamarin. He was in his twenties. There is a plaque with his name and that of another name, Britter, who also drowned in that accident. The memorial plaque is still standing. It was erected on the beach, facing the spot where it happened.

My grandfather, Francis Nozaïc, with wife Julie and their first born, my father France.

Another sister of hers also died young and left three children, a daughter and two sons. As her husband had passed away before her, the children were adopted by the family after her death.

The girl May went to live with her aunt's family (Edith Brousse), and the two boys were raised by Grand-Père and Grand-Mère. Their names were Guy and Pierre Rougier.

Pierre died in an institution. He was only in his twenties and had suffered a fall that caused some brain damage, so he could not be taken care of at home.

Grand-Mère came to live in Australia about a year after her husband's death. She lives with her daughter, Lise Mamet, in Brisbane.

She is a grand lady Grand-Mère. Always cheerful, and God knows it would be justified if she was otherwise, for she has survived two of her children, Tonton Leon (of cancer in 1973) and one of her daughters, Marcienne in 1981 (leukemia, she was only 48). Her son-in-law (Dad), daughter-in-law (Madeline), a great-granddaughter (Pauline Maujean) and at the beginning of the year, in February, her grandson (our cousin) Loulou (Louis Arnulphy) of a car accident in South Africa. He was in his early thirties and unmarried. To date she has lost all her brothers and sisters, save one, Tante Edith Brousse, one year her senior.

Francis and Julie Nozaïc, with children France, Madeleine and baby Noel.

Grand-Mère has never been able to master the English language. Think of it. She was in her seventies when she came here. She had never learnt English before.

When she first arrived, a few times she spoke French to the poor strangers that would knock at the door.

Maman also never learnt English at school. She always tells me that she first learnt it watching television. She still speaks in broken English, but had no trouble even when she lived alone for many years after Papa's death.

As for myself, I have retained this strong accent. It is now that I am becoming conscious of it when my children remark on how funny it sounds to them.

It is sad in a way that I do not know much about my Nozaïc grandparents. Specially Grand-Père, for I was only a toddler when he died. I remember my Dad's tears when it happened but was much too young to be affected by it. I have vague recollections of an old man who used to visit and give us lollies after giving us a gentle pat on the head with his cane that he used to walk with.

My parents, France and Myriam Nozaïc.

I know that they lived in Beau Bassin while their family was growing up. He came from a family of nine children (see Nozaïc genealogy). He was born Francis Nozaïc on the 27th of February, 1886 and married Grand-Mère Julie Charoux on the 9th of October, 1909. In fact, a sister of his, Odette, married his brother-in-law, Clement Charoux (the poet).

I know that he used to work at the docks at some stage. They owned a house in Rose-Hill where he passed away about three months after suffering a stroke that left him paralysed. Maman tells me that she used to go and give Grand-Mère a hand to take care of him, as her daughters lived too far away on sugar estates. Grand-Mère lived for years with Tante Claude, her youngest daughter who later married a Frenchman, Rene Baudoin, her pen pal who came to Mauritius to visit and asked her to marry him. At one stage, Grand-Mère, Claude, Rene and their daughter Arianne, who was about ten at the time, came to Australia to live, but they could not get used to the climate and went back.

Grand-Mère suffered from cataract and had lost sight in one eye. To help the other one, she wore double thickness glasses.

Of all of us, I would say that Marielle is the one who looks the most like her as compared to photos of her in her younger days. Grand-Mère was close to 90 when she passed away in 1975.

Papa was her eldest. He was born on the 14th of April, 1911 and was followed by six children (see Nozaïc genealogy). He did his schooling in Beau Bassin and had to leave school before obtaining his senior, when his father lost his job and he had to go to work to support the family.

He first worked as a school teacher in a public school, teaching Creole children. When he found out he was not cut out to be a teacher, he had a go at journalism when he joined a local paper. I don't think he lasted very long, because apparently being short of news to report one day, he proceeded to tell of an incident that he witnessed on the road. He wrote about a cow pulling a cart and tumbling on the side of the road into the gutter. His boss was not amused. (Imagine, a gutter story!).

When his father regained employment, Papa went back to school and obtained his HSC. He then started his career working for the government. He started at the bottom as copier (no photo copy machines in those days). He was paid so much per line. Apparently he had a co-worker who was very good at writing elaborately in a flourishing manner as to use only three words per line. (How clever. I don't know if he kept his job though).

Papa gradually went up the ladder, doing extra studies and obtaining his diplomas of chartered accountant. (In fact, I was quite astonished of all his qualifications as stated on his resume when he left Mauritius).

He reached the top, as Registrar General, and was respected by many.

I am very proud of my father. He was a very straight man, conscientious. He hated waste of any sort. I remember him telling us that even a pin or a paper clip should not be wasted, for added up to other things, it saved the company a lot of money. He still had the Email mug that he used as a junior.

At one stage Dad used to give lessons in accountancy as extra work, to have a bit of extra money as he was raising his young family. He was a very caring man. When as children, we used to wake up in the middle of the night due to sickness or because of a nightmare, it was Dad we called.

Papa seemed very stern to our friends, but he had a sense of humour. Prior to birthdays, he would ask us, "What would you like for your birthday? A sweet little red nothing, or a blue one?"

At night when we heard the crickets in the bushes, he used to tell us that they were "yooyootes". Little people having a secret life amongst the flora.

We used to love listening to his stories that would make us shake of fright, yet we would ask for them to be retold again and again. Especially the one about the monkey's paw that I will tell you about in a minute, but first I must mention that when we were getting out of hand, he would ask us to stop, or else he would unscrew our heads and put them on top of his study cabinet. The story went like this:

"There was once a couple who had an only son. When he grew into a man, he went away to war, to the desolation of his poor parents.

"Later on, when they were told that he had died in action, their grief knew no bound. Especially the poor mother, who became very distraught.

"One day his wife was beside herself with grief and he racked his brains trying to think of something to cheer her up. He suddenly remembered about the time when he had done an old gypsy a favour, and in recognition she had given him a small box containing a monkey's paw, all dried up and shrivelled. And she had solemnly told him that it had some magic powers, that when invoked, would grant him three wishes.

"So he decided that now was a good time to test it. For after all, what did he have to lose? He was desperate.

"So he held his dear wife by the hand and took her to the front of the house, in the sitting room, where they sat side by side on the sofa and opening the box very slowly . . . he asked his wife to trust him and not to interrupt. He held the monkey's hand in the palm of his hand, and his wife uttered a scream that she soon muffled, remembering her husband's warning not to interfere.

"Staring at the paw, with its long nails, that looked like claws, he uttered the words (all of us children by then were sitting on the edge of our seats, and Dad took this deep voice to say): Please have mercy! Make our son live again!

"They waited patiently, not very sure of what to expect to happen next.

They were very quiet ... shhh! ... all ears! ... listening to every sound ... nothing! A bit impatient, the man made a second wish: Give us our son back! The paw quivered...

"They waited again ... this time ... they heard the cre-e-eaking of the iron gate as it moved on its hinges. Click! It shut! (Sound by Papa of a clanging gate). They heard footsteps! ... ever so faint at first, that went ploc! ploc! ploc! ... the sound of boots approaching! The husband and wife moved closer and held each other ... ploc! ploc! ploc! ... the sound of boots on the gravel path, leading to the house. They started to sweat! They had an eerie feeling! ... panic rose to their throat as they saw and heard the door knob slo-o- o-owly starting to turn! They felt that there was some supernatural being close! ... as the door was about to open! ... the wife quickly took hold of the monkey's paw and said: Make our son rest in peace!

"At this point, they both uttered a sigh of relief as the sound stopped, and they heard the receding sound of the boots on the gravel! ... ploc! ... ploc! ... ploc! And the gate to open up and close again, and all was at peace. Ever so quiet! And the mother finally realised that she had to let go. As long as her son was resting in peace, she would find the strength to carry on. After all, she still had her husband, and she would see her son one day."

I must confess that the last paragraph was added to the story by me, because I could not remember the ending. I suppose this stems from the fact that as children, we probably lost interest as soon as we realised that the danger was avoided. As you can imagine, we were spellbound by those stories.

Papa used to exercise every day. I can still see him in his boxer shorts, bare chested and doing push-ups. So it was every afternoon after work that we would interrupt with questions concerning our homework. (We were teenagers. Mum helped the petites).

He was ever so patient. Until one day when I suppose I must have pushed it too far when I asked him to give me some ideas about an English essay that I had to do on (would you believe it?) a conversation between a piano and a wall of the school's hall. (It suddenly clicked that the nun, our teacher, probably wanted to know what we were up to).

Anyway, one sentence that Papa helped me with went like this: Wall to piano - "What the hell are you doing here?"

Well! I was blissfully unaware, not being familiar with the English language, of the implication of that sentence, and was quite proud of the finished work until Mere Bernice called me quietly to her desk and in a whispering voice asked me how did I think of this sentence?

Not wanting to tell her that Dad had helped me, I said that I found it in the dictionary (would you believe? I must check if it is mentioned there!). She was quite civil about the matter and gently explained to me that young ladies did not use such language!

I wanted to say to her that it was not me talking but the d.... wall, but I was a good girl and was grateful that I had escaped some form of punishment.

Maman was born on the 9th day of May, 1924. She was named Myriam and used to be called Mimi by her family. She met Papa when she was only thirteen years old, but I was told that she looked older.

Papa was thirteen years her senior, and did not declare his love until a few years later. They got engaged when she was eighteen, and was married at nineteen on the 11th of January, 1943. Their first born, Ivan, came into the world eleven months after on the 16th of December of the same year.

Writing this book, I asked Maman for a few details about that special event in their life, their wedding. Mum sent me a letter with details of the reception etc. It is sad, but Mum has no photos of that special day because the photographer bungled up his job.

Quite a few things happened that nearly ruined their day according to Maman's account. First, there was a cyclone warning No. 3 (fairly important category), and the gusts of wind were so strong that they nearly flattened the type of marquee, a shelter where the wedding reception was to take place in the family garden, covered with coconut fronds and flowers. A salle verte as it was called. Luckily the cyclone moved away before they had to cancel it.

The next bad luck was that both my parents suffered an attack of malaria and burned up, not only with love, but high fever as well. Mum tells me that they had to sit down while the toast was being proposed, for their legs would not support them.

They were married at New Grove church. A certain Mrs Bestel sang the traditional "Ave Maria" de Gounault. My grandparents place where the reception took place was in Eau-Bleu (blue water) sugar estate.

Roger Mamet was the family friend who made the speech that feeling so wretched, they had to sit through. Fine pair.

At around nine, they left for their honeymoon to a deserted (private) island called Mouchoir Rouge, that had only one campement. How romantic. They were chauffeur driven by Bobonne, the family chauffeur who used to take her to school. Apparently Bobonne had celebrated a bit too much at the wedding and was over the limit, managing to get lost on the way, and finally they made it there.

Alas, the next day, they had to go back and put an end to the dreamed of honeymoon, as poor Papa's health got worse from malaria.

A week later when Papa had recovered, they went back to the island to fetch all their gear. And guess what? Irony of it all, all my Dad's handkerchiefs had been stolen. (Mouchoir rouge means "red handkerchief on red handkerchief island).

Ivan my brother suffered from gastro-enteritis when he was eleven month's old, and Mum was expecting her second child, Marielle.

Mum tells me that as Ivan could not keep anything in his stomach, she saved his life by giving him a teaspoon full of water every five minutes for 48 hours.

Maman is of the worrying type. It must be hereditary, because Grand-Mère was a worrier too, I am told. I am also guilty of it to a certain point, but try to modify it as I have had examples of Mum worrying herself sick, when everything turned out fine in the end. But still, sometimes the genes are stronger.

For instance, Maman used to fuss terribly over Sylvianne's health because she had a heart murmur as a child. Some of us became a bit jealous because of it and we always thought that Sylvianne was her favourite, until Mum told me that it was just because on the day that Sylvianne was diagnosed, she had heard about a little girl who was born on the same day as her and had died of the same ailment.

So she became overly anxious about it, thus all the fuss to us. Poor Maman would wake up in the middle of the night and go and check if she was still breathing. Apparently, for fear of being ridiculed, she kept it secret. I must mention that luckily nothing bad came of it. As she grew up the murmur healed itself. The only thing is that in those days it was thought that to keep her healthy she should gain some more weight. As a result, Sylvianne has this weight problem caused by an eating disorder.

On the other hand, I used to be skinny as a child. As a teenager, Ivan used to say that I was like a piece of string with two knots, one for the boobs and one for the knees! To get back at me when I offended them, my sisters called me verre (worm).

I could not finish this chapter without telling you about Tante Julie, a special great aunt that I was very fond of as she used to visit us almost every day.

Tante Julie was my grandmother's (Arnulphy) youngest sister. Apparently she was quite a beauty. (I literally mean it!). Rose-Marie, my sister, looks very much like her with olive skin and very fine features, striking black eyes and hair.

Tante Julie became quite thin in her older days and she always dressed in fitted skirts and high heel shoes that I absolutely adored.

She was a chain smoker. She even beat Maman, who smoked a lot herself! (Not Dad!).

Tante Julie is the person who introduced me to the magic world of books. She was a book addict, but only of romance types though. As I don't think she had anything to boast about in that department, it served its purpose and I am sure it was a blessed escape.

She revelled reading the ones written by "Delly", a version of the modern "Mills and Boon" and more sugary.

Julie also loved to tell spicy jokes. She would laugh so much while telling them, that sitting down she would bend over and touch the floor with one hand while the other one held the permanent cigarette. Just looking at her was enough to make you laugh. I don't mean it in a mocking way. She also went to the movies every week and would give us her own colourful account of it.

She loved dogs and had about four pekinese, you know, the shaggy ones whose eyes are covered by their fur. So when we visited her, we would be greeted by the dogs that would playfully leap on us when she opened her front door.

Once while visiting her, we all decided to go and climb Colline Candos, a hill not very far from her place. It was during school holidays and quite early in the morning. Dad was at work and so was her husband. Most of us females, including Maman, Tante Julie and the nénenne and her younger son Eric took a full day to go up and down. At some places, it was so steep that we were on our hands and knees. But did we laugh. When we reached the top we had some tomato and peanut butter sandwiches and tomango juice (some type of cordial). I would say that this was the most strenuous adventure of my life, but it was worth it.

I will conclude this family chapter by telling you the meaning of Nozaïc. A Breton name, Noz means night and ahic - it is thought that was how it was originally spelt - means summer song. In French it is "chant de la petite nuit" (short summer night's song).

The first Nozaïc to come to Mauritius to live was Louis Nozaïc, who was born in Britanny in 1731. He married Marie- Jeanne Trauden.

Louis arrived in the colony on the ship "Les Deux Amies" (The Two Friends) in 1773. He was 42 years old and was accompanied by his young son, Etienne who was only five at the time.

I got all this information from a census form dated in the 1800s. There is no information on that form about his wife, Jeanne, so I wonder if she did come to Mauritius and passed away before the census or perhaps died in Britanny or passed away on board ship. At this stage I am waiting on some information concerning this matter.

Papa was very interested in his family genealogy and his job facilitated all the information he had gathered. Like all the birth and marriage certificates of every single one dating to the first.

It is interesting to note that the young son, François Etienne Nozaïc got married when he was nearly twenty-one to Anne Marie Bulle who was only fourteen years old at the time.

The man that Papa succeeded as Registrar General, Mr Raoul Brouard was a descendant of that union. He even gave Papa a photograph of his grandmother, a Jeanne Nozaïc.

It has been so interesting going through all these papers. It was a bit like detective work, but I enjoyed every minute of it.

The first Maujean to arrive in the colony was Nicolas Maujean, who was born in Metz, Departement de la Rochelle. He travelled on board "Les Deux Cousins" (The Two Cousins) in 1784. Unfortunately there is no record to show how old he was at the time. I am presently waiting on information as I said earlier, so I cannot wait.

Following is a brief history of the Nozaïc generations.

1st Generation:
Louis Nozaïc - Marine carpenter, born in Vannes (Morbihan District) Britany, in 1731. Passed away in Port Louis, Ile de France, on the 10th of March, 1792.

Louis arrived at Isle de France in 1773, at the age of 42 on board the ship "Les Deux Amies" (The Two Friends) accompanied by his son François Etienne, aged 5. I presume he was a widower as there is no mention of his wife Jeanne (nee Trauden) on a census list in my possession.

2nd Generation:
François Etienne Nozaïc - Born in Port Louis (Britany) on the 17th of June, 1768 in the parish of St Radegonde. Arrived in this colony with his father in 1773 aged five as mentioned above.

He was married at 21 on the 16th of January, 1789 to fourteen-year-old Marie-Anne Bulle, daughter of Louis Bulle and Jeanne Louise Perrin. The marriage took place in Flacq.

The witnesses were: Savois W. Perrin and Guillaume Pierre Perrin, Mathieu Jacques Renaux and Thoreas Reland, maternal uncles of the bride.

Their union produced five children:

Louis Noazic. Born 3-8-1790, deceased 28-10-1792.

Marie-Louise Nozaïc. Married Nicholas François Brouard at Flacq on 25-5-1810.

François Nozaïc. Born 17-1-1795, deceased 21-6-1797 at Flacq.

Edouard François Etienne Nozaïc. Born in Flacq on 28-11-1797. Married Suzanne Aglaé Peltier.

Jeanne Louise Nozaïc. Born 6-2-1802. Married Guillaume Honoré Brouard, son of Ambroise Brouard and Marie-Jeanne Bressin, in Flacq in 1820.

François Etienne took the Oath of Allegiance to the British monarch, George III in 1810 in Flacq when the British took possession of the island, Isle de France, that year.

The oath read like this:

"Nous Jurons fidelité, obeissance et soumission à sa Majesté George III, Roi de Grande Bretagne et d'Irlande, et au governement Anglais dans cette colonie."

Translation: We pledge fidelity, obediance and submission to his majesty George III, King of Great Britain and Ireland, and to the British Government of this colony.

The oath was signed by my ancestor at the Sunray Hotel of Mauritius. The inhabitants of Isle de France had a choice to either leave the island and go back to France with their financial possessions or stay and take the Oath of Allegiance to the new government.

François Etienne's wife, Marie-Anne passed away on the 11th of March, 1802, possibly from complications resulting from giving birth to her daughter, Jeanne Louise, five weeks earlier. She was 27 years old.

3rd Generation:
Edouard François Etienne Nozaïc - Born 28-11-1797, died 9-1-1840. He was 23 years old when he married 21-year-old Suzanne Aglaé Peltier, daughter of Louis Peltier and Marie-Françoise Castel. The marriage took place in Flacq on the 18th of April, 1820.

Witnesses to this event were:
Edouard Perrin, 65 years old, great uncle of the bridegroom; Nicolas François Brouard, 44 years old, brother-in-law of the groom; François Marie Privol, 67 years old, and Guillaume Castel, 62 years old, uncles of the bride.

Their union produced three children that I know of:
Edouard François Alphonse Nozaïc. Born 9-2-1821.
Louis Evenor Nozaïc. Born 24-8-1822. Deceased 27-7-1823.
Etienne Simon Selmour Nozaïc. Born 26-9-1826. Deceased 1-4-1827.

François Etienne passed away before the marriage of his son at the age of 43.

4th Generation:
Edouard François Alphonse Nozaïc - Born on the 9th of February, 1821. He was 19 years old when he married his cousin, Marie-Louise Angeline Perrin, daughter of Louis Edouard Perrin and Louise Tabardin in Flacq on the 20th of April, 1840 at 10 o'clock in the morning at St Julien church.

Witnesses to the wedding were:
M. Jean-Baptiste Perrin, 50 years old, uncle of the bride; François Ambroise Brouard, 25 years old, cousin of the bridegroom; Jean-Baptiste de Launay, 55 years old, maternal uncle of the bridegroom.

I don't know how many children their union produced.

5th Generation:
Edouard Felix Nozaïc - Born in Mauritius on the 2th of October, 1848. Passed away on the 17th of August, 1904 at the age of 56.

He was married to Marie Suzanne Jollivet, daughter of Isodore Jollivet and Angelique Laure Perrot, in the afternoon of Monday the 19th of June, 1876.

The groom was 27 years old and the bride 22.

On his marriage certificate his occupation is listed as Chief Douser.

Witnesses to the marriage were:

Laure Bussy de St Romain, estate manager of Plaine-Wilhems; Edouard Nozaïc, planter of st Wilhems; Pierre Antoine Jollivet, barrister of law in Port Louis; Louis Alphonse Lavoipierre, sworn broker.

Their union produced nine children including my grandfather, Francis Nozaïc.

Francis Noziac. Married Julie Charoux.
Felix Nozaïc. Married Isabelle de Fontenay (migrated to South Africa).
Raoul Nozaïc. Married Alice d'Hotman de Villiers (migrated to South Africa).
Odette Nozaïc. Married Clément Charoux (poet).
Giselle Nozaïc. Married Carl D'unienville.
Andree Nozaïc. Married Fernand Trebuchet.
Eva Nozaïc. Married Maxime Deschamps.
Marthe Nozaïc. Married Eugène Deschamps.
Edith Nozaïc. Spinster.

6th Generation:
Joseph Alphonse Armand Francis Nozaïc - My grandfather. He was born in Mauritius on Esperance Sugar Estate on the 29th of February, 1886.

At the age of 23 he married Marie Julie Charoux, daughter of Jules Charoux and Marie Clemence Bega on the 9th of October, 1909 at noon.

Their union produced 7 children:

Jules Felix Joseph France Nozaïc. My father.
Noel Nozaïc. Married Lily Mackie (divorced). Children: Jean Nozaïc (deceased); Noelle Nozaïc (South Africa); Guy Nozaïc (South Africa). Mario Nozaïc married Jeanine Mackie.
Madeleine Nozaïc. Married Pierre Masson (deceased).
Roland Nozaïc. Married Genevieve Suzor. Children: Christiane Nozaïc; Joelle Nozaïc; Françoise Nozaïc; Pascale Nozaïc; Suzelle Nozaïc married my cousin Leon Arnulphy, Australia.
Rose-May Nozaïc. Married Henry Masson (divorced). Children: Aubrey Masson (South Africa); Alain Masson (South Africa); Jacqueline Masson married Paul Descroizille and have one child, Isabelle Descroizille.

Thérèse Nozaïc. (My Godmother). Married Roger Doger de Speville. Children:
Roger de Speville married Catherine Bianchi.
Sylvain de Speville married Georgina Maurel (divorced) and their children: Denis de Speville, de facto to Roselyne Maujean, have one child, Krysten Emily Doger de Speville; Joséphine de Speville de facto to Paul Jorgensen and have one child, Marc Jorgensen (Queensland, Australia).
Daniel de Speville married charlotte Maurel.
Marianne de Speville married Robert Lemaire (Reunion Island). Children: Philippe Lemaire; Virginie Lemaire; Emanuela Lemaire.
Dominic de Speville married Wendy Hector (Australia).
Jean-Michel de Speville (Australia).
Claude Nozaïc. Married Rene Baudoin. Children: Arianne Baudouin married Eric Buonino (France) and had two daughters: Morgane and Maïle.

7th Generation - My father:
Jules Felix Joseph France Nozaïc - Born in Mauritius on the 14th April, 1911 in Beau Bassin. At the age of 32 he married Marie Zelie Myriam Arnulphy, daughter of Eugène and Zelie Arnulphy, when she was 19 years old on the 11th January, 1943.
They migrated to Australia in October, 1965.
They had seven children:
Ivan Nozaïc. Married Françoise Hoarau (born in Madagascar). Their children are: François, Joelle and Laïta.
Marielle Nozaïc. Married Yves Fay d'Herbe de Maudave. Their children are: Michael, Caroline and Sandra. Grandchildren: Cairo, Jordan, Alexandria, Grace, Liberty and Jeremy.
Micheline Nozaïc. Married Jean-Claude Maujean. Children: Pauline (deceased), Miriam, Dominic and Daniel.
Marie-Josée Nozaïc. (Myself). Married Philippe Maujean Jnr. Children: Patrick, Roselyne. Grandchild: Krysten Doger de Speville.
Sylvianne Nozaïc. Married Jean-Raymond Mallac. Children: Veronique, Corinne, Sophie and Tristan. Grandchild: Kayla Austin.
Marie-France Nozaïc. Married Gilles Mackie (divorced). Children: Gilles, Denis and Nicholas.
Rose-Marie Nozaïc. Married François Audibert. Children: Geraldine, Eric and Catherine.

8th Generation:
Paul France Ivan Nozaïc - My brother. He was born in Mauritius on the 16th December, 1943. He married Françoise Genevieve Hoarau in Melbourne, Australia on the 16th December, 1980 at the age of 37.

They have three children: François, Joelle and Laita.

9th Generation:
François Ivan Nozaïc - Born in Melbourne, Australia.

My father passed away on the 7th January, 1971 at the age of 59. My mother married Arthur Hogan on the 22nd November, 1987.

My aunt, Claude Nozaïc, told me about her great-great Grandmother, Elise Talbot-Bega, who allegedly had premonitory dreams on several occasions during her life.
This is her story as reported by her great Granddaughter (my Grandmother, Julie Charoux Nozaïc) to her daughter Tante Claude. (See Nozaïc genealogy).
From my calculations Elise must have been born between 1797 and 1800.
Young Elise lived at a time when there were slaves on the island. She loved nature and was quite friendly with the young natives that lived on her family's property in the District of Pamplemousses.
At 15 Elise had a dream where she saw this man that she had never met in real life who told her that soon some great happiness would befall her in the form of somebody coming from the sea.
Not very long after, while she was enjoying her time gathering flowers and collecting the freshly laid eggs on her property, she was called to the house for they had received a visitor.
Young Elise was a bit annoyed for at this age she felt she had better things to do than sit inside with some boring visitor.
As a dutiful daughter she did as she was asked and met this young man, Leopold Bega, a sea captain.
Apparently she was asked to sing for him and play the piano as was the custom in those days. Elise did not know the lyrics to any special song, so she improvised a song that started like this: "The young Elise, is she a good singer or not?".
She later married this sea captain.
Her second premonition happened while she was married with two children.
She saw a bearded man that she did not know (like in her first) who told her she would suffer a tragedy while she had her two children and expecting a third.
One night while her husband was at sea, she was woken up by the sound of church bells ringing for a funeral. She found it odd to happen in the middle of the night and opened the windows to make sure she was hearing right.

Page 73

She called her servant while she could still hear it and asked her if she could hear the bells, to which the servant answered "No!".

The Goelette "Le Solide" ("The Strong") never came back to return her husband. It had disappeared never to be found.

One night Elise had a third dream. She saw a beach with debris lying about, like after a shipwreck. Men coming and going, a corpse lying on the beach covered except for the feet, and she heard a man talk to another in a tone of command, saying: "It's Captain Bega. Make sure to give him a proper burial."

She was expecting her third child. She remembered that other dream and was certain her husband would never come back.

She gave birth to a son, Leopold, after two older daughters.

She had three children to raise on her own. She had to do some type of work to survive.

She sewed christening bonnets that she used to sell to a lady who owned a shop in Port Louis. By this time she had gone back to the family home in Pamplemousses and used to travel to Port Louis in a carriage

One night she had a fourth dream. Again she saw the bearded man who said to her: "Here is the one who will change your fate, his name is Amédée". She saw this young man and his features stayed engraved in her mind.

One day while she was at the lady's shop delivering a new supply of bonnets, there was a knock on the door and a young man entered. Elise recognised the man of her dream while her hostess said: "May I present you my brother, Amédée".

As you know, he became her second husband.

Her two daughters, Olivia and Emilie became nuns at the Bon Perpetuel Secours convent in 1861 and 1863 as Sister Pacome and Sister Jerome.

From that second union, a daughter was born. She was named Elise Marmarot.

While she was old, Elise lived with her son Leopold Bega, in Beau Bassin. He had married his cousin, Françoise Hoarau.

Grandma used to visit her quite often at her grandparents place where she lived in a room of her own at the back of the house. Apparently she always had something interesting to hand out on those visits, be it a satin ribbon or a piece of lace that she would fetch from a large trunk.

Elise was buried at the cemetery of Bois Marchand not far from Port Louis. As a new highway going towards the north of the island passes through the cemetery, most graves have disappeared.

She still lives on, that young Elise, for her story has been brought to me some five generations later.

PERSONAL RECORD

```
NAME        J.P.J.F. NOZAIC, Registrar General, Government of Mauritius,
            retired.
AGE    55.  DATE OF BIRTH   14-4-1911.
NATIONALITY British.
ADDRESS     12 Rowena Road, Chadstone.
TELEPHONE No.  56-7188.
MARITAL STATUS  Married.
HEALTH  Good.
MAURITIUS GOVERNMENT SERVICE   1929 - 1965.
LAST APPOINTMENT  Registrar General, Head of Registrar'General's
                  Department.
                  (In MAURITIUS - a British Crown Colony - the
                  Registrar General is :
                     (a) Registrar of Births, Deaths and Marriages.
                     (b) Registrar of Lands and Mortgages.
                     (c) Registrar of Companies.
                     (d) Receiver of Registration and Succession Dues.)
LANGUAGES   Equal knowledge of ENGLISH and FRENCH.
EDUCATION   Certificates held :
            1. CAMBRIDGE SCHOOL CERTIFICATE
               (credit in 6 subjects, including English, and
               distinction in French).
            2. HIGHER CERTIFICATES OF THE LONDON CHAMBER OF COMMERCE :
               (i)   Book-Keeping and Accountancy
               (ii)  Commerce and Finance
               (iii) Banking and Currency
               (iv)  Company Law  (distinction)
               (v)   Commercial Law   -do-
               (vi)  Economics        -do-
               (vii) Shorthand.
            3. Intermediate Certificate of the ASSOCIATION OF
               CERTIFIED AND CORPORATE ACCOUNTANTS (LONDON).
PRESENT OCCUPATION   Private teacher of French.
POSITION SOUGHT                      Office Clerk.
                                     Might be useful to Accountant
                                     (public or private) or as French
                                     Correspondence Clerk, or Interpreter
                                     or Translator.

SALARY DESIRED  About        dollars.
ADDITIONAL INFORMATION  Pensioner of the Government of MAURITIUS.
                        Settled in AUSTRALIA in October, 1965.

   DATE .....................
                          SIGNATURE ...............................
                                     (Jules F.J.F. NOZAIC)
```

A copy of my Dad's personal record when he left Mauritius.

COLONIAL SECRETARY'S OFFICE
MAURITIUS

30th January, 1961.

My dear Nozaic,

    I should like to repeat in writing the verbal congratulations, which I was very happy to be able to pass on to you last week, on your promotion to be Registrar General. I offer you my warmest good wishes in your term of office in this important post. I know that Government can depend upon you to see that your Department remains an efficient and happy element in the Government machine.

Yours very sincerely,

Tom Vickers.

F. Nozaic Esq.,
  Registrar General,
    Port Louis.

A letter from the Colonial Secretary's Office congratulating my father on his appointment as Registrar General.

CHAPTER 7

Those great people of the past . . .
Berenger and Canton Families

My husband's grandmother, Josephine Pauline Canton, was born in Sainte-Marie (a dependance of Madagascar) on the 9th of August, 1883 at six o'clock in the morning. (I have a copy of the birth certificate written in old French).

Her father, Paul Esprit Canton was then retired as port captain of St Marie, a penal colony. He was born in Cannes, France and was Capitaine au Long Cours (a sea captain) when he met his wife from Mauritius, Elodie Boulay. I have a medal with both their names engraved in commemoration of their wedding, with the date 27th of December, 1865.

When your great-great-grandmother (Pauline) was born, her parents were then quite old in a way, as stated on the birth certificate. He was sixty-one and herself forty-two.

Now I realise why she was orphaned so young (about twelve). As a result her sister Louise (who never married and was called Tantine by her nephews) and herself went to Mauritius to live with some relatives of theirs. The family of Tristan Avis. (I forgot to mention another sister, Marie, who also went to Mauritius with them).

From all the information I received from Tante Jeanne (D'Unienville) prior to her death this year, Pauline did not have an easy life as she lost many brothers and sisters.

Her eldest brother was Pierre Canton. Born in Sainte-Marie he died of poisoning by the natives when fairly young.

Then came Louise who I mentioned before. She was followed by another son, Joseph, who was also poisoned and died as a result. He was followed by Pauline.

Pauline married your great-great-grandfather, Jean Honore Raoul Berenger on the 23rd of February, 1911.

Pauline Berenger (nee Canton)

He was also a sea captain. (I have a copy of his certificate of competency as Master in the merchant navy. That was obtained on the 8th of March, 1902. All the information concerning him goes like this (again Tante Jeanne D'Unienville provided me with the details).

Jean Honoré Raoul Berenger was born on the 20th of May, 1882. He was the fourth in line of eight children to Marie (nee Basset) and Jean Honore Nemour Berenger.

His mother was first married to a Mr Boulle (Mauritian). She had a daughter from that union called Blanche. (Blanche married Hippolyte Montigny and later on they went to Singapore to live).

After the death of her first husband, Marie remarried to Jean Honore Nemour Berenger. Their children were as follows:

Louise Berenger: Died of typhoid when she was fifteen years old.

Paul Berenger: Died when only fourteen of some hematurique fever.

Gaston Berenger: Born in 1880. Married a girl of the Henkins family. He died in Marseilles, France in 1929 as a result of a factory accident.

Raoul Berenger: Your grandfather. Born 20th February, 1882. Died at sea on the 13th March, 1938.

Eliane Berenger: Born in France in 1884. Died in England.

Roger Berenger: Born and died in Marseilles, France. He also married a girl of the Henkins family.

Marcel Berenger: Born in France and had three daughters, Marie-Louise, André and Marcelle.

Fernande Berenger: Born in France. Later on moved to England on the request of her pen-friend to be a companion to her as she dreaded living alone after her husband's death. When the friend died, she left her mansion that they lived in with all her possessions to Tante Nan, as she was called.

Life has a strange twist sometimes, for little did she know that moving to England was to fulfill her destiny as when she was very old and was visiting her friend's grave, she was assassinated by a young man while her mansion was being ransacked. Later on when caught, the young man confessed that he got the idea after watching the movie "Clockwork Orange". This reminds me that I have never seen the movie and it would be interesting to see what it was all about. Tante Nan as she was affectionately called was also the writer that I mentioned before.

Coming back to your great-grandparents who had eight children, they also had their share of tragedies.

Marcelle Berenger: Born in Seychelles Island in July, 1913. She married Auguste Esnouf in 1936. Her children were Jacques Esnouf born in Kenya (Africa) in February, 1938; Francette, also born in Kenya in 1939; Raoul Esnouf, born in February, 1943 and Josée, born in September, 1945.

Jeanne Berenger: Born in Seychelles on the 28th of May, 1914. Died in Durban (South Africa) on the 27th of February, 1990. I met Tante Jeanne on her first visit to Australia in the 70's. She came a second time in the 80's accompanied by her daughter, Francine.

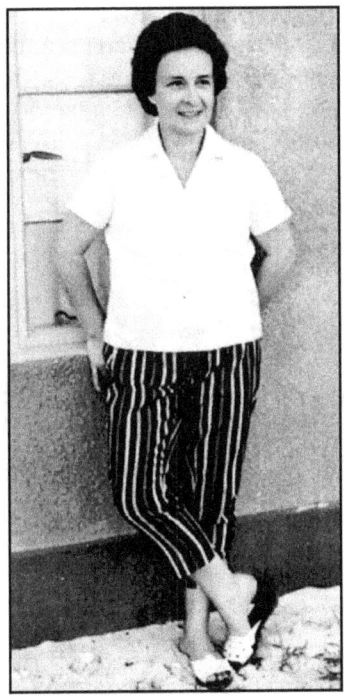

Yolande Berenger

She was a gentle-spoken woman, and I held her in great affection. I never met her late husband, Henri. He was a first cousin of my father, as his mother, Giselle Nozaïc was my grandfather's sister who married Carl D'Unienville. On Tante Jeanne's wedding that took place in Mauritius before they went to South Africa to live, Marielle my elder sister was a flower girl with Marcel Maujean as page boy. So, the rapport between the Nozaïcs and Maujeans started many years before the alliances. Tante Jeanne was also Popy's godmother. Tante Jeanne had a son, Jean-Henri, who married Diane Brokenshaw. Their children: Jean-Luc born 11th November, 1979; Nicole born 14th February, 1981 and Leandra born 20th March, 1983.

Yolande Berenger: Born on Seychelles Island on 1st February, 1916. Tante Yol lives in Cairns. She used to be a school teacher in Mauritius and ran her own school, Ecole Berenger, in Curepipe. She taught all her nephews during their primary years. Until they got married, her sisters Jeanne, Paule and Violette taught at the school. Tante Yol is like a second mother to Popy. Especially as he used to board at her place while attending St Joseph's school in Curepipe. It is sad that she never married and bore children as she would have been a perfect mother. What she missed she ful- filled by nurturing all the babies of the family. The first one, Pauline, was the apple of her eyes. When she first worked in Australia and could afford it, she used to dote on her and all the rest of them with clothes and toys. Tante Yol used to work hard and was very much appreciated at Vulcan, a factory producing heaters where she worked on the assembly line at Burwood in Victoria. Later on when the Maujean families moved up north to Cairns, she also followed and used to live with Roger and her sister Paule.

The Under-Secretary of State for War presents his compliments and by Command of the Army Council has the honour to transmit the enclosed Awards granted for service during the war of 1939-45.

John Nemour Berenger and the notice he received from the War Department regarding his awards for service during WWII.

Now Tante Yol lives in a flat on her own as she has for the last twelve years. Unfortunately she suffers of diabetes and is in poor health at the moment after suffering a stroke last December that partially paralysed her right side. Luckily after numerous physiotherapy sessions, she has regained much, but she still has difficulty in writing so she uses a tape recorder to communicate with the family overseas.

Nemour Berenger: Known as Uncle John. Born on Seychelles Island on the 5th October, 1917. He left Mauritius in 1938 when he was twenty years old, the same year that his father was lost at sea, to find work and be able to help his mother financially as she still had some young children to raise on her own. John went to Kenya where he first worked as a photographer until the Second World War broke out and he enlisted in the armed forces. He was part of the East African Reconnaissance Regiment. Part of the First Squadron, then No. 2 Regiment. John fought the war in armoured cars. Of his regiment, a third lost their lives. John gave me some of the medals he obtained as a result. After the war, he settled in Kenya and started an apprenticeship as a fitter. He later married Eleanor Riley, a Scottish nurse he had met during the war, in 1953. In the 1960s they came to Australia to live. They never had children. It is at their place in Victoria that the two Maujean families stayed on their arrival until the time they found a job and could move out to their house. Later on John and Aunty Eleanor moved to Cairns, from Brisbane, the same year that Roselyne was born, 1975. They bought a house in Melaleuca Street, Manoora, where Uncle John still lives on his own after Eleanor's death in 1989.

Jessie Berenger: Born in Seychelles on 16th September, 1919. Died in Mauritius on 21st January, 1934 when she was only fourteen years old.

Jessie Berenger

Sisters Violette and Lily Berenger

The whole family had gone on a picnic to the beach at Souillac.

A bus was chartered for the special occasion, as a first cousin of the children, René Montigny, was on vacation in Mauritius from France where he was a champion swimmer. The drama happened when René was showing his cousin Jessie how to swim. They were caught in a current and drifted out to sea. Apparently René could have saved himself, but going after Jessie to help, he lost his life also. The bodies were never found. Jessie's father forced a native who owned a boat to take him to sea to rescue them. Seeing the danger, the fisherman hit him on the head and knocked him unconscious.

Yolande and Violette tell me that it was terrible for them to be standing motionless on the beach and watch them gradually disappear out of sight. Yolande tells me that a priest later came and sent a blessing towards the sea. How sad it must have been for the family to leave their loved ones behind. On the bus that morning, Jessie had told them about the dream she had the

Violette Maujean (nee Berenger)

night before that she was going to die, and she commented: "Anyway, I am not scared to die, because I received communion this morning". At the special memorial mass that the nuns of the convent she attended had organised, they issued a photo of her with the French inscription underneath that read: "Je n'ai pas peur de mourir! J'ai communié ce matin!". The translation means "I do not fear death! I received holy communion this morning!". Rene Montigny was in his early forties and fortunately was a bachelor.

Paule Berenger: Tante Toto, born in Mauritius on 28th August, 1921. Married Roger Maujean.

Lily Berenger: Born in Mauritius on the 9th January, 1924. Died the 8th December, 1942. Lily was only 18 years old when she died of peritonitis. When she was operated on, it was too late. She regained consciousness and passed away with her family around her. I was told that Lily was a girl full of life. She used to share a room with her younger sister by one year, Violette. Apparently they even dressed alike and thus were very close. They had all been to the movies the night before her death and she started feeling ill.

As she had been eating mangoes during the day, they thought she was suffering of indigestion. When the doctor was called as her condition worsened, he sent her straight to hospital for an operation. There were no antibiotics in those days, and the infection had spread. Violette had her senior exams the next day and Lily told her not to worry, she wouldn't be able to have them the next day as she probably was aware of her condition. It is sad to note that her death occured just four years after their Dad disappeared at sea. Poor mother!

Violette Berenger: Born in Mauritius on the 3rd July, 1925 (your great-grandmother). She married Louis Philippe Maujean on the 10th November, 1947.

It is worth mentioning that Raoul Berenger was shipwrecked twice before the final one when he lost his life.

It was on the way back from Africa with a load of cattle on board the "Agnar" as chief officer under Captain Loiseau. They were caught in a cyclone just after leaving Madagascar. The authorities did not find out until the end of the year (1938), when a warship on transit in Mauritius alerted the Rogers Company that it had witnessed the sinking of a steamer on the
13th March. I have a newspaper clipping dating back to 1938. I think it came from an African newspaper.

As mentioned in that newspaper clip, Raoul Berenger was the captain of the steamer "Cigale" that sank between Mauritius and Reunion in 1924 with great loss of life.

I believe as it is the norm, there was an inquest after which Captain Berenger was demoted, after some relatives pressed charges.

However, apparently later on he cleared his name. As it happened such a long time ago, the details are a bit sketchy. What Violette knows is that the steamer was carrying a cargo of petrol, and apparently before the travel, somebody had approached him asking to travel on board the ship incognito, as he could not afford to pay and was prepared to work on board ship. Captain Berenger refused.

It is believed that the same man was a stowaway who probably lit a cigarette that started the explosion. When the captain was a survivor, seeing that many people lost their lives, it was probably contested that a captain should be the last one to leave his ship.

It is very hard to really know what happens when fire is involved. He might have been obstructed on one side as it must have happened very fast.

In 1935 he survived a second one as second-in-charge on the barque "Diego" near L'ile D'aigle (Eagle Island). There was a book written about it by Father Roger Dussercle, a missionary priest of Mauritius who used to travel to the islands of the Chagos Archipelago and was a passenger on board. I have the book and read it a few months ago.

Unfortunately it is written in French. However, there is an English report of the matter that I will write for you.

Beforehand, I will mention that they were going to Eagle Island to take the few natives left to another island after the government of Mauritius had decided to evacuate the island. The ship was destroyed in a storm off the coast and with the help of a native they reached the island where they stayed for months before being found. They built a raft and Raoul Berenger went with two natives to another island to find food. In an incident where the mast broke away, he had a finger severed at the first phalenge. He fainted with the pain. He had only two natives with him, so they had to turn back and start again at a later date, being successful this time.

This is the report concerning the loss of S.V. "Diego" at Eagle Island on June 20th, 1935 at 7 pm on a voyage from Port Louis to Eagle Island, Eagle Island to Salomon Island, Salomon Island to Eagle Island, Eagle Island to Diego Garcia and back to Eagle Island. From that island we intended to go to Peros Banhos and thence to Port Louis, Mauritius.

"We left Diego Garcia on June 18th at 2 pm. On the 19th at 9.30 am we passed in sight of Six Island and reached Eagle Island the same day at 2 pm and dropped the port anchor in the usual anchorage in seven fathoms of water. Weather fine and clear since our departure from Diego Garcia with gentle south-easterly winds. Soon after anchoring, I started to take up cargo to 5 pm. On June 20th weather was dull, cloudy and rainy with variable eastery winds. At 2 pm wind shifted suddenly to north-west without any warning; we then let go starboard anchor. At 2.30 pm fresh wind was blowing from north-west with rough sea running from the same direction, vessel being then on a lee shore started to drag her two anchors. A spare bower anchor was therefore let and we slacked away the cables of the two other bower anchors as much as was safe. Soundings were taken and we found six fathoms of water aft and vessel was drawing 14 feet aft. At 5 pm wire holding the spare anchor parted, wind and sea were increasing and vessel kept dragging her two anchors. High sea was then running and vessel was in a critical position. As we were close into shoal water, it was impossible to slack away any more chain and it being impossible to get under weight, life belts were distributed to all passengers and to each member of the crew. At 5.45 pm vessel dragged her anchors and struck the ground twice between the mizzen mast and stern-post causing the rudder to lift about 4 inches, although soundings taken at the time showed 3 fathoms. Soon afterwards north-west wind died down but heavy north-west sea still running. At 6.30 pm ship still heading, wind shifted to south-east, we set all sails and as she started to gather headway we hove up anchors. No sooner were the anchors aweigh that the south-east wind suddenly died down and with the heavy sea running, vessel sheered to starboard and was driven ashore broadside on, bumping heavily as she grounded, sea breaking all over the vessel. By 7 pm vessel had listed heavily to port. Three life-boats out of four were washed away by the sea and hold and cabins were flooded. As there was no hope of saving the vessel, rockets and distress signals were fired. A line was taken ashore in a small pirogue sent by the manager, and as soon as it was made fast ashore, children, women, male passengers and afterwards the crew were landed. This work was performed with the utmost difficulty; at midnight the last members of the crew left the ship. She had then a list of about 60 degrees to port and tremendous waves were breaking over her. I have to congratulate all the members of the crew who did their very best and acted bravely, also a labourer named Tallat who managed to manoeuvre by himself that small pirogue mentioned above in heavy surf, and thus saved the life of everybody on board. I may add that all of us left the ship with only the clothes we had on. On June 21st at 7 am weather was fine and clear with fresh south-easterly winds. All the cabins on deck had been washed away and any amount of wreckage floating about and carried away in a southwesterly direction.

October 4th 1935
J. H. Mazoué
(Captain)

There were 15 crewmen and 15 passengers. Captain J. H. Mazoué, Captain R. Bérenger and Rev. Father Roger Dussercle S SP on board.

In April 1936, the nautical magazine of Glasgow, Scotland published the article below about Arthur Tallat the labourer who saved the entire crew by his heroism. I think it is interesting to read:

HONOUR WHERE HONOUR IS DUE!

Often, the deeds of greatest heroism pass almost unnoticed by the general public because they happen to have been performed in out-of-the-way places. Such is the case with the saving of an entire ship crew by a single individual, Arthur Tallat, at Eagle Island in the Chagos Archipelago.

The barque, "Diégo", was driven ashore, broadside on a lee shore in a heavy sea. Seas broke over the vessel and the lifeboats were smashed and carried away. Tallat set out from the shore in a small 15 feet pirogue, and after battling for two hours in such conditions that his pirogue was capsized several times in the high sea that was running, he reached the wreck.

He then took a line from the ship to the shore and by this established connection by a hawser along which he pulled his boat backwards and forwards taking two persons at a time until the thirty who were on board the wreck were brought to safety.

For this act of sustained gallantry, he has been awarded Lloyds' Silver

Medal and never was it better earned. Such is heroism.

The diploma and medal were offered to him personally by Governor Jackson at the beginning of May.

When Arthur Tallat received his medal, the entire crew and passengers were sitting in the front rows.

On the 13th of October, 10 days after the survivors were reunited with their family (making it 4 months spent on their own, nobody iin Mauritius aware of their feat), Father Dussercle celebrated a special mass of thanksgiving in Port Louis in his parish church of St François Xavier; as they had promised Our Lady they would do if they survived, at the foot of the Grand- Mas at the beginning of their ordeal.

There is mention in the book by the priest of a note especially written for his wife that your great-grandfather handed him with the promise to give it to his wife in case he did not return from his mission (when going on a makeshift raft to another island to get food).

I have a photo of the captain, your great-grandfather and Father Dussercle, taken after their rescue, and also of the raft and the ship the "MacPhee Clan" who discovered them on the island so many months later and notified the authorities in Mauritius.

How terrible it must have been for your great-grandmother, Pauline, with no news of her husband. They probably all thought they were dead.

The "Diego" was the last of its kind used in Mauritius (it was a barque).

Isn't it sad? We cannot argue a man's destiny, for nearly three years later Raoul Berenger met his maker on the 13th March, 1938.

As the newspaper clip that I found while reading the book is so old and dated March 26th, 1938 I think by precaution I should write down its content, just in case.

CYCLONE FEARED TO HAVE
CLAIMED COASTER

CATTLE-LADEN SHIP WOULD EASILY FOUNDER

THIRTY-FOUR ABOARD: NO NEWS FOR TWO WEEKS
Port Louis, Mauritius
Saturday

Hope has been abandoned for the safety of the small steamer "Agnar", which left Vohemar (Madagascar) on March 10 to Port Louis with a crew of 31 and three passengers and a cargo of cattle.

The "Agnar" last communicated by wireless with Mauritius on Saturday, March 12, on the night when a cyclone was reported in her region.

It is believed that she foundered.
WIDE EXPERIENCE

The "Agnar" was commanded by Captain Loiseau, who has had much experience of these seas, and had as chief officer, Captain Berenger who commanded the steamer "Cigale", which carrying a cargo of petrol was destroyed by fire with great loss of life between Mauritius and Reunion in 1924. The "Agnar" was 400 miles north-west of Mauritius when last heard of by wireless. Various steamers on the route report no sign of her.

The shipping correspondent of the Natal Daily News writes: The accompanying map indicates the path of the cyclone, in the centre of which the "Agnar" is believed to have foundered. The path indicated was arrived at from reports and positions given by the "Dunbar Castle ", which experienced the aftermath or tail end of the cyclone passing ahead of her when coming to Durban from Mauritius.

LAST POSITION

A radio message of March 21 from Mauritius asked the "Dunbar Castle" to keep a look out for the "Agnar" which was then overdue there and gave her last wirelessed positions on March 12

Capitaine Jean Honore Raoul Berenger.

MAURITIUS.

BY HIS EXCELLENCY THE GOVERNOR

CERTIFICATE OF COMPETENCY

AS

MASTER

To *Jean Honoré Raoul Berenger*

WHEREAS you have been found duly qualified to fulfil the duties of Master in the Merchant Service, I do hereby, in pursuance of Her late Majesty's Order in Council, dated the ninth day of May, 1891; issued under the provisions of the Merchant Shipping (Colonial) Act of 1869; and in accordance with Ordinances No. 15 of 1887; and No. 18 of 1888; and in pursuance of Section 745 (1) (a) of the Merchant Shipping Act, 1894; grant you this Certificate of Competency.

GIVEN under my Hand and seal at Mauritius, this 8th day of March 1912.

Board of Examiners:
(Sd) H. Scrugg
(Sd) M. McDonald
(Sd) J. La Cay
(Sd) A. Gratte

Signed by Order of His Excellency the Governor.

(Sd) E. Smith
Colonial Secretary.

Registered at the Port Office, Port-Louis,
this 8th day of March 19...

Capitaine Jean Honore Raoul Berenger's Certificate of Competency as Master.

The three mast barque "Diégo".

The makeshift raft that was used by Capitaine Berenger to try and get help after being shipwrecked.

In the background is the "Macphee Clan" that rescued the survivors from "Eagle Island".

Three of the survivors from the "Diego" – from left – Father Dussercle, Capitaine Mazoue and Capitaine Raoul Berenger.

R. P. ROGER DUSSERCLE S. SP.

ARCHIPEL DE CHAGOS

EN MISSION

DIÉGO — SIX ILES — PÉROS

Septembre — Novembre 1934

* *

PORT-LOUIS — ILE MAURICE

THE GENERAL PRINTING & STATIONERY CY LTD

T. Esclapon, Administrateur

MCMXXXV

PRÉFACE

Le Père Roger Dussercle, missionnaire de la Compagnie du Saint-Esprit, curé du Saint-François-Xavier, l'une des trois grandes paroisses de la ville de Port-Louis, dans l'Ile Maurice, répondit, en 1933, à l'appel de Sa Grâce Mgr James Leen, archevêque-évêque du diocèse, pour assurer le ministère apostolique dans l'archipel de Chagos, lointaines petites îles peuplées de plusieurs containes d'habitants et situées à quelque douze cents milles au nord de l'Ile Maurice.*

Sa Grâce, dans la lettre-préface dont elle honora le premier ouvrage du Père Dussercle †, rappelait justement que le diocèse de Port-Louis ne se compose pas seulement de florissantes paroisses où les œuvres sont abondantes et où le chiffre des communions pour une année dépasse cent mille, mais jusqu'à de petites communautés de fidèles dispersés sur des Iles lointaines difficiles à atteindre par la nature et la rareté des communications.

* Le R. P. Cléret de Langavant - aujourd'hui S. E. Mgr de Langavant, évêque de Saint-Denis de la Réunion, était chargé spécialement des Iles d'Agaléga.

† L'ARCHIPEL DE CHAGOS, EN MISSION.

Curé de Saint François-Xavier, chaque année il confie sa paroisse et son église à un discret dévouement confraternel, sur la houle océane où les corsaires de l'Ile de France promenaient jadis leur menace, parmi vents et marées, tempêtes et cyclones, sur son trois mâts barque, il bourlingue.

S'en aller à l'aventure sur un navire marchant au vent du ciel, roulé, secoué, parmi marins véritables, marinés et tannés, et le soleil et les étoiles, la mâture et la manœuvre, la salure et l'embrun, naviguer des semaines à la recherche de mystérieux archipels où des gens vivent solitaires, en marge du siècle, sous les cocotiers, le beau rêve missionnaire...

Ce rêve-là, le P. Dussercle l'a réalisé, qui a mérité par ses croisières le titre émouvant de "missionnaire de la mer". Sur un bâtiment à voiles, à l'instar de nos hardis ancêtres créoles il sillonne la Mer des Indes, mais non plus en guête de gloire et de riche butin; il a troqué le pavillon de l'écumeur contre le drapeau papal. Ce n'est pas la guerre qu'il porte, mais la paix, au nom de son maître le Christ. Il visite des vingtaines d'îles dont personne ne sait bien où elles sont, à part des capitaines loups de mer qui, deux ou troisfois l'an,

Pour la mission de choix, il fallait un prêtre jeune et solide, insoucieux des périls de la mer et de l'aventure, un soldat de Dieu qui fût à la fois un marin et un poète: le P. Roger Dussercle en avait comme on dit "de la graine," étant de ce pays de Granville, sur les côtes normandes, à l'entrée de la baie du Mont Saint Michel, qui voit partir tous les ans les barques pour la grande pêche, de ce département de la Manche qui a donné et qui donne encore à la France de grands marins, voire des amiraux, à l'Eglise de saints prêtres et d'éminents prélats.

Après les études secondaires à Notre-Dame d'Avranches, en 1920, à dix-huit ans, Roger Dussercle entre chez les Pères du Saint-Esprit. Deux ans plus tard, le service militaire au Maroc en guerre. En 1926, l'ordination; l'année suivante, l'arrivée dans le diocèse de Port-Louis.

Professeur de français au séminaire diocésain Père Laval, le P. Dussercle compose une histoire littéraire que l'Alliance française régionale inscrit à son programme d'études; vicaire successivement de la paroisse Saint-Louis et de l'Immaculée, ses dons de musicien et de compositeur en firent le maître de chapelle de la Cathédrale.

hantent ces parages pour les sociétés huilières. Il navigue, connaît des péripéties nombreuses, les longs calmes plats, les coups de vent, le pittoresque des établissements lointains, les camps rustiques sous les palmes balancées, les cérémonies liturgiques en plein air; rythmées par la voix sans cesse toute proche de l'océan, ou dans de touchantes chapelles rudimentaires, -la vie singulièrement animée d'un prospecteur d'âmes et de terres.

C'est le second de ses beaux voyages accomplis en prêtre, en observateur et en artiste que le Père Dussercle nous donne aujourd'hui. Bel ouvrage, en vérité, où s'enferment non pas seulement le journal de route tour à tour verveux, grave ou attendri, du missionnaire, mais encore, sous une forme familière et attachante, la plus instructive documentation, offerte comme sans y penser; toujours exacte, souvent complétée par des cartes et des croquis dont le récit s'illumine...

Quel guide merveilleux que le P. Dussercle, sur sa barque DIEGO, parmi les atolls, de Diégo Garcia à Péros Banhos, en passant par Salomon, les Six Iles, l'Ile d'Aigle, et de nombreux îlots minuscules. Nous applaudissons aux succès apostoliques du religieux, nous nous amusons des chansons du cru, d'une directe et singulière saveur, recueillies par le voyageur; simples et naïves, des lèvres mêmes des rudes marins créoles, chants de travail scandant la manœuvre ou répertoire qu'on égrène sur le pont, le long de la veillée nocturne, sous le brasillement de la croix du Sud.

Ce livre dans sa simplicité et sa vérité est attrayant plus que les plus compliqués romans d'aventures. Je ne sais point de lecture plus propre à réjouir le cœur et à satisfaire l'esprit. Une impression de vie totale s'en dégage. Le plus riche, ce n'est pas Rothschild ou Rockfeller, mais le missionnaire distribuant l'Hostie aux îles perdues de la mer.

Le Pére Dussercle aujourd'hui ou demain remettra à la voile. D'autres fois encore, infatigable, un suroît, je pense, par-dessus la soutane, il s'en ira, pèlerin passionné, à la conquête évangélique parmi les "îlots". Nos vœux et ceux de tous ses amis et lecteurs l'accompagneront dans ses nouveaux périples qui nous donneront, j'espère, des livres encore, frères des premiers, éloquents, amusés, aérés comme celui-ci du grand souffle double de la mer et de la foi.

CLÉMENT CHAROUX.

From Island to Continent   *Marie-Josée Maujean*

CYCLONE FEARED TO HAVE CLAIMED COASTER

Cattle-laden Ship Would Easily Founder

THIRTY-FOUR ABOARD: NO NEWS FOR TWO WEEKS

PORT LOUIS (MAURITIUS), Saturday.

Hope has been abandoned for the safety of the small steamer, Agnar, which left Vohemar (Madagascar) on March 10 for Port Louis with a crew of 31 and three passengers, and a cargo of cattle.

The Agnar last communicated by wireless with Mauritius on Saturday, March 12, on the night when a cyclone was reported in her region.

It is believed that she foundered.

WIDE EXPERIENCE

The Agnar was commanded by Captain Llovseau, who has had much experience of these seas, and had as chief officer, Captain Berenger, who commanded the steamer *Kale*, which, carrying a cargo of petrol, was destroyed by fire with great loss of life between Mauritius and Reunion in 1924.

The Agnar was 400 miles northwest of Mauritius when last heard of by wireless.

Various steamers on the route report no sign of her.

The shipping correspondent of the Natal Daily News writes:—

The accompanying map indicates the path of the cyclone, in the centre of which the Agnar is believed to have foundered. The path indicated was arrived at from reports and positions given by the Dunbar Castle, which experienced the aftermath or tail-end of the cyclone passing ahead of her when coming to Durban from Mauritius.

LAST POSITION

A radio message on March 21 from Mauritius asked the Dunbar Castle to keep a look out for the Agnar which was then overdue there and gave her last wirelessed position on March 12

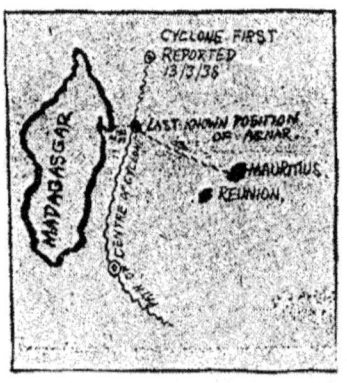

" STILL NEED BRITAIN "

A newspaper clipping of the disappearance of the ship "Lagner".

CHAPTER 8

Those great people of the past . . .
Maujean Family

The first Maujean to arrive in Mauritius was Nicolas Maujean who was born in the Departement de la Moselle at Metz in the Lorraine region of northeast France. He travelled on board the ship "Les Deux Cousins" (The Two Cousins) and arrived in the colony in 1784.
Your great grandfather, Louis Philippe, was the son of Louis Marcel Maujean (factory manager) who was born at Quatre-Bornes, Mauritius, on the fifteenth of September, 1891 at nine o'clock in the morning.
He fought during the First World War (1914) and served for Africa where he was living at the time, in the South African cavalry against the German dependencies of East Africa. The medals that he received as a result were later given to Jean-Claude, his grandchild.
At the age of 25, he was married in Mauritius to Miriam D'Hotman de Villiers, daughter of Joseph François Gaston and Marguerite (nee Mamet) on the 24th February, 1917. He went back to South Africa with his new bride and their first child, Marcel, was born the following year on Tongaat sugar estate in Natal, on the 19th August, 1918. Poor child passed away between the age of seven and nine of a brain tumour caused by a fall. In all they must have spent about six years over there, judging by the date of their children's births.
Their second son was called Roger (Louis Roger) as all Maujean boys of that generation and the next were called. (We changed it where this new generation is concerned because in Australia, the first name counts, so it would have caused some confusion as it did with my husband Louis Philippe junior and his father, Louis Philippe senior, especially since they dealt with the same bank. So we broke the tradition with Patrick).
Uncle Roger was born on the 10th October, 1919 in South Africa. He married Paule Bérenger, Violette's sister in Mauritius, where all their children were born.

As mentioned before, they came to Australia to live in 1965. Uncle Roger passed away on the 9th March, 1991. Even though his death was a release for him as he suffered of poor health for numerous years, it has left a great void, and he is missed by many as he loved people, and was always surrounded by them.

Roger was cremated and his ashes will be kept at the White Rock Cemetery where Aunty Eleanor Berenger was buried, and his son-in-law's ashes are also kept (Glenn Cowans).

I do not think I mentioned before, Pauline Maujean, his granddaughter, is buried at the Martyn Street cemetery in Cairns.

If it is a consolation, I truly believe that they are all together, probably celebrating when a new family soul arrives up there.

Some people find it macabre talking about death, but after all, we are here for such a short time.

Like my Dad used to say to us when we grieved someone's passing, "We are only like birds going from one place to the other". "Des oiseaux de passage", like in transit if you like. It is sad for the ones that are left behind, but after all, after the normal grieving, we have the consolation of knowing that we will be reunited one day. That's what our faith is all about.

The Maujean family at the wedding of Christine Maujean to Glenn Cowans. Standing from left – Jean-Claude, Roger, Christine, Glenn with son Shannon, Chantal, Paule and Paul. Kneeling is Marcel.

Maujean Family

Coming back to the Maujean family, the third son, Louis Pierre was also born in South Africa in 1920. He was known as Pierrot, after living in Mauritius during his youth. He later went back to South Africa and married fairly late in life, a Mauritian, Thérèse D'Abadie, and they had three children, two girls, one called Martine and the other Geocelyne, and a son, Jean-Pierre. They all live in South Africa. (Pierrot passed away exactly a month after Roger's death).

The following year, their first daughter, Daisy, was born on the 28th February, 1921. Daisy lived in Mauritius all her life. She married Gabriel (Gaby) Lionnet and they have three children, Noel, Marc and Gilles. Gilles married Caroline Monplé. Their children are Loic and Anais Lionnet.

Their fifth child, a boy they named Hervé, was stillborn.

Their first child to be born in Mauritius was Philippe, my father-in-law, on the 4th July, 1924 at Rose-Hill.

And their last, another daughter, Aliette, who married Hervé Mayer. Their children are: Rivaltz (bachelor); Clifford, married to Sylvie Régnard with children Diane and Natasha Mayer; Marie-Anne to Alain Lamusse, children Stephane, Fabrice and Christophe Lamusse.

My father-in-law, Philippe, attended school at a catholic convent where he was a boarder from a very young age.

He met his future wife, Violette when he was only sixteen years old.

At the age of seventeen, he had his whole left leg amputated following a shooting accident. It occurred after a hunting trip. His brothers and he were playing at bouncing stones on a railway track when one of the stones hit the trigger of a gun that had been left lying on the track (nobody knows how it got there) and Philippe was shot in the leg. By the time he was driven back home one and a half miles away, it was 5.30 in the evening.

The sugar estate's male nurse in charge of the infirmary had to get a special permit from the nearest police station to be able to drive him to the town's hospital, as it was during the war and there was a curfew at night. By the time they were able to do so it was already 11 o'clock at night, and gangrene had started to set in.

Philippe told me that when it first happened he did not feel any pain. But a few seconds after the initial shock the pain started.

Unfortunately the leg could not be saved and it had to be amputated. What a terrible tragedy! So young! But Philippe was not one to be overcome by this.

Three months later he went to South Africa accompanied by Gaby Lionnet, his brother-in-law, to have an artificial leg fitted.

It was April 1942, and they travelled on a small cargo ship the "Zambesia". A few days after departing Mauritius, Philippe's stump became purulent.

My parents-in-law, Philippe and Violette Maujean celebrated their wedding on the 10th November, 1947.

There was no doctor on board, so when he realised that the infection stemmed from a small bone fragment that was pushing to the surface, he cut it out himself, a cut half and inch deep and about one inch wide using a scalpel belonging to the captain's medical kit.

His mother had kept that bone fragment and was later buried with it as was her wish.

Philippe spent three months in South Africa. On his return his mother was very disappointed to see him disembark without wearing the new leg as he had found it too painful at first to walk with.

Later on, seeing his mother's tears and thinking back that she had sold a diamond ring of hers to raise enough money for all the expenses, he forced himself to get used to it by wearing the leg ten minutes at a time at first and then gradually increasing the length of time, until finally after three months he was wearing it permanently.

From then on, although he suffered much discomfort, he lived as normal a life as possible.

The Cygne (The Swan) that Philippe Maujean co-owned with his brother Roger and brother-in-law Gaby.

He rode a motorcycle and drove his car. As there were no automatic cars in those days, he had a special hand accelerator attached to it.

Philippe enjoyed fishing and later on, as part-owner of the fishing boat "Le Cygne" (The Swan) that his brother Roger and brother-in-law Gaby had bought in partnership with him, he would be seen hopping along on board on one leg during their numerous fishing expeditions that they enjoyed at weekends.

He could also swim and in fact, he never let this handicap stop him from achieving anything he wanted to do.

After they were married in November 1947, Philippe and Violette first lived at "Maison Blanche" (the White House), an annexe of the Beau-Plan sugar estate that I mentioned in a previous chapter.

Philippe worked in Beau-Plan sugar estate as a clerk under the supervision of Mr Jean Chasteau de Balyon who made the speech at their wedding. I have a copy of it in French that I translated to English. (Jean Chasteau and his wife had seven children. He lost his wife at the birth of his youngest son. Later on, when all his children were grown up, he became a priest. He is currently in charge of my ex home town, Notre-Dame Du Rosaire, parish in Quatre-Bornes).

Philippe and Violette's first born, a son Philippe junior (Popy, my husband) was born a year later on November the 26th, three months premature. It was a home birth. Popy is such an impatient man that when he tries to rush me sometimes, which annoys me, I remind him that patience is not his greatest virtue as he could not even wait to be born!

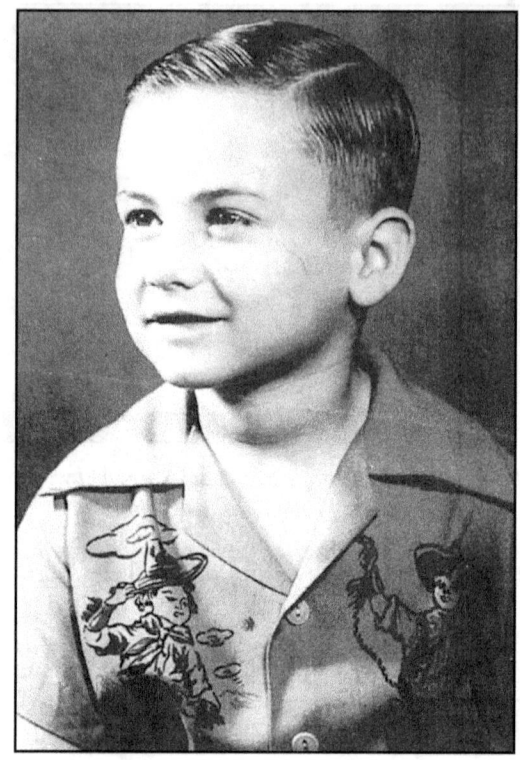

Philippe "Popy" Maujean as a young five-year- old and later to be my husband.

Apparently he was such a chatterbox as a toddler that the family doctor used to call him "Radio".

Philippe and Violette later on moved to Beau-Plan to live. They had two other children, a daughter Monique and a second son Cyril who was affectionately called "Bouboule". (I believe it stems from the fact that he was such a chubby baby).

When Popy was about 10 years old, his father was cleaning and oiling a gun when he accidentally shot himself in the hand that was resting on the barrel. He believed the gun was unloaded. Popy tells me that he was in an adjoining room at the time when he heard the shot and did not hear a sound from his father. He thought that he had been killed and went and locked himself in the bathroom until he heard him speak. Since then, understandably, Violette did not want any gun in the house. Luckily, Philippe did not lose his hand. He had numerous operations and skin graft on the back of his hand.

Maujean Family

Philippe and Violette Maujean's house on Beau-Plan Sugar Estate.

They lived at Beau-Plan until they left Mauritius for Australia in 1965, at a period when the exodus was truly on the way, as Mauritius was going through such political and racial unrest. Troops had been sent to the island from England to try stopping the violence that had erupted, beginning with the murder of my mother's first cousin, Robert Brousse.

It was especially unsafe on sugar estates. Later on a curfew was in order after it used to be such a risk driving at night you never knew what could be hurled at you. Numerous were the people who had their cars damaged while travelling through far-away villages.

On sugar estates, families had to keep guard during the night in case they were attacked by some of the blacks. To make it more convenient, about 3 or 4 families would be at the one house and they would organise a shift for two to stay on guard all through the night.

The Maujean's gardener, Madoo, had warned them not to open the door to him if he was to knock at their door some time at night, as he was being pressured by the mob.

It is a sad thing when life comes to a point when you are in a situation where you do not even feel safe in your own home.

So it is not surprising that so many families left secure jobs and relatives to go to a safe place where at least they knew their children would be able to carve themselves a secure and peaceful life.

Roger and Paule Maujean who lived next door to them also came to the conclusion that it was time to leave.

Australia, such a vast and new country, had a lot to offer.

Nicholas Maujean — Born at Metz (Department of La Rochelle) in 1756, son of Nicholas Maujean and Catherine Né Peultier. Arrived in Mauritius (then known as Isle de France) in 1784 aged 28 on board the ship "Les Deux Cousins with Captain Carreau.
He passed away on the 2nd November, 1820 (a widower residing at his son's place for several years) at ten-thirty in the evening.

Claude Nicolas Amédée Maujean - Born at Moka (Isle de France) at 3.30 am on the 29th November, 1793.
He married Marie Geneviève Coralie Treize at Port Louis on the 4th February, 1824. She was born in Port Louis, the daughter of Louis Treize and Adelaide Dureau (divorced). It was a morning event.
Witnesses to the marriage were the bride's father, Mr Treize; the bride's mother, Adélaide Dureau; the bride's uncle, Jacques Dureau de Vaulconte; Jean-François Chrestien, aged 56 years; Professor Louis Auguste Bettand, aged 34; the bride's brother, Captain Theodore Folin of the Merchant Navy, aged 31.
Their union produced a son.
Claude Maujean passed away at 8 pm on the 9th August, 1873 at Beau Bassin aged 86 years.

Louis Adolphe Amédée Maujean — Born at Moka on the 8th April, 1832. A trader, he married Henriette Ringuet, divorced wife of Victor Benoit Florens. Henriette was the daughter of Pierre Ringuet and Marie-Louise Gillot.
The marriage took place at Port Louis on the Monday afternoon of the 6th June, 1853.
The groom was 21 years old and the bride 26.
There were four witnessess to the ceremony. François Gustave Trebuchet, uncle on the mother's side to the bridegroom, a surgeon dentist, 40 years of age; Louis Auguste Montenot, uncle on the mother's side to the bridegroom, a proprietor, 34 years of age; Henry Aristide Ringuet, first cousin to the bride, an usher, 31 years of age; Charles Gillot, uncle to the bride on the mother's side, a clerk, 24 years of age.
Their union produced a son.
Louis Maujean passed away in Port Louis at 11 pm on the 18th February, 1882.

Louis Amédée Maujean — Born in Port Louis on the 19th January, 1861.

Married in Port Louis to Alice Marie Amelie Marot, daughter of Elysée Armand Marot and Mathilde Louise Rougier Lagane.

It was a morning wedding on Monday the 30th July, 1888. The groom was 27 years old, a professor at the Royal College.

Witnesses were Alfred Messeroy, Rector of the Royal College; Edouard Rougier Lagane.

Their union produced a son.

Louis Marcel Maujean — Born at Quatre Bornes, Mauritius, at 9 am on the 15th September, 1891.

He married Marie Françoise Josephine Miriam D'Hotman de Villiers in Rose Hill, Mauritius on the 24th February, 1917 at 4 pm.

Louis was 24 years old and his bride, 21, was born in 1896, the daughter of Joseph François Gaston D'Hotman de Villiers and Marguerite Marie Mamet. The bride came from a family of eleven children.

Their union produced five children including three sons, Roger, Pierre and Philippe and two daughters, Daisy and Aliette.

Daisy married Gabriel Lionnet. They had three sons, Noel, single; Marc; Gilles, married to Caroline Montplé.

Marcel and Miriam Maujean

Aliette married Hervé Mayer. They had three children. Rivaltz, single (15-5-1953); Marie Anne (8-5-1954) married to Alain Lamusse, and their three sons, Stephane (15-8-1981), Fabrice (9-7-1984) and Christophe (19-2-1991) all living in Mauritius.

Clifford married to Sylvie Régnard, and their children Diane (20-2-1981), Natasha (8-11-1983) and Kevin (9-8-1991).

Marcel Maujean passed away at Beau Climat sugar estate on the 20th July, 1962.

Miriam Maujean passed away in 1951 aged 54 years.

Louis Philippe Maujean — Born Rose-Hill, Mauritius on 3rd July, 1924.

He married Marie Jeanne Violette Bérenger, daughter of Captain Jean Honore Raoul Berenger and Joséphine Pauline Canton (from Madagascar). The wedding took place in Curepipe on the 10th November, 1947.

They came to Australia in August, 1965.

They had three children, Louis Philippe, Marie Monique and Louis Cyril.

Monique married John Harris and had three children: Scott, Kristian and Michael. The family at present reside in Cairns.

Cyril married Chantal Mackie and also had three children: Michael, Christopher and Belinda. They reside in Brisbane.

Louis Philippe Maujean — Born in Pamplemousses in Mauritius at 4.50 am on the 26th November, 1948.

Came to Australia in August, 1965 on board the Northern Star.

Married Marie-Josée Nozaïc, daughter of Jules Felix Joseph France Nozaïc and Marie Zelie Myriam Arnulphy, at the Sacred Heart Catholic Church, Oakleigh, Victoria on Saturday, 30th August, 1969. Both the bride and groom were a few months short of their 21st birthday.

Their union produced two children: Patrick and Roselyne.

The Maujean family vault in Pamplemousses cemetery, Mauritius

CHAPTER 9

The Tender Years
Christmas, Maiden Cyclone

My early memories of Christmas are a mixture of delicious expectation, apprehension and delight.
To this day, that special smell of pine from a Christmas tree sends me back to my childhood when the fun would start about a week beforehand with the decorating of the tree (a real one!).
It would be a family affair. We would all help hang the pretty coloured decorations and every night it was magic when it was all lit up and created a special atmosphere of anticipation.
Come Christmas eve, we were allowed on this special time of the year to fire off crackers and the younger ones or the faint-hearted (like me) lit sparklers.
From about 5 o'clock in the afternoon onwards, the whole island sounded like a battle field by the noise of all families celebrating with a good supply of crackers bought at the local Chinese shop that did a roaring trade by their sale.
Strange, but I never heard of a child being hurt by one of them. I suppose it was well supervised by the adults.
At around seven or so, just before dinner, Santa Claus would call at home.
I remember being very apprehensive when I would hear his loud "Ho, Ho, Ho", and Santa (usually an uncle) would walk into the salon and demand a song from the shaking little ones who with a trembling voice would be brave enough to make an effort at singing "Petit Papa Noel", encouraged by the Nénenne and the parents.
After all, one had to. Otherwise that scary old man with the white beard (reminded me of Bluebeard the pirate) might decide not to give you any presents if you refused.

I would sing the last note with relief and be rewarded with lollies and balloons.

After listening to all of us sing (what a patient man) Santa would say farewell without forgetting to remind us to put our shoes under the tree before going to bed.

After dinner, excitement was at its peak. It was the only night of the year when we would go to our bed of our own accord (naively thinking the quicker we went to bed the sooner we would have our presents) after reverently putting our shoes under the sparkling tree.

We were told to keep our eyes shut. So the head was full of dreams, with little faces all scrunched up eagerly waiting for Morphey to embrace them.

On waking up the next morning, a cardinal rule was not to go into the lounge where the tree was unless our parents took us there. It would not stop us from having a peek though.

We would not dare wake our parents outright, but we made sure there was sufficient noise to do so.

Then ... oh! ... delight of delight! We would be taken to Ali Baba's cave.

I can't even remember the routine of eating a proper meal that day, save for chocolates, marzipan and nougats.

As we got older, there would be the gathering at Grand-Mère's place where the grandparents, uncles, aunts and cousins would sit together for the traditional Christmas dinner.

Just as well there were domestics, otherwise it would have been too much to cook for so many of us.

From the age of seven onwards, after making my first communion, I always attended midnight mass with my family.

Before mass, there used to be a type of concert, called Tableau Vivant, a reenactment of that first Christmas. Once, Marielle and Micheline as well as our cousin Danielle, took part in one of them. They were "angels". They dressed in a white robe and I especially remember their wings made of cardboard with tissue paper.

Usually mass would be celebrated in the open on a raised platform that can be seen by the congregation sitting on the lawn all around. We had our special candle lit up as well.

New Years Day was also very special. After attending mass in the morning, the whole family would go visiting. This would be the only day of the year we would visit far away relatives, bed-ridden old ladies, great aunts of ours that would scare us children a little or some special people that my parents considered like family, people they were grateful to know. We would drink numerous cups of tea and have biscuits after being complimented by so and so for our good behaviour and be commented upon by old ladies who thought it was their duty to find a striking point in our feature to compliment us.

If you were not very pretty, or in one word, plain, they commented on what a lovely smile you had. Not that she lacked in prettiness, Marielle was told once how lovely her teeth looked by an unimaginative person.

Then you would also meet the originals of the family. It fascinated me. There was the one who had a passion for clocks and watches.

He had a collection of them partly demolished that he was trying to bring back to their original state. I don't know if he ever did.

There was a cousin of my mother on the Arnulphy side, Maxime Griffiths, who was a genius with his hands. He could turn a piece of wood into anything he wished.

He made beautiful sculptures, he could paint and draw and he made beautiful furniture. Maxime was a Bob Hope look alike. (Bob Hope, American comedian, for all of you who may read this book in 50 years time).

He was a bachelor who had a lot of success chasing women. He used to travel by taxi. He would visit us about twice a year and we children always enjoyed his visits. He would make a point to show an interest in us and always brought a box of "Montelimar" nougats to be shared amongst us.

Sometimes his sisters would visit us too. Hilda was Micheline's godmother. She had her own school in Curepipe.

I have always loved ballet. I used to dance in front of relatives sometimes. (Not that I volunteered. I was asked to. I must mention that I never had any tuition). Once after my performance, Hilda commented that I had a natural talent that should be encouraged.

Mum answered that her Dad had said that he would not like to see his grandchild performing on the stage. This was the old fashioned outlook.

Anyway, my parents could not afford it. But I used to dream. Every year I would wish for dancing shoes as a Xmas present. Alas, I never got them.

Once, my aunts Jacqueline and Annie, made me a tutu and they applied makeup to my face and tied my hair up like a proper ballet dancer. Afterwards I danced for them and my grandparents and some visiting friends. Boy, was I proud of myself. (I was lucky enough to attend 3 performances by the Russian Bolshoi Ballet in 1974. It was terrific. I went with my father-in-law, who also loves ballet).

Every year when we would all be sitting around the table on New Years day, Grand-Mère would comment: "This is my last year amongst you." Today she is still alive and will turn 96 in two months time.

Easter also would be well celebrated. The only time of year when we would have a leg of ham specially cooked for the occasion. Chicken roast, green peas and baked potatoes.

On easter morning we would as usual exchange easter eggs. Beautiful chocolate ones (not hollow in the middle). Some came with a plastic coloured kangaroo and the egg placed in its pouch.

Afterwards it would be mass at Notre-Dame De Lourdes, driven there by the same taxi owned by an Indian who used to drive us to church every Sunday for years.

In the end Papa didn't even have to call him. He knew those special occasions and without fault he would be waiting in front of our house. It went on until Papa bought a brand new Vauxhall.

Every Sunday after mass, we used to go to the markets. I was always begging my parents to buy me some Indian type of earings that they sold there. I called them "anneaux piments" (chilli earings). They were gold dangling ones. I thought they looked beautiful. I must mention that I would have needed to have my ears pierced. Anyway, I never got them. I would have looked ridiculous wearing them.

The Maiden Cup in Mauritius is a horse racing event that could be compared to the Melbourne Cup of Australia. It is the first race of the racing season.

It is held at the Champ de Mars hippodrome, set at the foot of a mountain range.

There were some Australian jockeys taking part. I especially remember the surname of one who was Gilmore. My aunt Lise Mamet who is a dressmaker, used to do well sewing for the jockeys wives. Even though she barely spoke English, Tante Lise managed to somehow communicate with them.

There is one incident that I hope Tante Lise won't be offended by me mentioning is the time she wanted to make the lady understand that a pink rose would be the epitome of fashion if added to a certain dress. She proceeded to do so by saying "A pink, pink would look nice". (Pink is the colour rose in French).

The Champ de Mars is where the M.T.B. Mauritius Turf Club was founded in 1812. It is the oldest club after the British Jockey Club. If you were part of the M.T.B. you could have your private booth in the stands.

Our family did not, so we attended in the grounds. To us kids it was magic. The crowd was very colourful, a mixture of races of all ages from toddlers to the elderly.

Merchants would take the opportunity to sell their wares ranging from food to artisana.

There would be the smell of fried chilli cakes (gateaux piments) mixed with that of dahl puree and a redolence of spices. What used to delight us as children were the colourful windmills made of plastic and also the painted horses on wheels made out of tin that you would hold with a long wooden handle to push forward.

Christmas, Maiden Cyclone

I never went there very often with my family, as it would have cost them a small fortune. But I used to be invited by my cousins. I suppose it had the same attraction to us children as the show would have here.

The Champ de Mars is not used solely for the races, but also for parades of troops on special occasions as the Queen's birthday for instance.

Working for the government as Registrar General, Papa had to take part every year in the grand parade in honour of Queen Elizabeth II.

I remember him, dressed in full regalia, with a sword at the side etc. They also used to be invited to the Reduit (house of the Governor) to formal receptions when there was some dignitary visiting the island. When Princess Margaret came to Mauritius, my parents got to meet her. She was young and unmarried at the time.

Her visit to the island started some game for us children when we would play at being a princess. We all had our turn. We would dress into our mother's clothes and wear some knee high socks in place of gloves. Mum's high heel shoes and a chapeau pot (flower pot hat) as was the fashion in those days. Then all the sisters, brothers and cousins would form a line on each side of the corridor and Princess Margaret would walk in between in a very dignified way, moving the arm ever so slowly doing the royal salute by moving the arm back and forth while the crowd would cheer and applaud. The game lasted for about 6 months after she left Mauritius.

We certainly were never bored as children, even though we never went out very much as my father did not own a car for a long time.

We did not have television as I was growing up. Families used to sit and have conversations in those days. Television did not come to Mauritius until 1963.

We would sit in the salon on those days that my parents did not play belotte, and after dinner listen to the radio. Papa was a keen participant of the English Pool Football. Sometimes at night he would listen to the results of matches and we also heard Big Ben in the background, while he tuned to London.

The first time I watched television was at my boyfriend's place (Popy). Papa drove all the way from our place to the Maujeans, a fair distance apart. It was an episode of Dr Kildare with Richard Chamberlain. We thought he was "it". We even enjoyed watching commercials. I must say that the episode was in English, so we did not catch everything they were saying.

When I was eleven years old, Mauritius was hit by cyclone Carol in February 1960, only two weeks after Alice had already prepared the path for destruction.

Call it coincidence? Every fifteen years, for a long time, the island has suffered a severe cyclone according to its history, dating from 1915 - 1930 - 1945 - 1960 - 1975.

Every year there would be cyclone warnings or actual threats as the cyclone would pass very near to the coast. As a rule we loved it as children as we would see in this the occasion to miss a few days of school, plus all the extras like eating by candlelight when power was cut off and being fed "biscuits cabins" (sao biscuits) in the security of a strong house.

In some ways it was a break of routine. Little did we know of the true potential of a cyclone of Carol's calibre when it hit the island with full force. It started out with the usual warnings on the radio until it was raised to a warning No. 3, meaning it was coming straight for us at around 6.30 pm.

My dad was applying some masking tape to the windows when Tonton Rico called to ask him if we wanted to spend the cyclone at their place. Papa refused politely and carried on with the usual precautions.

I remember when the radio announcer issued a top priority warning from Mr Davey in charge of the weather bureau and wished the community good luck.

Papa and Ivan brought mattresses into Marielle's room for all of us would sleep together close to the younger children's bedroom.

Our house before the cyclone "Carol" struck.

As it turned out, we did not sleep a wink because as the night progressed, so did the force of the wind gusts. It was a bit scary actually because we could not see outside, being so dark.

There was the constant roar of the wind and when the gusts would blow, it would rattle the windows. At one stage we heard a sort of whistling noise and that's when Papa took Ivan who was around 16 at the time, for an inspection of the other rooms. Apparently the roof was starting to lift up and there was water in the ceiling. We had buckets at different parts of the room to catch the dripping water.

On another inspection of the house, they found that the ceiling had started to cave in. That's when we all went to the back bedroom (the petites). It must have been critical, for at one stage Papa and Maman started to pray aloud and made us join them.

I must point out that although we knew there was some danger we weren't really scared. I remember Marielle having a nervous laugh (which

A photo of myself standing in front of our house after cyclone "Carol" struck.

she does not) and Micheline tells me that Marie-France said that she did not want to die in her funny way as she was only five at the time. (It is interesting to note how every one remembers a certain situation with a different perspective).

At this stage it was impossible for us to venture outside as the gusts were too strong. At the weather bureau they recorded a wind velocity of 250 miles an hour before the machine broke. (It was stronger than Tracey that affected Darwin in 1974).

We were praying for the wind to decrease so that we could escape to the neighbours.

By now it was daybreak. We saw the "pit latrine" (outside toilet for domestics) being blown away, whole. A gust of wind approached and lifted the whole contraption that went flying past our window. We could not believe it.

Shortly after the gusts started to decrease announcing the eye of the cyclone, the calm. When this happens, the gusts are also further apart, we managed to go to the neighbours, The Sampson family. It was the only house in our neighbourhood who hadn't suffered any damage. Two other families had also taken refuge there. There was about 25 of us in the one house. The calm lasted for two hours, which gives you an idea of the diameter of the cyclone.

I can still remember the stillness. It was stiflingly hot. We felt oppressed. We were shocked when we first lay eyes on our surroundings at daybreak. It was complete chaos outside. Debris everywhere. Papa walked to our place to assess the damage.

Our poor dog, Loulou was pinned under the rubble as part of walls had collapsed. He was trapped and howling, already sick with distemper before. Papa picked his revolver to shoot him to release him of his misery but he could not release the trigger and asked Mr Samson to do it as he did not have the heart to do it himself.

Us children weren't allowed near the house as a precaution. Soon we were all inside the neighbour's house as ripples of wind started to be felt announcing the tail of the cyclone.

It is only now that I can start to think what must have gone through my parent's minds. The worry of wondering if the Samson's house would be strong enough to withstand some more battering. Luckily for us it did.

Unfortunately all the neighbouring houses were further demolished as Carol finished what she had started out to do.

As the wind gusts gradually started, there was still a sightseer, a young man of Indian origin riding a bicycle. He had been caught unaware and was furiously pedalling on his way home.

We watched with disbelief when he was literally picked up, bicycle and all and like the latrine was blown away by a gust of wind and deposited parallel to the road in our yard just in front of our garage wall still standing at the time. He just had time to pick up his bicycle and run before that same wall fell to the ground. We all let out a sigh of relief that he was so lucky to have avoided disaster by a split second.

As the wind picked up, being daylight this time, we were able to see debris flying by. Galvanised sheets of metal seemed to peel off houses and looked like crunched up paper being cast about.

We were lucky that not a single pane was broken.

Soon it was dark again and we did succumb to sleep this time, exhausted. I remember about 10 of us children sprawled wherever we could on a double bed.

I don't think our poor parents slept though. The only food we had was a roast duck that the Rouillon's grandfather managed somehow to share around. I'll never forget that morning, when we woke up and had a look outside. Disaster. Our house (a rented one) was razed to the ground except for a wall panel on one side. It looked as if it had been hit by a bomb. A heap of rubble. A large beam had fallen across that small room where we stayed last. We escaped in time otherwise we could have been killed.

All we had left was the clothes we were wearing. There were sheets wrapped up around telegraph poles.

Mum and Dad had done their monthly grocery shopping the previous week. Well, it was all mixed up and to be seen wherever you could walk.

Washing powder had foamed, mixed with lentils and rice and flour. My father's glass cabinet where he kept all his treasured books, especially his pride and joy, a leather bound collection of books about the two world wars. His prize books that he had kept since a schoolboy. Everything was ruined.

Luckily he salvaged the family photo album as well as the others that contained mementos of their European tour. Along the years, Papa had formed the habit of every now and then, slipping a note in between pages of a book so that he could be pleasantly surprised by them some day. Luckily for him he did retrieve some that were seen floating about. God knows, he needed them now.

Everything of sentimental value was gone. Gone all the wedding and first communion presents, school books, clothes, everything.

That morning, the whole family including grandparents, aunts and uncles rallied around us and helped with any salvaging work. Us children seemed to walk aimlessly, shocked I suppose.

One aunt sent some clothes to share among us.

All of a sudden our life as a family was disrupted.

Mum and Dad went to Tante Jacqueline's place with the three youngest.

Ivan went to his friend's place (Gilbert Baudot). Marielle went to the Nozaïc cousins. Micheline and I went to Grand-Mère Arnulphy's place.

That was the only arrangement possible as there were no houses for rent. Poor Marielle had to cancel the party for her fifteenth birthday that was going to be a grand affair as is the custom in Mauritius. It was to take place on the 4th of March, the following week.

Even though Grand-Mère and the rest did all they could to make life as pleasant as possible for us, I still missed my parents terribly. Specially at night, when I would go to bed and feel totally miserable.

The nuns at our convent school helped us with books and let us wear casual clothes for a while.

As we had 45 minutes break for lunch, I used to run to my aunt's place to see Mum every day. I would only have time to have a drink and exchange a few words then it would be time to say goodbye and run back to school.

Finally after about six weeks, Papa was offered a bungalow at the seaside at Grand-Baie by a business colleague. We were all so happy at the news. It had been arranged with the school that we would be away for a while as it was too far for us to travel to school.

Imagine. At the beach. And no school to boot.

The campement was a double-storey one furnished rustically. It was all white and looked straight onto the beach. There was a balcony on top and it was quite a novelty to go up and down the staircase.

We were so happy to be a family again. Poor Papa still went to work though. He would travel by bus.

My aunt Annie and Rita, their cousin, came to spend a few weeks with us. We were making the most of it, when our joy was short-lived as in the middle of the second week, Maman started to be sick with a high fever.

She became delirious and got worse. By then she couldn't keep any food down. That's when Tonton Henri (Baritauld) helped take Mum to hospital. His car was his pride and joy and it was always immaculate. Well, on the way Mum was sick in it.

As it turned out Mum suffered from jaundice. She spent a few days in hospital and luckily when she got better, Papa had found us a house to rent in Quatre-Burnes at walking distance from school.

We lived there for a couple of years. That was the time when the puberty blues were starting and I fell in love for the first time.

He was one of Ivan's friends and I don't think he was even aware of my existence until the day when he came around with a group of friends, and they were sitting and talking when Paulo asked Sylvianne to call me.

I walked into the garage, all 4 ft 10 inches of me, in a decisive manner and Paulo said, "alla ti fi, content Roland". (Boys used to speak Creole when amongst themselves). Translation: "Here's the girl who's in love with

Roland". Well, I pivoted on my heels and exited in a flash, to walk inside the house where I had a tantrum. I saw red. Apparently I kept turning around in Mum's bedroom saying Oh my God. Oh my God. How cruel. I don't think I dared glance at that boy afterwards. I think it was a case where embarrassment took over infatuation.

Like I mentioned before, I was not very tall, and I was fairly skinny. Horror, my boobs started to grow. And they grew and grew.

One day, typical brother Ivan asked me if I was wearing falsies. I must mention that in those days, it was the fashion to wear padded bras that looked like cones, they were so pointy.

These were the awkward years, lonely years in fact, when I used to be a great deal on my own as the three eldest went to surprise parties that I was too young to be invited to and the petites to birthday parties that I had outgrown.

That's when I took a passion to reading and I used to have a diary. I filled three exercise books of them. Alas. A few years later, in Australia, they just disappeared and I have a suspicion that they fell prey to Papa's hands who used to burn anything that he thought was discarded in the newly acquired incinerator.

In his eagerness to get rid of the rubbish, he even threw in a set of teaspoons that Maman had just purchased.

In those days it was very hard for parents to talk to their children about the birds and the bees. Even though Maman was fairly open as compared to other mothers, I couldn't really speak to her about everything like my daughter Roselyne does nowadays.

I had a suspicion that something special happened to a girl when she was around 12 or so, but nothing specific was mentioned to me. I guessed when it happened to my older sisters because of all the whispering among the grown-ups and they missed school that day when they did not look sick to me.

Later on, one of my friends told me that she thought she suffered from cancer and was scared to tell her mother about it.

I learnt about the facts of life from a book called "Anne-Marie". The story of a teenage girl who used to write letters to her married older sister and ask her about life.

There was a similar book for boys called "Dany". I had to wait a little bit longer to read that one as my sisters thought that I was not yet ready for it.

I laugh now when I remember a conversation that I had with my cousin Françoise and thinking she was so knowledgeable about those things. She once was very proud to tell me that she had heard that something special happened on the honeymoon, that the husband deposited a seed into his wife and that sometimes something came of it and sometimes nothing. If it did not work there was no baby.

I was about twelve and a half at the time. It is a bit hard to literally translate, it sounded so funny in French by the way she described it.

It was the sixties, rock'n'roll had just started. Parents thought that such a dance was outrageous. We used to wear white glossy lipstick and tease our hair. Real tight slacks were in fashion with huge, in fact the longer the better, jumpers.

I will never forget when I had my first high heel shoes. They were not so high, just court shoes. I wore them to the movies and wow! I was so proud of them and kept looking at my feet. I was about 13 then. I was allowed to wear a pale lipstick, and the first party I went to was for my cousin Danielle's 15th birthday. I was in love again with another of Ivan's friends. Again it was platonic. I was too young for him. I was only 13, he was 18.

At that party there was a special dance to set the mood and get everyone to dance. All the girls had to give a piece of jewellery that was placed on a tray and all the boys had to choose one and dance with the owner. Well, by accident, he picked my bracelet. I'll never forget that dance. It was to a song of Ray Charles, "I Can't Stop Loving You". Talk about swooning.

I used to go past him every afternoon on the way back from school. Our paths would cross, you see . . .

From a distance, walking towards each other my heart would skip a bit until we'd come close enough to say "Hi" and that would be it.

I think today's generation is missing out on a lot. There was not such a rush to grow up then, and we were full of ideals.

I attended high school at a Loreto convent in Quatre-Bornes. School in those days was quite different to my childrens. We did not have all the excursions and dances that they do now.

From high school girls went to convents and boys to a college run by brothers. So it was quite an event when the college bus went past the convent every morning. You should have heard the cheers and whistling.

The main event so to speak was when the college had their annual sports day. It was the place where boy meets girl and many a romance was started or ended that day.

For most young people, sport was the last thing they were interested in that day.

School was also very serious business. We did not have options of subjects like they do today.

Apart for form 4-5 you were not forced to do trigonometry or chemistry, otherwise we had to do the lot: history, geography, literature English and French, Latin, maths, religion. When I applied myself I did fairly well, otherwise I must admit that I did not take school seriously enough.

We were assessed by our tests every semester and the system of points. The total defined how we were ranked.

When the principal (a nun) and the prefect would walk into the classroom to announce the first three and then the report books were distributed to the whole class, it was a very serious affair indeed. I was second once (for the first year of high school). I also found myself in the middle or at the end.

Poor Papa was forever trying to encourage us into studying. Ivan and Marielle passed their Cambridge senior tests. Micheline and I never completed our schooling as we had finished form 3 and did not go back to school when we arrived in Australia. We started in the workforce instead. I suppose it was the equivalent of grade 10.

We used to have to study everything by heart. We had so much homework that we did not finish until 9 or 10 pm every night.

The day at school would start by morning prayer in the school chapel, and at the beginning of every period the teacher would say a short prayer.

Every Friday afternoon there would be a special benediction when hymns were sung and incense was burnt.

I used to be very shy at school. I hated to be called to the blackboard, especially during Latin period when Melle Leblanc would call everyone in turn to do a translation in front of the whole class. That's when my mind would go blank.

Every year we had to sit for the inter loretto exams. It took place in the hall with all the high school grades sitting together, and the teachers would walk through the aisles to check that everything was in order. The results would be published in the newspaper and this decided whether or not you moved to a higher grade the following year.

Once I missed on some of them as I was too sick to attend after the extraction of a tooth that was so hard to pull out as the roots were crossed that the dentist had to saw it off and do an incision in the gum.

Well, you should have seen me after that ordeal. Not only had it been terribly painful, but I felt at one stage that the dentist was going to dislocate my jaw in the process. My whole face and neck swelled up and no kidding, I spent nearly a week in bed with a high fever on antibiotics.

A year later I suffered an absess as there was still a small piece of root left that caused an infection. I had to be operated on. At first the doctor thought that it was the saliva gland causing all the trouble, thus causing my parents a great deal of worry.

As it turned out I was operated on just in time as the absess had filtered and nearly reached the jaw bone. This operation has left a fairly long scar under my right hand jaw.

Page 119

I was the only one in the family to have an operation. Not bad when you think of all nine of us. Plus, in those days, doctors used to pull out tonsils and perform an appendictomy at the drop of a hat.

Another incident that happened to me when I was about eight years old was the time when I was cleaning out the dried lentils before cooking (because in those days there were still pieces of straw or dirt mixed in) and I was holding the vanne (a circular straw dish that you place the grains on and shake to separate the unwanted bits). As I was doing so, Ivan was flicking some lentil pods at me to annoy me. At one stage one went into my ear. I tried to pull it out with my finger at first but it was too deep. Maman tried to pull it out using a tweezer to no avail.

It was a public holiday so they had to take me to Candos hospital. On the way I was remembering the story I heard of someone having a major operation when a grain of maize got into his ear and it germinated.
To make a long story short, it finally came out after the doctor syringed my ear.

Chapter 10

Cupid Strikes

The year was 1963. We had just moved house again and our address was at Cossigny Avenue in Quatre-Bornes. Our last prior to leaving Mauritius.
It was the same year when Beatlemania took hold of the world. The radio would constantly blare out those songs that I must admit, took me a while to get used to. Those four young men from Liverpool with their Cockney accent sounded far from harmonious as compared to Elvis Presley or Cliff Richard.

I must first mention that somehow when young people would meet, one question that always popped up in the conversation was Elvis or Cliff? I personally was a Cliff Richard fan, even though I enjoyed Elvis's songs. A cousin of mine, Marianne, was mad about Elvis, a source of constant teasing from her many brothers.

The Beatles not only caused quite a stir by their music but also for the fact that for a long time in history men had had short hair, and they turned it around by having shoulder (not even that), should I say collar length hair.

When we first saw their photo in Le Cerneen, our newspaper, they looked something close to aliens to us. All the boys of our generation until then had short back and sides (hair)!

We were far from knowing then, how far they would go as to revolutionise the music world and be as popular now, twenty-seven years later.

1963 is also the year when things started to change for me. I was growing up.

I was now invited to parties after turning fifteen. Somehow it was like a free pass to adult status. I went to my first real new years eve party at Constance sugar estate. I had a beautiful green dress made by Maman. It was of a shiny material and quite low in the back as was the fashion in those days.

We went accompanied by our parents. In those days, parents and teenagers mixed.

Luckily for me I did not lack in partners and danced all night. Never mind if one of them tried to impress me by lying in saying that he was a sailor from a French ship (as I learned from Gilbert, our friend).

In those days it used to be a dishonour if you did not get asked to dance. It was called "faire tapisserie". (Like being part of a wallpaper. I think the expression here is "a wallflower").

That same year also had its sad part as it was when American President John Fitzgerald Kennedy was assassinated in Texas. I can still remember how we were stunned when we first heard of it on the radio.

We had followed the President's political career and family life through the French magazine Paris Match over the years. We felt for Jackie and her two young children. So popular was the man that it shocked the world.

President Kennedy and his wife Jacqueline were on an official tour of Texas when he was shot as the motorcade was passing through the main street of Dallas. The Governor was also shot but not fatally. The President died later on in the afternoon at 1 pm while undergoing surgery to remove a bullet from his brain.

Lee Harvey Oswald was later arrested for his murder but three days later he was himself shot by Jack Ruby. To this day no one really knows for sure who shot the President. There have been all sorts of allegations but the mystery remains.

Who knows? Perhaps one day the truth will be known. Meanwhile, it remains a tragedy that put an end to the life of a great man and politician admired by many.

For my fifteenth birthday, also in November, I was given a watch by my parents. My first one. My godmother gave me a gold signet ring as was customary. Unfortunately I did not have a special party (dance), but still it was special for all the close family was invited and wished me well.

Popy, my future husband was also turning fifteen that year. I had not met him yet but knew his sister Monique who was in the same grade as myself. Plus, she had started out to be Ivan's girlfriend.

I had a dream that I was invited to Popy's party and somehow we hit it off.

As it turned out I did get invited, but apparently it was reluctantly on his part as he had never been invited to any of our parties (surprise parties, they were called).

Nothing special happened on that day. He danced with me once. I thought he was quite cute. I already knew Marcel and Jean-Claude (his cousins), as they were friends of Ivan who went to the same college of St Esprit, while Popy attended another one in Curepipe, St Joseph's.

Cupid Strikes

A few months later we were invited to Tante Jacqueline's place for a new years eve party.

Ivan and the elder sisters had planned to go to some nightclub and so I was the only one to accompany Maman and Papa.

I'll never forget that evening. I was wearing white, below the knee, tight corsaire as was the fashion in those days and a sailor type top. I thought I looked okay, with my teased up hairstyle and real pale pink, almost white, frosty lipstick.

Popy also came with his parents that night.

As it turned out it was the start of our romance as we danced mostly with each other that night.

Gilles, my future brother-in-law, was also present and as he later joked reckoned that Popy, his friend, got to me first.

It was a very romantic night that I won't elaborate much on as it is described in one of the following chapters.

As it was, during the school holidays one day I received a phone call from him inviting me to his bungalow at Trou-Aux-Biches, the following Sunday.

Popy suggested that I ask his cousin Marcel for a lift in his sports car, as he used to drive there every Sunday and usually asked Marielle and Micheline to join him.

Well, believe me, it was a bit of an ordeal for me to ask Marcel as he had once admitted to Maman, being frank as to how he felt, that there were two of her daughters that he could not stand, Marie-Josée and Marie-France. We annoyed him, he reckoned.

So I had to swallow my pride so to speak and ask. I can't describe the relief when he agreed.

That day we went sailing in "Malesh", the boat Marcel owned in partnership with my brother Ivan and mutual friend, Gilbert. It was previously owned by a Dutchman, thus the name.

It was a beautiful day and I enjoyed myself except for the time that I felt so embarrassed and felt clumsy when with the movement I spilt some of the contents of the Coke bottle I was drinking onto the front of my T-shirt.

We left each other that day with the promise to see each other again. I can't describe how I felt, when going back to start a new year of schooling, his sister, Monique, handed me a letter from him. My first love letter so to speak. In between classes, I tried to read it, my head buried into my desk for fear of being caught.

Alas, I never managed to go through the length of it, so could not wait to get home where I locked myself in the "loo" and my heart pounding, I read and re-read the contents.

Page 123

I dared not speak to Maman about it in case she'd put a stop to my receiving following ones. Plus, knowing my sisters, they would probably have tried to read it.

In that letter, he was asking me would I go to another surprise party that was to take place the following Saturday.

During those years until we all left Mauritius, there would be a surprise party almost every week. It would be on a Friday or Saturday evening.

Every family brought a contribution in way of soft drink and savouries (gadjacks, as we called them).

Usually the person organising it would make a list beforehand of all the guests and plan accordingly what was required in way of food and drinks.

Boys would bring a couple of beers, but would never get drunk. It was considered a disgrace to get drunk. It happened on some occasions that one "got sick", in which case he would go home. Those who got deliberately drunk would never be invited again.

Girls never touched any. After all, we would not dare as we had been warned that we should beware the effects of alcohol. We usually had lectures from the parents when we reached an age where we would start going to parties.

They were rules that "nice girls" never broke or you would earn yourself a "reputation". "You are not to hold hands when you've just met". (Actually, not unless you are going steady). "If a boy asks you to go outside with him to get some 'fresh air' (because, after all, it is pretty stuffy inside, what with the crowd in a room full of smoke), you should refuse outright! A decent girl never, never goes outside with a boy, otherwise her reputation is finished on the spot!"

Another "no-no" was to dance cheek to cheek with a boy you had just met. I must confess that I broke that one once to the tune of "Spanish Harlem" by Englebert Humperdinck. Anyway, I did not dare repeat the experience because my sisters reported the episode to Maman the next morning.

After such a lecture concerning my virtue, I decided that definitely a few moments of bliss wasn't worth the hours of guilt.

Another time when I was reprimanded concerning matters of the heart was when Papa caught Popy and I kissing in the kitchen. (It was broad daylight too! How daring!). It was just before he was about to leave to catch the bus that would take him to school on a Monday morning.

Papa did not say a word to me at first. He decided to let Maman deal with it after telling her.

After spending an agonising day wondering if I would still have a roof to sleep under come tonight, I was confronted with it.

Maman set the "case", Papa joined in to give the "verdict" after decision of the jury (the two of them) that I would not be allowed to spend any time at all, not even a day, at the Maujean's place during the coming school holidays. I was reminded that nice girls behaved themselves.

It was okay for boys, they did not have a reputation to think of. If it was now, my daughter Roselyne would say, "How sexist!". Which is true. But I'm afraid that's how it was in those days.

After all, my parents were doing their duty. No matter what, every generation disagrees with imposed rules. Such is life. One has to conform to the present society.

I must point out that we kissed after months of knowing each other.

The first present that I received from Popy was for my sixteenth birthday. It consisted of a bracelet (that I've still got, but it's gone dark) and a "single" record of Cliff Richard where he sang "Bachelor Boy" and on the verso "The Next Time". Was he trying to tell me something, I wonder? I suppose it would suit his Sagitarian personality well. Life was great in those days. Not a care in the world.

We had a great group of friends. All the Maujean clan, Paulo Berenger related to them, Michel Maujean, Alain Pastor (our first cousin), our close friend, almost a second brother to us, Gilbert Baudot (we called him Baudot Rose for his pink cheeks), and Yves Fayd'Herbe (future brother-in-law).

Between all of us and a group of school friends we'd rage at the parties where the light was subdued by coloured cellophane paper being wrapped around it.

The "Twist" was in fashion in those days and we listened to both French singers like Johnny Halliday and Sylvie Vartan as well as British and American pop singers.

The song "Bobby's Girl" was very popular, and I used to sing it by saying "I want to be Popy's girl".

At school during lunch hours we were a close group of girls consisting of Monique (my future sister-in-law), Marielle Lailvaux and Jasmine Masson (who were cousins to each other and with their parents later emigrated to South Africa).

Little did we know that the following year would bring a change to our peaceful lives.

The quest for independence from Great Britain had started, thus causing political turmoil.

The future looked bleak indeed. One by one our friends started to leave the island, either on their own as they were old enough to fly of their own wings or with their family to distant places such as South Africa, England, Australia, and some who could not bear to abandon their French customs, to New Caledonia.

Numerous were the farewell parties.

Alain and Yves were the first ones to leave. The first to South Africa and the latter to Australia accompanied by his father and brother, Marcel.

It was such a farewell party for Beaudot Rose that Popy and I actually spoke of our future life together. At the time his parents were looking towards the New Hebrides to settle and he promised me if they were to leave Mauritius, he would send for me after saving some money.

As it turned out after thinking of South Africa next as a destination, his parents finally settled for Australia to my delight, as Papa had already applied for permits of residence for our family from the Australian Emigration Office in Canberra.

It took a few months until we learned that we had been accepted.

As to decide where to go in Australia, Papa had written to several Mauritian families living in Sydney and Melbourne and after receiving their opinion on those places, opted for Melbourne where it looked more promising concerning job availability and the number of Mauritian families already established there that somehow would alleviate the loneliness of the early days.

Wherever you went in those days the conversation would always turn to Australia or South Africa.

Somehow there would be people for and against leaving Mauritius. Especially the older generation would be against it. Imagine, they were too old, dear souls, to leave everything behind and start anew, and feared losing their loved ones. As a result, tempers would flare from all the suppressed emotions.

There would also be the ones that could leave, but did not see that there was anything to worry about, that things would come back to normal.

In one word, human nature being what it is, some just could not accept and respect another's opinion, thus causing the unnecessary arguments that they were the loser for, as all suffered for it in the end.

It is only now being an adult, that I can have an idea of what it must have been like for my parents having to take such a step and leave their parents (that they knew they would probably never see again).

My grandfather (Maman's side) passed away just five months after our departure. It must not have been easy to leave a lifetime of memories, the warm security of family and friends for the unknown of a distant land where even its language and customs were foreign to them.

I suppose what must have given them the courage to burn all bridges behind, so to speak, was the knowledge that it was all for the best interest of their children. It was time to turn a new leaf, like their forefathers, those courageous Breton sailors had done nearly two centuries before when they set sail from Britanny towards their destiny on that tiny island in the Indian Ocean, "Isle de France" which later became Mauritius.

CHAPTER 11

The Deep Blue Sea!

Being Mauritian descendants of sailors from Britanny and being surrounded by its unfurling waves, is it any wonder that I should consecrate a whole chapter to the sea.
Since my early childhood when my parents had rented a campement right on the beach, I have wonderful memories of lazy days spent by the sea.
Sunny mornings were spent searching for bigornos and tec-tecs (molluscs) that would later on be concocted into appetising bouillons served for lunch by the nénennes. Not to mention the beautifully coloured sea shells that we collected of various shapes and sizes, some quite big like the one that I remember Grand-Mère using for darning socks and sleeves, that when pressed to the ear would give you the impression of hearing the shaw-ah-ah of waves gently breaking onto the shore.
Usually at mid-morning we would be taken for a spin on the water in a pirogue with Papa and a fisherman who would row the boat. To us kids it was magic to see those beautiful tropical fish through the clear water below.
Maman was adamant that we should not swim for two hours after lunch, so we used to spend time as children, sitting under the filaos, pretending to make tea by filling some discarded tins with filaos seeds and water that we would set to boil in the midday sun.
Then it would be time for a nap, where most of the time as the bed adjoined a window, we would be more interested as to the goings-on outside than actually sleeping. At the time there was no electricity at the beach, so at night kerosene lamps were lit that made the place look cosy and cast shadows onto the walls.
I liked it at night when snugly tucked in bed, everything was silent except for the sound of the waves crashing on the beach, and the sound of the wind through the filaos that was a constant wa-a-ah.

On one occasion that we were spending a month at the beach at a campement that Grand-Père and Grand-Mère rented, Micheline and I, as it was thought the sea air would do us good as we suffered from bouts of tonsolitis, played "cavalier" on the beach with Jean-Claude and Paul Maujean who had come with their parents, Roger and Paule, to visit for the evening. The game consists of being piggy-backed trying to throw down adversaries.

Little did Micheline know that she had met her future husband, Jean-Claude. We also met Yolande during that sojourn. It is a pity that I am not a very good swimmer. In fact I am a bit apprehensive of the deep. I am sure it stems from the fact that Maman was very protective of us whenever we happened to be in water; quite natural when you think that there were seven of us to account for and also due to an incident where I was concerned that caused quite a lot of anxiety at the time.

Monique Maujean at Trou Aux Biches in northern Mauritius.

The Deep Blue Sea

We were spending the day at the beach at some relative's campement and we children were in the water as our parents were playing cards inside while we were supervised by a nénenne (a young one) sitting on the beach, who had been given all the recommendations to forbid any of us to wander from her gaze.

As it turned out, I became a bit bored after a while and decided to go and see what Ivan was doing, a few rocks away, fishing.

I never thought of asking the nénenne for permission and went on my merry way, unaware of what panic my action would cause a few moments later when Maman came on the beach to check on us.

As she usually did, she counted the number of children in the sea and ... horror! There was one missing. She realised that it was me and asked the young nénenne, "Where is Marie-Josée?" The reaction of the nénenne was to turn around and say, "But ... she was right there! She was right there a minute ago!"

Well, that's when pandemonium broke out, I was later told. The alarm was given that I had disappeared. All the adults formed a search party and scattered in all directions.

I was sitting on a rock next to Ivan, blissfully unaware of the storm I had caused when Tonton "Allen" appeared in front of us and said to me, "Your Mum is going to kill you!" You can imagine how I felt when told of the anxiety I had caused. Back at the campement I found Maman in tears. They were all relieved to see me walking in but Maman's relief soon turned to scorn and I learnt a lesson that day.

Alas, children being children do not always think of consequences. A few years later my poor mother received another shock to the system when Ivan, being the proud owner of "Malesh" that I mentioned in the previous chapter, had a bit of a mishap at sea one afternoon when the mast broke and it was feared they would go adrift. Ivan, Marcel, Jean-Claude, Robert Masson and Gilbert Baudot were on the boat that day.

Seeing that it was getting late and Ivan should have been back by then, Maman rang Beau-Plan's sugar estate where the Maujean's lived and first talked to the security officer who prior to transferring the call without knowing who she was, told her that the Maujean's were involved in a drama at sea, and some people had been sent to rescue them.

Understandably, Maman was shocked. She was beside herself. They drove to the estate straight away where they were told the proper story and learnt that another boat had gone to their rescue. As it turned out, with a makeshift mast they were on their way back when the boat reached them. They didn't get home until midnight.

The story was in the paper the next day and they all had a tale to tell.

Page 129

Maman was all relieved and attributed the happy ending to "Our Lady of the Sacred Heart" for whom she has a great devotion and has all of us under her care since we were children.

The Maujean's have always been involved in fishing. In fact, they owned the game fishing boat "Le Cygne", a 30 ft by 10 ft boat that the two brothers Philippe and Roger owned in partnership with their brother-in-law, Gaby Lionnet.

"Le Cygne" (The Swan) was designed by Jacques d'Unienville and built by Roger Dupre, Philippe, Gaby and Roger (mainly motor installation). It took twenty-two months to build and was launched in 1950. It was built in Philippe's backyard in Beau-Plan. They all derived great enjoyment catching pelagic fish like marlins, tunas, bonitos and so on.

Violette, Philippe's wife, enjoyed fishing as well and joined the men whenever she could. She once caught a shark weighing about two hundred and fifty pounds.

Philippe can boast about a marlin close to two hundred pounds and a sailfish that might have been a record breaker had he not been disqualified because of a rod breakage. It weighed 125 pounds.

Violette Maujean with a yellow-fin tuna caught off the coast of Mauritius.

The Deep Blue Sea

One of Roger's prize catches was a marlin of around 350 pounds. Popy, (my husband), was about ten years old when he caught a bonito close to 25 pounds. He enjoyed fishing but unfortunately those expeditions were marred by vicious bouts of sea-sickness.

Luckily now he does not suffer from it, only on occasions where he has celebrated a bit too much the night before.

Ivan, my brother, took part in many fishing expeditions with friends, like St Brandon, off-shore from Mauritius.

He was also a keen spear-fisherman. Papa never had much opportunity in taking part in game fishing. He was quite happy going in a pirogue or sitting patiently on a rock, rod in hand, waiting for that big one. That's what I call real dedication.

His dream was that when he could retire, he would live by the sea. Alas, it was not to be. On one of his diving expeditions with his cousin Roger,

Philippe (my husband) with a 200lb shark caught in the northern waters of Mauritius.

Ivan once came upon a shipwreck that he asked Papa to investigate for him. Thus a copy of such investigation. (Please note the way that people spoke in those days! Believe me, it is no mistake on my part!).

Minutes of the proceedings of the "Mauritius Marine Board" in reference to the loss of the ship "Caprera" of the Burthen of 597 tons. William Thomas, commander, on the "Whale Rock", Cannonier Point, Mauritius, on the night of 9th February, 1866.

The board met at the post office on the 19th February, 1866, and was composed of the following members:-

D. Wales Esquire, Harbour Master and President.

H. Adam Esquire, President Chamber of Commerce. Jas. Fraser Esquire, Lloyd's Agent.

T. H. Mullens, Surveyor to the "Mauritius Marine Insurance Company".

J. P. Ellis, Surveyor to the "Melbourne, Victoria Insurance Coy".

Assisted by:-

Captain Thurtell, of the barque "Chatham" and Cptn Richards of the ship "Solway".

Appeared before the board:-

William Thomas, Master; Andrew Jamieson, Mate; Alex. J. Rainey, Second Mate; James Carey, Seaman - all of the "Caprera".

William Thomas, sworn:-

I was the Master of the ship "Caprera", she was built at St Andrews, New Brunswick in 1864 and classed five years A.I. in the Veritas. At the time of her loss, she was coming from the Chinchas Islands to Mauritius with a cargo of guano. I have been Master since 1847 and passed my examinations in 1850. This is my first voyage to the Mauritius. I have been in Australia, India, China and North America. I never lost a vessel before my running ashore. I abandoned one at sea. In coming to Mauritius, I had no sailing instructions. I had a chart which I produce. It was published in 1836 and there are no lights marked on it. When at Chinchas I made enquiries of other captains bound to the Mauritius. I was told to come round the north end of the island, that there was a good light off the harbour, but no-one told me that there were lights on Flat Island and Cannonier Point. My mate had never been at the Mauritius, but two of the seamen had.

We came in between Flat Island and the Quoin at 6 pm. We were between those two islands, a little to the westward of the Quoin. The wind was NE, the ship running about 6 mph. The lights were lighted on Flat Island and Cannonier Point at about half past six. There was a second light at Cannonier Point, a red light.

It was a very distinct light, as bright as a vessel's side light.

That red light was to the eastward, Cannonier Point light about two ship's length. From information given by one of the seamen, I was under the impression that these two lights were at the entrance of Port Louis. I hauled to the southward for the purpose of anchoring near these two lights and got a cast of the head. The mate called out, "There is very little water. Hard a port the helm". This was done immediately and the vessel's head was well off the land, when she struck and remained fast. Her stern, however, was carried out to the NW. The courses from 6 o'clock to 8 were W, WSW and SW by W. The vessel was under easy sail after passing the Quoin. That is, the main sail and foretop gallant sail were taken in.

I attribute my vessel's position when it became dark to a strong current against me. I considered that I was well round Cannonier Point, when unfortunately I was still to the northward of it.

I should have hove my vessel to and waited till daylight, only I was afraid of driving too far to leeward and not getting up again.

From the time I saw the light on Cannonier Point, I was under the impression that it was the light off the mouth of the harbour. It appeared to me to be at least 16 or 18 miles distant, and the red light seen afterwards confirmed me in what I now feel was a great error.

Before leaving Callas I made enquiry not only of the British Consul, but of many other persons for more recent charts than mine of 1836, and for sailing instructions, but I could procure nothing of the sort.

I owned one quarter of the Caprera; 16/64ths. I think that she is insured for 6000 pounds currency, about 4800 pounds sterling, but I cannot state it with certainty. There are four other owners besides me. They all live in St John's in New Brunswick. I don't know whether the freight is insured or not. When at Callas, I drew for my disbursements on the owners instead of drawing against the freight of my charter party entitled me to do. I did so because the rate was more favourable. The "Caprera" cost to sea on her first voyage about 5400 pounds sterling, that was without coppering, spare stores or classification.

(Signed) W. M. Thomas.

Andrew Jamieson:-
I was Chief Mate of the "Caprera" at the time of her loss. I have been 31 years at sea. This is my first visit to the Mauritius. It was my watch on deck from 6 to 8 on the night that the ship was lost.

I saw the lights on Flat Island and Cannonier Point shortly after sunset; but I had no idea that the latter light was on Cannonier Point. I was under the impression that it was 15 miles distant, and (from James Carey's statement) that it was one of the lights off Port Louis. I looked over the Mercantile Navy list of lights with great care during the voyage and found both Flat Island

and Grand Port lights, but no mention of any other lights on the Mauritius coast.

(Signed) A. W. Jamieson.

(The Mercantile Navy list of 1864 being examined by Mr Jamieson's statement was found to be correct).

Alexander Griffith Rainey:-

I was 2nd Mate of the "Caprera". I have been 6 years at sea. This is my first voyage as 2nd Mate. I remember coming between Flat Island and the Quoin on the 9th February. I was never at Mauritius before I saw both Flat Island and Cannonier Point lights. Just after they were lighted, I thought Cannonier Point light was between 15 to 18 miles from us. I noticed anoth- er light to the eastward of Cannonier Point light. It was a small light. It appeared to be too large for a house light. I had heard Carey say that there were two lights at the entrance of the port and supposed that the light I saw might be one of them. I did not however pay much attention, being engaged shortening sail at the time. It was a bright light, rather deeper in colour that Cannonier Point light, but not a red light.

(Signed) A. G. Rainey.

James Carey (sworn):-

I was a Seaman on board the "Caprera". I have been at the Mauritius on two previous occasions. Once in the "Mount Stuart Elphinstone" about 6 and a half years since, and once in the "Croesus " about 3 and a half years since. Since the Captain asked me about the lights, I told him that he would first see one light, and that when off the harbour he would see two at the same time. I said nothing about distances, when running to the SW I saw a light to the eastward of Cannonier Point light, but I cannot say what its colour was.

James Carey.

Mark

(This witness was asked many more questions, but his answers were those of a very ignorant man, and threw no light whatever on the enquiry. It was evident to the board that he knew nothing whatever about the Mauritius).

REPORT

The "Caprera" was nearly a new ship of 597 tons burthen, she appears to have been worth, when coppered and stored, 6500 pounds. The Captain owned one-quarter of her, and as stated in his evidence she is insured for only 4800 pounds, and the freight not insured at all. He must be a heavy loser by her loss.

The "Caprera" lay about a month at the Chinchas Islands taking in guano and sailed thence to Mauritius on the 20th November, 1865. There were other vessels at the Chinchas bound to the Mauritius whilst the "Caprera" was loading which may be mentioned, the "Agnes" and "John Banfield". Mr Thomas, who has been a Master since 1847, and whose certificate is dated 1850 had never been at the Mauritius, neither had any of his officers. There was however, one of the crew who had been there, twice within the last 7 years, and who unfortunately was relied on as an authority with regard to it, whilst in reality, he knew little or nothing about the place.

On leaving Callas for the Mauritius, the commander had no sailing instructions for approaching the island, beyond what he gleaned from conversations with other commanders of vessels. He had, however, Laurie's chart of Mauritius and Bourbon, published May 10th, 1836. That chart is by no means a bad one, and is on a tolerably large scale, but no lights are marked on it.

There are 5 lights on the coast of the Mauritius, 3 of which are first class lights and 2 are harbour lights. The first class lights are: "Ile Aux Fouquets" or Grand Port light, situated on an island on the edge of the reef, on the east side of the island of Mauritius. It is a white light, fixed and visible, 18 miles from the deck of a vessel of 600 tons. (Flat Island light (revolving) is white and is visible 32 miles, and Cannonier Point light (fixed) is visible, 10 miles. This latter light is on a low point at the NW extremity of the Mauritius and was placed there to warn ships of the reef in its vicinity, and the "Whale" a dangerous detached rock to the northward of it. Cannonier Point light is also a white light, but on a certain bearing changes from white to red when vessels are to the south of it, thus change indicates that vessels are too near the reef that extends along the coast between Cannonier Point and Port Louis.

The anchorage off Port Louis is pointed out by two lights of inferior power, one green, the other red, visible from 6 to 7 miles, which shine over arcs of the horizon of a certain number of degrees, and the place where the colours intersect is the best anchorage, in short the Mauritius coast is admirably lighted and is as safe to approach by night as any coast in the world, only it is not advisable to attempt anchoring off the port at night, unless well acquainted. Neither is there any advantage in doing so, as no communication with the shore is permissible, till a vessel has received clearance, which is only given during the day. Flat Island, Cannonier Point and the harbour lights were first lighted in 1855 and Isle Aux Fouquets lights in 1864, consequently did not appear on the chart which Captain Thomas had, which as before mentioned was published in 1836, but he learnt at Callas, or the Chinchas that there was a light on Flat Island, and on examining the commercial code of signals and Mercantile Navy list for 1864, he found that there was another light on Isle Aux Fouquets, Grand Port.

Though strange to say, there was no mention made in that publication of Cannonier Point light, or of the harbour lights. He also obtained whilst at Callas and the Chinchas, some general information as to the manner of approaching the island, but failed in getting any printed sailing instructions.

The "Caprera" voyage was prosperous to the 9th of February, on which day she arrived on the east coast of Mauritius, and passed by the usual track between Flat Island and the Quoin about 6 pm. Shortly afterwards, whilst steering a WSW course to round Cannonier Point it became dusk, and the lights on Flat Island and Cannonier

Point were lighted up. From this moment, all was error. Nearly all on board appear to have been strangely deceived with regard to the distance of Cannonier Point light, which although only about 3 and a half miles off, was variously estimated at from 15 to 20. It bore about south when first lighted, and an hour later it had not altered its bearing.

There was in fact a strong tide setting to the ESE of which the captain knew nothing, and although there was a 6 knot breeze and the vessel was skipping fast through the water, she was in reality making but little headway, and as the distance run by log placed her at half past 8, a long way to the SW of Cannonier Point.

Captain Thomas and indeed all on board, were perfectly deceived as to the "Caprera's" real position. The information given by the seaman, Carey, who having been twice before at the Mauritius, was supposed to know all about it, was entirely erroneous. He knew nothing of a light on Cannonier Point, though he remembered that there was one on Flat Island and also that there were lights at the entrance of the port, and as another bright light was seen near the Cannonier Point light, he declared, on being questioned by the captain that he recognised them as the harbour lights, and that there was now nothing further to be done but to come to an anchor as the vessel was off the port or harbour. The lead was passed along and the ship steered directly on the light, as the lead was hove. The mate called out that there was very little water, the helm was at once put hard on a port, and the vessel's head was off the land, when she struck on the "Whale Rock", and a few hours after was full of water and a total wreck, thus were lost a vessel and cargo which may be valued together at 16,000 pounds.

The night was fine and clear, the position of the vessel at 7 pm was perfectly well known, not withstanding which, only two hours later, the "Caprera" was wrecked almost in sight of her port of destination.

This loss is to be attributed to various reasons, and not to the want of proper sailing instructions, the board cannot help thinking that had Captain Thomas taken more trouble to obtain such instructions when at Chinchas or Callas, he might have obtained them.

There were several vessels at the Chinchas bound to the Mauritius. Surely the existence of lights that have been established for 2 years must have been known to some of these commanders or officers, or a copy from Hobeburg or some other book of sailing instructions of the manner to approach the Mauritius, might have been obtained.

Another reason is the strange omission in the commercial code of signals and Mercantile Navy list of 1864, of Cannonier Point light and the harbour lights which have been in use for 2 years, whilst Grand-Port light which has only been lighted one year and 10 months, is mentioned.

The velocity of the tides may be given as a third reason of which, however, the Captain ought not to have been altogether ignorant, although he had no regular instructions for on the chart he was navigating by, will be found between the north end of Mauritius and the Quoin de Mire, two important notifications: "Heavy race with ebb tide". Commonly 3 miles an hour which ought to have put him on his guard in a place of which he knew nothing whatever of the direction or velocity of the tides.

A fourth reason was the erroneous information given by the seaman Carey, coupled with the fact of a second bright light being seen on the shore, to which all the witnesses testify, and which proceeded doubtless from some private house lit up with globes, in the manner usual in the Mauritius. These bright lights are to be seen on all parts of the coast of Mauritius, and are unavoidable in a country where doors and windows are generally kept open, but it is difficult to believe that there was hardly any difference in the appearance of the second light seen, and a first class light, only 3 miles distant also having determined that the light was 15 to 20 miles distant when first seen, and Carey knowing nothing whatever about a light at Cannonier Point. It was natural to believe his statement that the lights seen were off the port, all these circumstances contributed more or less to the loss of the "Caprera".

But on the other hand, the captain being on a strange coast ought to have been more than usually cautious. He ought to have known how generally erroneous are statements made by uneducated persons, that all such statements ought to be taken with great reserve. How was it that although from half past 6 till the vessel had only altered her position four miles, it was supposed that she had run, 15, and with so high and distinct, an island and the Quoin almost close to them, the whole time. For when she struck, it was only 2 and a half miles off. No bearing lights or land were taken. It was presumed from the first that the lights were the harbour lights, and all that was done was done on that conviction. Surely a commander of ordinary prudence, would have been satisfied with making his voyage to Flat Island successfully and once to the westward of it would have endeavoured to keep in its neighbourhood till daylight, when he might approach the port with confidence.

If Captain Thomas knew nothing of lights ahead, at least there was the Flat Island light, and with its aid, there would have been no difficulty with a commanding breeze in maintaining the vessel's position, and there was a commanding breeze.

The board therefore are unanimously of opinion, that Captain Thomas acted with great rashness and imprudence, not to say carelessness, in continuing his voyage by night after passing Flat Island. He says he feared falling to Leeward of the island and not being able to work up to it again. It is well that everyone bound to this port should know that there is no difficulty whatever in getting to windward. Ships come in from the westward continually. All the cattle ships, all the Bourbon ships, almost all the traders from the Cape make the land from the leeward and have no difficulty in working up to it, and large vessels just showing their royals above the horizon at daylight, work up against easterly winds and anchor by sunset.

The board having carefully considered these arguments are of opinion that Captain Thomas's certificate should be suspended for 6 months from the date of the publication of this decision and suspend it accordingly.

This decision of the Mauritius Marine Board was stated in open court as the Act directs, on the twenty-sixth day of February, 1866.

N.B. - The board would respectfully suggest that as notifications of new lights and dangers are sent to British Consuls all over the world, it should be made imperative on commanders of vessels to provide themselves with such information at every foreign port they may sail from and in the event of loss, be prepared to furnish proof if necessary, that they had done so.

J.P.E.
Initial D.W.

CHAPTER 12

Points of Interest . . .
Jardin of Pamplemousses, Paul and Virginie
Pirates and Corsairs

If you ever go to Mauritius, a must is the botanical garden in the Pamplemousses district (very close to Beau-Plan sugar estate). It's main founder was Pierre Poivre. Even though his surname means pepper, a spice, it has nothing to do with its discovery. But Poivre did risk his life on many occasions for importations of other spices from India that the Dutch who had a monopoly on the trade of spices (that were prized as gold at the time) punished by capital punishment any underground dealer who was caught.

Pierre Poivre was also an "Intendant du Roi", the King's representative, if that is the right word for it, and an excellent administrator.
At one stage the garden was described as the most beautiful, unusual, rich and resourceful one in the world.

Walking through the garden amongst the natural beauty of some century old trees, some even dating to the time of Labourdonnais, you will come upon a grave and be moved by the inscription "Virginie". Some people mistake the Colonne Lienard monument for the grave of "Paul et Virginie", a novel written by a notorious French author, Jacques Henri Bernardin de St Pierre, in 1787.

Bernardin was inspired after his stay in Isle de France from 1768 to 1770.

The novel has been translated into many languages. In London it was known as "Paul and Mary", as well as in America. It has been appreciated by numerous audiences across the world in the form of poetry, music and dance as ballets and operas. It obtained success at a time of history when romanticism was much sought, after so much blood had been spilt. The novel was also very much appreciated for its vivid description of nature.

The story takes place at the first half of the eighteenth century in Isle de France where a young nobleman has just settled from Paris.

Mr Latour, as he is called, is killed in the course of a mission to Madagascar and leaves behind a young pregnant wife who later gives birth to a daughter, Virginie.

Mrs Latour's only possession was a small parcel of land and a young Creole woman (slave).

Providence makes her meet a young woman of Breton origin who is unmarried and has a son after being jilted by her lover. His name is Paul. She has no one but an old African slave, Domingue.

The two women become close friends and their children grow up together and fall in love.

It is a pure and innocent love. One day, Mrs Latour is visited by the Governor, Mahé de Labourdonnais, who hands her a letter from a rich relative in Paris who requests that Virginie be sent to her to acquire a proper education.

Virginie must leave and the pair are desolate!

At some stage in France, her aunt wants her to marry a rich nobleman, but Virginie refuses.

In the end after spending three years over there, she realises that she cannot live without Paul and decides to go back, to the joy of her loved ones back home.

She comes back on the St Géran and as the ship comes close to shore, it is hurled against the reefs during a storm and poor Paul who is standing on shore waiting for his beloved tries without success to go to her rescue and the waves throw him back on the beach, unconscious.

People everywhere on board, realising the danger, take off their clothes (bulky ones) and jump overboard. A naked sailor approaches Virginie and asks her to remove her garments so that he can save her, but she is such that she cannot bring herself to do it and the sailor has to go without her.

The St Géran sinks! There is the funeral of Virginie and Paul dies two months after of a broken heart.

I read the book many years ago and was moved by it. (I am a terrible romantic!).

Some people believed that the novel was based on a true story, for apparently when the St Géran did sink in August, 1744, off the coast of Amber Island at the northern end, close to Mauritius, two young ladies were on board: Mesdemoiselles de Mallet and Caillou, who were engaged to two officers: Messieurs de Peyramon and de Longchamp.

Like the heroine, Virginie, they would not undress to be saved and their fiances stayed on board and they all perished.

Jardin of Pamplemousses, Paul and Virginie, Pirates and Corsairs

As I mentioned in an earlier chapter, the St Géran had on board machinery for the first sugar mill, ordered by the Governor, Mahé de Labourdonnais.

Divers discovered the wreck in the late sixties. An amateur diver, my cousin Roger de Speville, and some friends discovered some pieces left of the machinery that was for the Villebague sugar estate, and also a large number of Spanish coins dating to 1740. The St Géran carried fifteen barrels of those coins. They also discovered the bell that rang to call the passengers to rally on deck on that tragic night so many years ago.

One cute story that I think is worth mentioning, as the gentleman in question bears the same surname as my brother-in- law, Jean-Raymond, is the one about a certain Eloi Mallac, a young handsome man born in Isle de France, established in Paris a few years after the novel, Paul and Virginie had known enormous success over there.

He was at a grand ball at the Tuileries and many distinguished guests were present, notably a reknown author, Prosper Merimee, who when asked by his dinner companion, the Marquise B........ about this handsome young man, was answered: "But he is the son of Paul and Virginie. Remember how she had to go to Paris?". The Marquise believed him and asked to be introduced.

Soon, all through the ballroom people were whispering: "He is the son of Paul and Virginie!".

On meeting him, Madame la Marquise, the voice full of emotion, said to the bewildered Eloi, "I am so happy to meet you. I cried so much for your parents. Especially for your poor mother".

Prosper Merimee could hardly restrain his laughter.

The story has it that Eloi Mallac, having also some outstanding qualities, became the Prefect of Nievre. He was also the lover of the Duchesse d'A........., who bore him three daughters. In private, some people called them "Les Mal-Acquises", which literally means: the (mal: wrong) (acquises: acquired) - the wrongly acquired daughters!

Before closing this chapter on Mauritius, it is worth mentioning that the island at the time of French occupation was in an area where corsairs and pirates were often seen and carried out their treasure hunts. One of those famous corsairs was Robert Surcouf who was born in St Malo (1773-1827). (An ancestor, Louis Noel Delphine Arnulphy, was a corsair who served on "La Clarisse" with Rober Surcouf as captain in 1807).

Those corsairs are not to be confused with pirates, as they carried their chase after receiving their orders from the government with a sealed letter of approval, where pirates carried their own acquirement of treasure for their own benefit and were cruel to whoever fell prey to them.

A corsair was required to give half of his booty to the king.

No doubt some hid most of the booty in some secret location, before coming back to port with only a small part of what they captured. It is also likely that some corsairs died taking the knowledge or the location of these buried treasures with them to the grave.

It is believed that accordingly, numerous treasures have been buried on and around Mauritius. I believe that there are still people who go on lucrative treasure hunts.

As a young girl, I can remember hearing about a certain Mrs S........, who had many prominent people interested in a search for some buried treasure that she would lead with a concentrated frenzy, pendulum in hand! Of course nothing was found.

There are rumours that a long time ago, whatever was there, had been discovered by a few families that made their fortune this way.

And it was all kept hush hush, of course. Who knows?

No matter what, it has added a certain mystery that makes the charm of the island and sets some imaginations running wild!

CHAPTER 13

Pot-Pourri and Farewell!

As I am getting close to the final chapter concerning that island of mine, there are some precious and colourful memories that I think are worth mentioning as they are like the all- important outlining threads that form a tapestry, the story of my life.

The comparison stems from the fact that I was quite impressed once by a priest who referred to every persons life as looking at the back of a tapestry where all the knots and criss-crosses that do not make any sense of the picture and yet are so important to the gradual work taking shape on the reverse to give that final, successful picture.

As children, we used to spend a lot of time at weekends and during school holidays at Tante Lise Mamet's place. She was Maman's oldest sister whose husband was Tonton Henri, and their children were as follows: Danielle (between Micheline and Marielle's age), Marc-Henri (my best friend), Marie-Anne (Sylvianne's age), and Christine (the same age as Marie- France).

Being a dressmaker, Tante Lise was very fashion conscious, and had her daughters perfectly groomed for every occasion. (She was only twelve when she sewed her own dress as a flower girl at a wedding).

She would give the final inspection before departure for the Sunday morning's mass and somehow I always felt that there was the final little "something" missing where I was concerned, as being from such a large number of daughters, we were reasonably dressed. But with no trimmings. In fact, I think that sometimes Maman could not keep track of who needed what in way of socks etc., as it was more or less a case of first in, first served policy.

As children we were a bit intimidated by the grown-ups, for after all, they used to go out a lot and would leave us in the care of the nénennes. Such a nénenne was Marthe at Tante Lise's. She worked in their household for years.

In fact, I have known Marthe for as long as I can remember. She was good at keeping us in check and soothed the children's little hurts and pains.

Tonton Henri had an artifical leg as his leg was amputated below the knee as a result of a shooting accident on a hunting party when he was fairly young. He used to keep a spare wooden leg in the bathroom that used to scare the hell out of us when we would be confronted by it in the dark during one of our numerous hide and seek games.

The Mamet's house was on a huge property belonging to Tonton Henri's brother, Roger, and there were three houses built on it. One huge one, of weatherboard of colonial style, a smaller one for his mother and unmarried sister, Marga, and Tante Lises's house. The latter two were separated by a canal, about 4 ft wide and 2 to 3 ft deep, that went through the whole property and finished about a mile away into a dam. There was a small bridge to go across, but we used to jump over.

There was plenty of room for us to give free vent to our energy when we used to ride bikes or play numerous games like children do, everywhere.

At the edge of the property, near my cousin's place where there was a dentist surgery, was a huge tree that we used to climb on and have full view of the poor patient on the torture chair.

We used to make faces at our cousins or relatives when they happened to be sitting on the other side, and thought that we could get away with it as Tante Marcienne used to work there. As it turned out, we got into trouble and were forbidden access to the tree.

There was a senile old lady, Tante Marguerite van der Meersch, their great aunt who was bedridden and lived in a one bedroom sleep-out on the property. Sometimes Tante Marguerite could remember her younger days and gave us some interesting insight into her life then. Like when they used to travel in carriages, etc. She had some pictures of saints on her walls and used to crochet some tiny little doilies that she would stick next to the pictures. To her they were like flowers, I suppose. Poor soul! We used to make fun of her. How cruel youth can be.

Sometimes we used to hide under her huge high poster bed, and she would threaten us with her chamber pot.

Tante Marga was a milliner. She was very much in demand and catered for the high society. She followed the latest fashion from Paris.

To our delight, she used to give us some scrap of materials, smooth velvets, lace and gauze, and we used to sew some hats for our dolls.

We used to spend hours, to our parents content, totally absorbed in our creativity. Tante Marga had a good sense of humour and travelled a lot. She had a lot to offer to us children in her anecdotes that would make us double up with laughter.

Pot-Pourri and Farewell

The Mamets now live in Brisbane. All the children are married and have children except for Marco. When we were children we reckoned that we were going to marry each other when grown up.

My father's younger brother, Tonton Roland and Tante Genevieve Nozaïc only had daughters. In fact, five of them.

We were closest to those two sets of cousins, as all the others lived on sugar estates and we would only see them at special occasions. People like the Arnulphy's, Jacques and LouLou (Roger). Jacques is married and lives in South Africa and LouLou was killed last year in a car accident.

Leon (Zoum as he is affectionately called) is the only son of Tonton Leon and Tante Monique Arnulphy. Tonton Leon passed away a few years back in Melbourne, and Tante Monique has remarried to Brian Jackson. They all live in Brisbane now.

Zoum is interested, like me, in our family genealogy. He regularly comes and visits us in Cairns.

We also see the Mamet's whenever we go to Brisbane. Our Nozaïc cousins are Christiane, Joelle, Françoise (my age), Pascale and Suzelle. They are all career orientated, and travel a lot. Suzelle, I believe has a beautiful voice and has sung in operas while living in South Africa. She is now married to Leon Arnulphy, my cousin.

All the others still live in Mauritius. Some of our de Speville cousins (Tante Therese is Papa's sister) now also live in Australia with Daniel and wife Charlotte and Sylvain's son and daughter, Denis and Josephine living in Kuranda.

For a long time, Papa did not own a car, as I mentioned earlier, so we only went out when asked by other cousins or friends. On the other hand, when we did buy one a couple of years prior to leaving the island, we used to go out every Saturday and Sunday.

Saturday mornings usually were spent doing some shopping in Port Louis, the capital and attending "Tele-Box", a novelty in the sense that it was like a jukebox with a picture.

There was a special song by a comedian, Fernand Renaud, "Et Vlan Passe Moi L'Eponge" (And Wham! Pass Me The Sponge) - you really can't translate it - that had Papa in stitches.

We used to favour "La Plus Belle Pour Aller Danser" (Looking My Best To Go Dancing) by Sylvie Vartan and "Le Jour Le Plus Long" by Dalida. It was at the back of a Chinese shop, and this was what we had been waiting for all week.

On Sundays, Papa used to drive us to Flic en Flac for a picnic at the beach. We would set out at around four o'clock (after the afternoon nap) and stay there until sunset.

Later on, Popy used to come with us when he used to visit.

Once he even succeeded to convince my serious Dad to race another car on the only highway of the island at the time.

Papa and Popy got on well. On those numerous weekends that Popy used to spend at our place, we used to go to the local cinema on Sunday afternoons. Poor Popy. I was not allowed to go on my own with him, so we had to be accompanied by one or two sisters.

It was at the "Rio" cinema, where all the youths of the district would meet. Afterwards it would be goodbye for another week as he had to catch the bus to Yolande's place, his aunt with whom he boarded during school weeks. Poor Tante "Yol" spent a small fortune while he was courting me!

Popy left Mauritius two months before me. Actually it was only two days before his departure that I heard of the news and I was quite distraught at the prospect. It was in June 1965. He gave me a photo of his in a frame that I religiously kept next to my bed.

Popy and his father were the first to leave in their family, as his mother and Monique and Cyril were to catch a plane later on to meet them when the cargo ship they travelled on (the Boundary) arrived in Durban.

I will never forget that day when we went to see them off. As the ship slowly moved away from shore and I was left standing there, waving until my love was only a small dot on the horizon.

A view from the ship of family and friends who came to say farewell to Popy and his father on their voyage to Australia via South Africa.

Pot-Pourri and Farewell

Popy used to write to me twice a week and vice-versa. I've still got the letters. It does you good sometimes to just sit and let yourself be carried away on the distant shore of memories by reading them again.

Even though I missed him terribly, there was little time left to brood, as so many things had to be done prior to leaving ourselves.

First it was all the injections against yellow fever and smallpox. Passport photos to be taken, shopping expeditions to buy some warm clothes.

We were delighted when Maman bought us a pair of stockings to wear with our new high heel shoes.

Maman sewed us some coats, "manteaux" as we called them, out of suede material.

Marielle's choice was a woven black and white coat, while Micheline wore a green one and for myself, of course, it had to be red!

At night we were invited to our numerous relatives to dinner, and they all wanted to farewell us with a memorable meal of venison or crayfish with red sauce that our palates would be denied for the rest of our lives.

As a sixteen-year-old of course, I was nostalgic of leaving people and friends behind, but also there was a sense of adventure! A "the sky is the limit" feeling, with Popy at the far end waiting for me! And my head full of dreams after reading his accounts of such different and exciting places.

Photo taken the day before we left for Australia at my Arnulphy grandparents place in Rose-Hill.

Micheline was also waiting to see Jean-Claude again. Ivan had already left, in fact, on the same day as our cousin Genevieve and her two small sons, accompanied by her brother Jean-Raymond Mallac, with all their painful memories to start anew.

Little did we know that day, that Jean-Raymond was to become our brother-in-law a few years later.

They all left by Qantas and we were to follow on the fifth of October. After saying goodbye to all the tearful domestics, selling all the furniture
and packing all the crockeries and things, all the treasured mementos (we were each allowed to take some favoured books but were still limited) the crates were finally ready to be shipped away.

We went to my grandparent's place (Arnulphy) and Micheline and I used to sleep at Volcy and Rita Monnier's (Mum's uncle and cousin) place at night. Marielle stayed at the Nozaïc cousins place. Poor thing. She was so reluctant to leave.

She found it very hard as she had started to work in an office and loved her job and had made many friends. Her future had started. I think she was also very much interested in some guy and the prospects looked very promising. She wanted to stay behind but Papa would not have a bar of it. She was twenty years old mind you. But in those days, girls were not as assertive.

We were to leave on a Monday morning, the 4th of October, 1965. As it turned out, there was a delay of 24 hours and we left on the fifth.

A family farewell for the Maujean and Nozaic families at Roger and Paule Maujean's house on Beau-Plan Sugar Estate.

Pot-Pourri and Farewell

We were all gathered at the airport at 6 o'clock in the morning, donning our newly made coats and feeling very chic.

Papa drove his car for the last time before handing the keys to one of his former colleagues who bought it.

All the aunts and uncles and cousins were there that morning, save for the older ones. Grand-Père and Grand-Mère Arnulphy had all privately said their goodbyes.

My two grandmothers had not said their final adieu, for Grand-Mère Nozaïc did come to Australia a few years later to stay, but could not adapt to the climate and returned to her native land.

As for Grand-Mère Arnulphy, she is still going strong in Australia. Little did we know that Grand-Père was near the end of his final journey.

In all aspects, when a new leaf is turning, comes a time when it is best to look forward, concentrating on the road ahead leading towards our destiny.

Ivan, my brother, ready to depart for Australia from Plaissance airport.

Nozaic family members at Plaissance airport to farewell us on our departure for Australia.

Part 2

Australia – The Promised Land

CHAPTER 14

Australia! ... Here we come!

It was the fifth of October, 1965. The whole family was gathered at Plaisance airport.

We donned our new coats sewed by Maman, as the air was cool being early in the morning, six o'clock to be precise.

I was especially proud of my new pair of stockings and high heel shoes that I wore for the first time. I thought that they contributed to make me look so 'chic' and grown-up for the occasion.

The 'petites', my younger sisters, could not wait for the moment to set foot on board the aeroplane. I might add that it was going to be a first for all of us.

I remember Maman telling me about the first time she set eyes on one. It was the first aeroplane to fly over Mauritius. When it flew over the Saint-Hubert sugar estate where she lived as a child, it was a great event very much anticipated by the whole family, excitedly posted at the upstairs windows at the scheduled time.

The small aeroplane coming from Reunion Island flew over from the direction of Mahebourg village.

Maman told me they were quite disappointed when the whole experience amounted to nothing more than sighting a black dot moving slowly across the sky accompanied by a roaring sound. As she was eight years old at the time I figure that this event took place around the year 1932.

However, a few years later while Maman was attending a regatta at Mahebourg, they were pleasantly surprised by the appearance of three aeroplanes that flew over the area at a reasonably low altitude.

To this day Maman is fascinated by the sight of one and feels compelled to go outside to have a peek whenever she hears it's roar.

It must not have been easy for my parents when the time for departure was announced.

Page 153

I remember passing from one set of arms to another when all the relatives gave us a final hug and a kiss. A few tears were shed, especially when saying goodbye to our Nozaïc and Mamet cousins. Personally it was the separation from Françoise (Nozaïc) and Marco (Mamet), cousins and close friends.

This voyage from Mauritius to Melbourne, our final destination, lasted seventeen hours.

At first we were all excited for the first few hours of novelty but it became boring when hours on end we flew above the sea.

To be quite honest, I was a bit impatient to be reunited with Popy. It was getting a bit tedious for Micheline and I to refresh our make-up as we wanted to look our best for our sweethearts.

It was around five in the afternoon when the plane landed at Cocos Island for refuelling.

We spent about two hours on this island that only had a few inhabitants. It was good to stretch our legs by having a stroll on the beach before being advised that dinner would be served.

Dinner! we exclaimed, and Papa had to explain to us that the British custom was quite different to ours. Dinner at home would be no early than eight in the evening, you see. As we were not familiar with the Australian way of calling lunch dinner, I wonder if indeed it was not so — as after all there is a time difference of six hours between Mauritius and Australia.

The restaurant faced the sea and we had a New Zealand waiter to attend to our needs and the eight of us sat at the table.

Marielle was the first to test her knowledge in the English department when she wanted a glass of water. After much explanation to the poor man who was not familiar with the Mauritian accent, her wish was granted to which she humorously replied 'cinq sous' (sank soo), which means 'five cents' to thank you! That poor man did not know what we were all about when we burst out laughing.

It was the first time when we started to realise the wisdom in Papa almost forcing us into having English reading sessions a few months prior to leaving. We were not amused at the time.

The resuming flight to Perth where we landed around 2 am was quite boring as it was night, save for the soup of kangaroo tail that was served for supper.

Poor Marielle did not have much rest as she suffered badly of travel sickness, a fact that did not help things as she was reluctant to leave Mauritius.

An incident caused me much anxiety as we were in transit at Perth airport. I had lost my visa. Somehow I could picture myself being left behind and having to catch a plane on my own to Melbourne.

(My dramatic nature!). Of course nothing of the sort happened after Papa had a talk to the officials.

Australia! ... Here We Come!

Later on Marielle confessed that she had simply taken mine out of my handy bag while I was in the powder room. As it was getting close to the time of being reunited with Popy I was quite lenient towards her.

At daybreak we took turns in sitting near the window as we flew over Australia, all of us wanting to watch the scenery unfolding below.

How exciting it was! The land was so vast and yet everything looked so minute from the distance. Farms and houses looked like doll houses and the sheep like mice on a green carpet.

When we flew over the suburbs of Melbourne it looked so orderly. At last! The big moment had arrived and we landed as Essendon airport.

Micheline and I walked on the tarmac, our eyes like radars scanning the awaiting crowd in search of a glimpse of the two lover boys.

Alas, disappointment set in when we could not find them and were told by my brother Ivan and friend, Yves Fayd'herbe that they could not make it this day as they had already had time off work the previous day when they had come to the airport to be told that the plane had a 24 hour delay.

It seemed to take ages passing through immigration. All the suitcases had to be searched. Papa had lots of documents to produce for inspection.

The first thing that startled us when stepping out of the building was to see a white man sweeping the pavement. We weren't used to seeing that!

There were two cars to drive us to our house. My parents and the petites travelled with Ivan and the rest of us went with Yves.

It was peak hour traffic around eight in the morning. Our eyes weren't big enough to take it all in - the highways and tall buildings - in fact everything! It was all so new, we even took pleasure at passers-by.

Finally we arrived at our new abode in Forest Hill, a double storey house with an upstairs patio. Ivan told us that we would be living upstairs while the owners occupied the bottom flat.

Nicole Leblanc, a compatriot who had come to Australia a couple of years before with her young family and who knew my parents, had gone to the trouble of hanging a huge banner in the entrance hall that read:

"Welcome to your new home".

It was a lovely house, fully furnished with all modern amenities.

When we saw the washing machine, we could not help thinking of the poor 'bibi' (domestic) back home who used to hand wash our clothes on a special slab outside the house and the 'dobi' (Indian name), a young man who would call every now and then to collect the linen to be laundered. It would be delivered a couple of weeks later looking impecable and crisp as Maman would take an inventory of the stock by consulting her special notebook where every item would have been listed.

After enjoying our first 'morning tea' that consisted of a delicious cake baked by Nicole, our landlord, a Mr Wright, came up to get acquainted.

Page 155

Well, you should have seen the expression on his face when we all shook his hand, especially the girls! Ivan had to explain to us later that it was not the custom in Australia to shake hands with females.

Mr Wright said 'Good die, to die'. After seeing the blank looks on our faces, Ivan said 'Good day, today'.

As he pointed out the various electrical appliances to Maman, chit-chatting all the while, we could see that our poor mother could not understand a word, but being polite would nod and say 'yes' a few times (knowing that it would be explained to her by Papa).

She was not amused when Papa told her she would find herself in dire situations if she answered 'yes' to everything. (Maman's knowledge of the English language amounted to some basic words taught by a tutor when she was a child).

Later on all eight of us walked across the main road to the nearby shopping centre, whose name could be seen flashing in neon lights.

It was time for some grocery shopping and it was an adventure that we were all eager to experience. It was so different from Mauritius where there were no shopping centres as such, only the 'magasins', shops that were of one level in different towns. (Shops where you could barter, I might add).

That 'Safeway' was so spacious and clean. Even the trolleys were new to us and we thought that the trolley boys looked quite impressive with their attire of white tunic and hat.

It was quite a change from the bazaar where it was so crowded and you had trouble making your way to the various stalls where the Indians sold their products, each trying to catch the attention of prospective buyers by yelling out the exaggerated value of their goods in a boastful manner. It was so exciting and a bit weird using the new currency of pound, shilling and pence that luckily we were familiar with when doing our maths homework.

It was the same when we went to Box Hill, an adjoining suburb, later on, driven by Yves.

We went past a store and Marielle exclaimed 'Colez' for 'Coles'. Micheline and I were quite flattered when two young men from the local post office walked past us and said 'hello'. In Mauritius, strangers never addressed each other in the streets.

On our return there was a stranger in the house, accompanied by the landlord. We all greeted him by shaking his hand. He was flabbergasted, as was Mr Wright, who's jaw dropped. We had done it again! He was there to fix the washing machine. A point for saying 'Habits (good or bad) die hard'.

The salon (lounge room) was chaotic. Imagine, everyone trying to speak at the same time.

To an outsider it would look as if there was a great debate going on, or

Australia! ... Here We Come!

worse, some heated arguments. For you see, there were a few voices being raised and a lot of arm and hand movements. In fact it was not so, just a normal Mauritian gathering as the whole Mauritian community had come to say their welcome.

Excitement was at its peak, as everyone wanted to give his or her impression of the new country and catch up with news from the distant ones. Needless to say my joy at being reunited with Popy. For the occasion he had brought me a present — a beauty case — a novelty that delighted me.
As the evening progressed, we all got dispersed into various rooms according to our age group. The two Maujean, Arnulphy, Mamet and Leblanc families were there.

The children knew no bounds to their cavorting in the absence of nénennes. To us teenagers it was great to exchange our recent experiences.
Everyone left fairly early though, as they realised that we were very much in need of sleep after such a long journey and very eventful day.

You can imagine Papa's shock the next day on waking up to find out that it was one o'clock in the afternoon. That's right, we had overslept.
Ivan had left early to go to work and did not have the heart to wake us up. He used to work for the 'Dunlop' company in Box Hill preferring an outdoor job to being cooped up in an office that he was qualified for, having obtained his senior Cambridge certificate.

The next day or so, Nicole Leblanc helped us to find a job. Papa was going to have to wait a while and intended to have a part-time job as a French tutor. So Nicole took Marielle, Micheline and I to Box Hill as she thought we could gain employment as shop assistants.

We were at first disappointed at having our hopes of working in an office and earning fourteen pounds dashed, as we had been misinformed on the matter and were later told that we would earn less, Micheline and I being juniors. Unfortunately we weren't even successful that day as we were given the advice to wait a while until we had more practice in the language.

So we ended up gaining employment in a dressing gown factory in Nunawading and started work a week later as machinists. I won't mention the name of the firm as we found out later that we were underpaid. I earned four pounds ten shillings as a seventeen-year-old and Micheline about five pounds 10 shillings being nineteen. ($8.50 and $10.50).

We would commute by bus in the morning and by train in the afternoon. Our supervisor was a certain Miss 'Pride' as we understood it to be. Now I would not bet on it. It took us a while to get used to the Aussie accent, having only experienced the Irish and Oxford English of our teachers so far.

This lady was elderly and looked a bit severe and intimidating with her gold rimmed spectacles.

A young flamboyant girl named Kate was very helpful to us and took great pain in explaining our job to us, stating the word for various parts of the sewing machine. Somehow the word 'spool' stuck in my mind.

That red haired girl was fascinated by the fact that we were French, even though we tried to tell here that we came from Mauritius and not from France. As it turned out they all understood Mauritius to be a place in France. Not many people had heard of tiny Mauritius in those days, so a combination of ignorance and our strong accent added to the confusion.

Working there was an eye-opener, meeting different ethnic groups and people of different social backgrounds. We had been so insulated in our own circle up to then. As a result we suffered a culture shock.

Just to give you a few examples, we could not understand how females irrespective of their age were called girls and addressed to in their christian name. It felt odd calling an elderly lady by her christian name.

After working there for a couple of months, the management asked me if I was interested in obtaining a trade as a fabric cutter, since they thought I had potential after helping Nancy cut out the patterns on numerous occasions. I accepted, however fate decided otherwise when I had to quit my job as we were moving house quite a fair distance away when Papa had bought one in Chadstone.

First Christmas in Australia for Mum, Dad, Rose-Marie and Marie-France.

Australia! ... Here We Come!

That house was of brick veneer and fairly small but it was well situated only some ten to fifteen minutes away from the local shopping centre and primary school where mass was celebrated. Every Sunday morning we used to walk to and fro as Papa did not have a car, being retired, and having to repay a loan to the bank out of his modest monthly pension from England. Sylvianne, Marie-France and Rose-Marie attended the Burwood Primary Catholic School.

Marielle and Micheline gained employment at 'Nicolas', a pharmaceutical company and worked there for a few years until they got married. Marielle even went on a date with the owner's son.

I obtained work at the nearby shopping centre in Myer as stock controller for the lingerie department.

I will never forget my job interview with the personnel officer, a young man of German origin. Replying to his questions concerning my family I said 'My father is on retire'. It caused me to blush when he politely corrected me.

I was very happy to be working in the same store as my boyfriend Popy, who worked in the paint department. My wages were doubled too as compared to the factory. Sometimes Popy and I managed to have coffee breaks and lunches together.

My job was very interesting and it was not monotonous. There were two of us in charge of four departments. When it got busy on the floor, we were called to serve the customers. A few months after the currency changed to dollars and cents. It was no problem to us as we were used to that system with rupees and cents. So we did very well, Popy and I, when Myers had special training classes for employees culminated by a test.

The Maujean's first house in Australia at Repton Road, East Malvern, Victoria.

Page 159

My sisters had made new friends at their school. The discipline was rigid. They were to behave impeccably even when out of school, while wearing the uniform.

Their peanut butter and tomato sandwich used to cause quite a stir at lunch time. I must point out that in those days other cultures had not yet influenced the Australian gastronomy. For instance there were no pizza parlours or Mexican food for take-away. Fish and chips and hamburgers were the norm. Wine was not widely consumed and friends were quite amazed that my younger sisters were allowed a small glass of wine at the dinner table.

Our new neighbours, the Fraser and Varani families were friendly and had children of our age.

Papa had a go at tutoring French for a while but stopped when he did not have enough students.

As he was bored staying at home, Papa obtained a job as a clerk. He worked for that firm until his death some five years later.

Meanwhile, the Maujean families had also bought their own house after renting one together in Malvern. Roger and Paule in Burwood and Philippe and Violette in Oakley.

Roger and Paule worked for a paint firm. Roger doing clerical work and Paule some spray painting which she gave up after a while to resume her former occupation of dressmaking, working for herself at home.
Jean-Claude was in the merchant navy and Paul attended Caulfield Technical College like his cousin Cyril.

Chantal and Christine also attended the Burwood Catholic Primary School.

Philippe worked for Lee Marden, a tobacco company, as a clerk and his wife Violette and daughter Monique worked for Coles in the Chadstone shopping centre. Monique later met John Harris, her future husband, also working in this store.

Their house in Oakleigh was across the road from a golf course that made the delights of Cyril, twelve at the time, who would fill most of his spare time exploring the surroundings before becoming a TV addict as they usually do at this age.

My uncle, Leon Arnulphy (Mum's brother) and his wife Monique, bought their house in Box Hill. Leon worked for Vulcan and Tante Monique with us at Nunawading.

Their son, Leon Junior, whom we affectionately call 'Zoum' was around fourteen and still going to school.

CHAPTER 15

Earlier Days ...
The Adventure Begins

Every weekend we used to go for drives to get to know our new country. Our first outing was to the Healesville Sanctuary. The whole crowd of Mauritians took us there. We felt like tourists with cameras and binoculars.

Beforehand we were told that it was a must, as we would have our first glimpse of a kangaroo and a koala, without forgetting the famous platypus.

We bought numerous souvenirs including badges, and cameras were clicking furiously as photos of us were taken next to various animal enclosures. Photos of importance were to be sent back home to relatives.

It reminds me now that we were like the Japanese tourists of nowadays who love to pose for photos.

On that day we tasted our first Australian pie - yuck! No offence. It was less than pleasing to the palate. I could not stomach this floating 'bouillon' (soup) of a filling. I admit that over the years I have acquired a taste for it. This little discomfort though did not stop us from enjoying our day.

That weekend was the first in a string of visits to the Myer Music Bowl, the botanical gardens, the museum, to country places like Wyala (a ghost town), once famous for gold, to Arthur's Seat and to beaches like Morrdialloc and Rosebud where we seemed to be spending a great deal of time doing the Australian salute - shooing flies away!

I think we got to know Victoria more than the Victorians themselves.

At the time Normie Rowe was a famous young pop singer, as well as Olivia Newton John, Ian Turpie, Pat Carroll and Lyn Rendall. Sometimes they would perform at the nearby shopping centre to our delight.

Sylvianne and Marie-France feature in a photo holding a portrait of Normie their idol. These idols appeared on the television program 'Go!'. I remember Denise Drysdale as a young 'go-go' dancer of the sixties.

In those days it was fun to own a TV set. (We never did in Mauritius). As soon as Maman had finished with the dishes (we got into the practical habit of having dinner early), as a family we would enjoy such shows as 'Lost in Space'. In the beginning we used to miss a few words here and there and really had to strain our ears. A similar situation would arise when answering the telephone. Popy tells me that at first he felt like running away each time the phone rang at work.

There are a few amusing anecdotes to tell in regard to the mastering of the English language. As was the case when my father-in-law asked for a 'slip', wanting to buy a pair of underpants. In Mauritius they were called 'slip', an English word, so we assumed it was the correct one.

Imagine Philippe walking to a sales assistant in Myers men's department and asking for 'slips', to which he was politely told to go upstairs. When he got to the ladies lingerie department he was a bit confused to say the least. He was approached by a female sales assistant who asked 'May I help you?'. After stating that he wanted to purchase a 'slip' he was asked 'What size, sir?'.

Myself and Philippe at Forest Hill, Victoria.

Philippe replied 'I don't know, it's for me!'. I wish I had been there to see her face. Philippe did get his underpants in the end.

A lady had asked for 'something in it', wanting motifed underpants as was the fashion in those days, after being shown a plain one by the sales assistant. Awful crimes had been committed when babies were put into an 'incinerator' instead of incubator for being underweight at birth. Lawnmowers turned into 'mohairs' and sheets into 's_ts', bikinis into 'biggy knees', the beach a 'bitch', ice-cream into 'I scream' and slacksuit into 'suit slack'.

An especially funny one but not concerning a Mauritian was a Dutch woman who was talking about marine stingers prevalent in northern waters who had so many 'testicles'. I must admit that even now, there are certain words that I avoid mentioning because of my strong accent. They might make me blush!

Sometimes it would be also funny in the French way as was the case when my brother-in-law Cyril, who as a child told his Mum 'Je n'aime pas les vegetables' (I don't like legumes — turning an English word into French).

We used to go out every Saturday night. A group of us would enjoy ice skating at the St Kilda rink. I admit that I was not very good at it but would be encouraged by the most experienced of the group who would hold my hand and slide me along, which quite often resulted in my landing on my derriere when they got carried away in their zeal. Embarrassing to say the least, but it was good fun.

It was a barrel of fun visiting the amusement park - Luna Park. Having a go at such rides as the big dipper when you felt your heart reaching up to your throat. I was even brave enough to try the 'Rotor' that left you looking like a dead lizard. Legs and arms spread apart, plastered to a wall turning at tremendous speed while the floor has been gradually dropped. It was also quite horrifying when coming to the end, the speed was decreased and you would feel yourself sliding down with the sensation that you would crash to your death.

It was quite funny actually to just watch people on this particular ride, for the males bell bottom trousers (as was the fashion in those days) would creep up. And as for females, the few who were brave enough to wear a skirt would become totally helpless at being fully exposed.

I attended my first ball as an employee of the Myer Emporium. It took place at the St Kilda 'Star Dust' ballroom. Popy and I were formally dressed for the occasion. He had bought himself a dinner suit (that he also wore for our wedding). I was quite pleased with the full length pink evening gown that Maman made me. I wore long elbow length gloves as was the fashion. (See photo).

It was a very enjoyable evening followed by many more. In those days it was quite popular to go to the drive-in theatres and quite cosy on winter nights to cuddle up to your boyfriend in the front seat of your car while watching the movies.

We did not suffer much on our first winter as it took a while for our body to acclimatise. I remember walking to work early in the morning wearing just a twinset (t-shirt and pullover) over a light skirt.

Even though we went out a lot, Popy and I managed to pay board to our parents, plus save some money towards a deposit on a house.

Six months or so after our arrival in Australia we were followed by many, who having heard how well we were doing in our new country, decided to emigrate.

Patrick Morel, cousin by marriage to my in-laws, could not afford all the fares for his family, so he came on his own and stayed with the Maujean's until he was settled in a job and could afford to bring his family over. They had three young daughters (one of them Josique was my bridesmaid a few years later).

Myself and Philippe all dressed up and ready to go to Myer Emporium Ball, Chadstone, Victoria.

The Adventure Begins

Patrick gained employment with the Broadmeadow's Ford company as a representative. He earned a good pay in those days, $80 per week. He is still working for them nowadays and close to retirement.

Tante Yol came a few months after on the 'Northern Star'.

The Mamet family followed and arrived on the ocean liner 'Australia'.

Grand-Mère (Arnulphy) and her unmarried daughter, Annie, also came.

Single men like Gilles Mackie and Robert Mallac came on their own. Gille's family followed a few months after. Later on they became part of our family when Gilles married my sister Marie-France, and Robert my cousin Danielle Mamet. These two arrived in 1966 on the ship 'Aurelia'.

From then on we often went to the Melbourne port to welcome new Mauritian immigrants. The 'Patris', an Italian ocean liner, brought thousands of Mauritian immigrants to Australia in the late sixties.

The creoles of Mauritius even composed a 'sega' called 'Alla Patris Allé' (When the Patris Leaves).

According to the 1986 census, there are 13,086 people born in Mauritius living in Australia - 6374 males, 6712 females.

There are 397 people living in Queensland - 187 males and 210 females. This information was obtained from Canberra and the Queensland Bureau of Statistics which I double checked.

We all helped these new families with accommodation until they gained employment and could afford living on their own.

As the Mauritian community grew, we used to have get-togethers on Saturday nights in our Chadstone garage.

Philippe's first car, a 1961 FB Holden.

Page 165

It always resulted in dancing enjoyed by both the older and younger generations. I think it served its pur- pose as to let off steam during the adapting period.

Our first new year's eve party took place in a sleep-out on the property of Patrick and Thérèse Morel. Many a tear were shed come midnight by the parents at the thought of loved ones so far away while they comforted each other. A drink of sherry was enjoyed and affordable in those days.

I used to spend many weekends at Popy's family until he reached his eighteenth birthday and obtained his driving license that same day, having already bought himself a car, a second-hand green and white Holden a few months before.

Once, Popy, unable to get a lift back home after visiting me at home, tried hitch-hiking. He was unsuccessful and had to walk all the way for some seven kilometres. Young love!

In those days there was a ballot system for recruiting young men to do their National Service in the army. I remember spending some anxious moments wondering if Popy would be called. Luckily he was not.

The night of our engagement, 17th February, 1967 at my parent's house in Chadstone, Victoria.

The Adventure Begins

His younger brother Cyril also missed out, but in Roger and Paule's family both Jean-Claude and Paul were called.

Popy and I were officially engaged on the 17th February, 1967. It was a special double engagement party for my sister Sylvianne and Jean-Raymond Mallac also became engaged. It was done the Mauritian way and we received lots of flower arrangements that filled the lounge. Unfortunately Popy was not feeling the best, suffering from influenza, causing him to refrain from most of the dancing when usually he is the life of the party. (Still is!).

I chose a diamond ring mounted on platinum. Sylvianne and I wore an Aline white lace dress, identical except for the colour of the underlay. She chose blue and myself a pink one.

We often arranged for our holidays with Popy's parents so we could travel interstate by car and thus get to know Australia.

We travelled to Canberra, Lakes Entrance, Sydney and Brisbane. We would get some knowledge about it by reading the various information supplied by the RACV (Royal Automobile Club of Victoria) booklet. It was also a good way to break the monotony as we travelled most of the day, only stopping for fuel, and would spend the night in a caravan park.

I must mention an event that took place in December 1965 when my brother-in-law, Jean-Raymond Mallac, was working as a teller at the Ormond branch of the ANZ Bank in Victoria.

It was before lunch time when two armed bandits held up the bank. They were Ryan and Walker, who ordered the manager and staff to lead them to the safe where they gathered all the loot and then locked them all up before fleeing.

Jean-Raymond tells me that luckily the thieves did not use the safe combination to lock the door thus permitting them a few minutes later to open it from the inside. These two men were later arrested after committing a series of criminal offences including the fatal shooting of a policeman. Jean-Raymond had to go to court as a witness. Subsequently they were tried and Ryan was sentenced to death after being charged for the murder of the policeman. He was the last person to be executed by hanging at the Pentridge Prison in Melbourne, and the last in Australia as the death penalty has been abolished since.

Jean-Raymond again was in the limelight a few years later when he became a football competition winner after coming the closest to guessing the score which won him $500. One of the conditions of the prize was he had to be interviewed by a newspaper journalist. Jean-Raymond was quite amused when reading the article as the reporter had made his own story that portrayed him as a French playboy.

A tragic event took place in those early days when my great uncle Volcy

Page 167

Monnier was struck by a car while crossing the road in front of the Mamet's residence where he lived with his daughter Rita since his arrival in Australia just two weeks before. Volcy was on his way to the local milk bar accompanied by his daughter and the Mamet girls early in the evening when the accident took place. He was grieviously hurt and passed away a few days later during the Easter weekend. Poor Rita had come to Australia a couple of years before her Dad and was so excited to be reunited with him. She was unmarried with no family of her own.

Tonton Volcy's death affected us all and I can still remember Papa that sad Easter morning comforting us by telling us not to feel sorry for him as he was at rest now, having eternal life as we all were 'des oiseaux de passages' like birds on a journey where this life on earth is just a preparation and it is always harder on the ones left behind. A separation until we meet again one day on the other side.

The whole Mauritian community attended his funeral and comforted his distraught daughter and his sister, Grand-Mère.

Volcy was laid to rest at the Springvale cemetery.

My poor parents! In the three years that followed they went through the organising and expense of four engagements and weddings. In fact Marielle was the first to get engaged, to Yves Fayd'herbe living in Sydney at the time which resulted in many long weekends spent interstate, driven by Popy.

I'll never forget our first time there when after enjoying a very busy three days we had trouble finding our way out to the main highway leading to Victoria. After driving in circles for ages, Popy was stopped by a policeman who was about to book him for doing a u-turn at a traffic light. After explaining his predicament the policeman took pity on us. (Popy reckons that it is the four females in the car that did it!). We were given police escort to the Hume Highway.

Marielle and Yves did not stay engaged very long as it was not practical being so far away from each other. So they got married and Marielle moved to Sydney.

My parents hired a marquee for the reception and decided to have caterers. The whole thing turned out a bit of a fiasco to their chagrin when first of all, coming back from the church they discovered that cups of coffee and tea were about to be served instead of the customary champagne. This was soon rectified but as the evening progressed, to their horror, the food was in short supply. Something quite incredible for the cost of it all.

They learned by their mistake for the following ones — Sylvianne's, Micheline's and mine — were held at some relative's large house and they took care of the catering themselves, which resulted in successful events, even though they catered for some seventy guests.

CHAPTER 16

Wedding Bells!
Happy Times and Tragedy!

The date was set for Saturday the 30th August, 1969 at five pm for my long awaited marriage to Louis Philippe Maujean junior at the Sacred Heart Catholic Church in Oakleigh, Victoria, after an eighteen months long engagement.

It rained that morning when Popy picked me up so we could attend mass together in the chapel of the Chadstone convent.

We did so as in those days it was not the norm to have a nuptial mass.

The day went fast after spending hours at the local hairdresser 'Umberto', having quite an elaborate coiffure that consisted of a curled chignon from which my long veil would stem.

I felt quite nervous when I had a moment to myself prior to getting dressed with the help of Tante Lise. The prospect of walking up the aisle with all eyes on me sent me into a panic that was soon dispersed with the arrival of Tante Lise to add a final touch to my attire.

My wedding dress was of a crepe material with long fitted lace sleeves. It was an A-line with a flat bow at the back from which stemmed a very long train bordered by scallops of lace. It had been a bargain as due to its small size — xx small — it had been reduced to $25. Even so, its length had to be altered by Tante Lise.

When my father-in-law photographed us prior to leaving for the church, he made me stand on a couple of thick encyclopaedias wanting to show the effect of the train spread out.

Patrick Morel served as chauffeur of the bridal car, his latest model white Ford decorated for the occasion.

My younger sister, Rose-Marie, was my only bridesmaid with Josique Morel as flower girl. They wore a long pink dress of very fine ribbed velvet with short sleeves and a fine velvet sash at the waistline.

Our wedding day, 30th August, 1969.

They both had their hair piled up into a chignon with tiny flowers inserted amongst the curls.

Everything seemed to happen so fast from then on. My walking up the aisle on the arms of my very proud and shiny-eyed Papa, meeting with Popy at the foot of the altar.

I remember the two of us holding hands clasped fast as if to support each other amongst all the fuss. (Later on in life it's a gesture that has proven great comfort at many distressing times).

My two brothers-in-law, Jean-Raymond and Jean-Claude served as witnesses who signed the registry while a male vocalist sang the 'Ave Maria' of Gounault and 'Panis Angelicus'.

When as best man, Jean-Claude, dressed in his army uniform had to procure our wedding rings, he suffered a few moments of panic when only retrieving Popy's from his pocket and not finding mine. A few minutes that seemed like hours lapsed before he realised that my ring had fitted inside he larger one.

Wedding Bells! Happy Times and Tragedy!

Jean-Claude Maujean and my sister, Rose-Marie join us at the altar.

We were a radiant couple walking down the aisle.

I will never forget that feeling of happiness while we sat in the car on the way to the reception that was to take place at the Mamet's house in Malvern.

A friend, Andrew Simpson, made the speech in our honour. It was quite humorous as it was on the theme of a boxing match between my Dad as 'Kid Franco' and the challenger 'Battling Philippe' for the championship. I've still got a copy of it but it's in French and would not produce the same effect after translation.

We departed for our honeymoon after a big send-off amidst the rackety noise produced by gravel-filled cans tied to the back of the car and a few spicy remarks written on its back window with lipstick. Quite embarrassing to say the least when stopping at traffic lights.

We spent our honeymoon at Lakes Entrance in Victoria.

After a couple of weeks we returned to 'our home' that consisted of half of an old timber house divided into two flats.

On our honeymoon at Lakes Entrance.

The house was in Seymour Drive, Camberwell. It was about 100 years old and quite quaint. On the front porch there was an old rusty rocking chair that Papa reckoned must surely belong to a ghost.

I loved its old fashioned kitchen with its old stove with cover on top. The back yard looked a bit spooky with lots of trees and shrubs. You could see the spiral of a church in the distance. There was a camelia bush in full bloom that added to the atmosphere.

I was a bit put out the following week when answering the door bell to the store delivery man of our recently purchased furniture, to be asked for my Mum, looking younger than my approaching 21st birthday.

It was also the time when we had bad news from Mauritius concerning my maternal aunt Jacqueline, who was gravely ill following an operation (mentioned in an earlier chapter).

On that second week I got sick with a bad case of influenza and had to stay in bed for a whole week. That's when we had recourse to Dr Patrick Lavoipierre, a newly appointed GP. I was his first compatriot patient. As Popy had to go to work to Frankston, a fair distance away thus having to leave early in the morning, he gave a key to the good doctor who would call every day to give me an injection.

Luckily for Popy the kitchen cupboards were laden with tin food as I had not yet become an experienced cook, as my dear husband could only just cook a boiled egg, so it saved him.

That house could not accommodate a washing machine as there was no laundry as such. I managed doing the washing in the bath tub, a frustrating experience sometimes, especially when the adjacent tenants would decide to have a shower at the same time, thus causing our water supply to be reduced to almost nil.

Wedding Bells! Happy Times and Tragedy!

We lived there for nearly nine months and I loved it. It was so cosy! We moved to my in-laws when they offered us Monique's bedroom after her wedding. It was practical as it would save us the rent money to help towards a deposit on our own home. They lived in Mulgrave, in a brand new Jennings house closer to Popy's work in the Glenn Waverley 'Colour Brush' store that he managed.

My parents became grandparents when a son, Michael, was born to Marielle and Yves. They moved back to Victoria when their baby was about nine months old. Sylvianne and Micheline gave birth, both to daughters, Veronique and Pauline, two months after Michael's birth on the 27th November, 1969. Veronique was born around nine o'clock in the evening of January 13th, 1970 while Pauline was born the following morning at 8 am. Unfortunately, the two mums weren't in the same hospital, causing my poor parents to travel between both. It was also a double amount of anxiety until being told that mothers and daughters were doing well!

Marie-France was engaged to Gilles and Rose-Marie had turned 15 the previous year which was a cause for celebration by having a party at the Mamet's place.

I was so proud of being an aunt and loved my nephew and nieces to death! I was God-mother to Veronique. I wanted to become a mother myself but unfortunately it was not to be for a few years yet.

During this period two incidents that caused us quite a shock and a certain amount of anxiety occurred.

The first was when Papa was knocked down by a car reversing from a driveway on his way to work one morning. Thank God he was not seriously hurt. As a result Papa suffered a dislocated shoulder that caused him much discomfort for the rest of his life. You can imagine our concern on first hearing about it.

The second one also could have ended in tragedy and this time affected my brother, Ivan. While living in Brisbane prior to joining the army, Ivan was working on the construction site of the AMP building in the city. As this letter he wrote to my parents is self explanatory, I have translated it for your benefit. It was not dated but took place around 1969.

Last Sunday.

Dear Mum and Dad,
I was very glad to receive your letter last Friday and to learn that all is well. It is a shame that you have not yet been able to use your fishing reel, Dad. I hope you will find the opportunity soon.
Your letter surprised me, not expecting one from you this week, seeing that I haven't written for a while.

Everything is OK here, nothing major to tell you. Oh, yes! A silly mishap that might interest you!

There are on the building site at work some large air-ducts that go vertically to distribute hot and cold air at different floor levels. The floor ducts from the 15th to the 24th have been erected by myself.

Last Friday at about 9.20 am, I was in the process of taking measurements at the 24th floor so that I could order the last section of one of the cold-air risers. I had covered all the pipe openings on that floor with some galvanised sheets, in order to stop the dust and humidity from affecting them. As I did not find anything more solid to cover them with, as a measure of precaution to prevent people from walking on top of them I had erected a railing.

So, on Friday morning I had gone to the inside of the railing to take some measurements when in a moment of inattention, I was caught in my own trap - I walked on the galvanised sheet. I heard a great noise and realised that it was giving way ... in front of my eyes I see the wall panels of the duct rush past and I feel the friction of air against my skin. I spread my arms and legs to try to slow the fall. A series of shocks and I am at the bottom. (See drawing).

I am stuck and I feel the walls of the duct pressing on my chest and I have some difficulty breathing. I tell myself to stay calm, otherwise I will run out of air. I move my hands and wriggle my fingers and toes. Nothing seems broken. Looking up I can see a square of light a long way through the darkness (the opening through which I fell nine stories up).

I cannot haul myself upward because of the narrowness and I have no place to lean my elbows on. The only way for me to get out of there is by being pulled up by a rope.

I call 'Anybody up there?'.

A voice answers 'What's the matter?', to which I reply 'I'm down the cold air riser. I'm alright. Send a rope.' ... 'OK!' comes the reply. Then I hear talking in Russian or some similar language and I think to myself that perhaps the fellow did not fully understand as I find that he is taking a long time.

I call again and many voices answer me. I hear 'It's Frenchie! He is down the riser! He is alright!'.

They send me a rope but first it's too short, so I say 'Hurry up with that rope! I want to get out before smoko!' It makes them laugh and also reassures them. The second rope tied to the first is also too short.

'Eh, Frenchie. We are leaving you now. It's smoko!'.

'You'd better send mine down then!'.

At last. After what seemed like an eternity the end of the rope reaches me. I give the signal and they start pulling me up.

Wedding Bells! Happy Times and Tragedy!

Mid-way, and being tired (me, not them), they stop and I brace myself against the wall making a stirrup of the rope to pass my foot through and stand up. Finally they pull me through and I come out of that hole, my hair full of dust, nose bleeding and my shirt in tatters.

I go down to the first-aid room where they rub disinfectant over two friction burns on my back while waiting for the ambulance.

In hospital I am interviewed by the Telegraph, a paper equivalent to the Melbourne Herald and also by a television crew of Channel Seven.

After putting three stitches in my elbow and making me do some movements and contortions, the doctor is satisfied that I don't suffer any broken bones and they let me go.

Arrival back at work and there is a great commotion about security on site. The safety committee is blamed, etc. Lucky no strike!

My boss has given me two days off work (full pay!) and work is going to compensate for replacement of the band and glass of my watch that got ripped off my arm taking some skin with it.

On Thursday night, no sleep whatsoever, with all the scratches and patches of skin left raw on my back stopping me from turning over.

Friday morning - joint pains all over!

Today, Sunday, I am still a bit sore but better! I will go back to work tomorrow. I was a bit surprised on the phone to hear that you had already heard of the incident. I did not expect it, so I tried to ring you to reassure you and be the first to tell you about it in case the paper mentioned it the next day. But to no avail.

So, I thought that I would surprise you with my beard! Too late!

A kiss to all of you.

Salame

Ivan

P.S. I send you a newspaper clip from here. It is probably the same photo as the one of Melbourne. Send it back to me with a copy of the Melbourne one, if possible.

After being unable to reach my parents, Ivan rang the Morel's place where he was told that my parents already knew.

Actually it was I who told them as that afternoon I got a shock myself on picking up the Herald to see a large photo of my brother on the front page with his name printed underneath. The headline read 'Man falls down eight floors'.

I thought, what if Papa sees it! It will kill him! So I thought of calling to their place first and find out somehow if he had already read the paper. When he hadn't, I told him that Ivan's photo was in the paper, and that he was alright after falling down some floors.

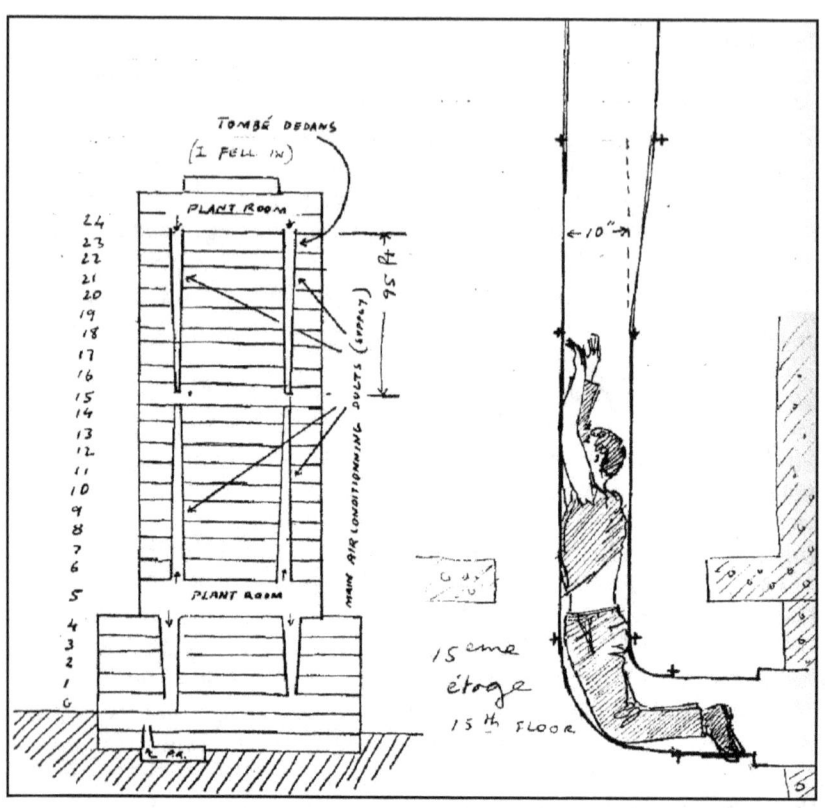

Drawing by my brother, Ivan, to describe his fall into an air-conditioning duct while working on a building in Brisbane.

It was still a shock to him as he could not believe that somebody could be alright after such a fall. He then read the paper.

Me telling Papa caused quite a stir in the family but I know that I said it the best way I could in view of the situation, for I felt that reading it in the paper with Ivan's photo would have caused a bigger shock since the headline did not say that he survived!

Papa could not wait for the time when his grandchildren would be old enough to listen to his stories. Unfortunately, it was never to happen. Fate had decided otherwise!

He only lived to see Marie-France being married, and in November his first grandchild — Michael — celebrate his first birthday.

Wedding Bells! Happy Times and Tragedy!

I'll never forget how his face lit up while showing us the photos, as he remarked how much Michael looked like him as a baby.

On new year's eve, 1970, there was the usual party in our garage and come midnight, while wishing each other a happy new year, he added, 'I hope this year will bring you a baby son'.

On the way home that night, sitting next to Popy driving, out of the blue I had this awful feeling thinking that my parents would be gone one day. A premonition, for a few days later Papa was taken to the Box Hill hospital in an ambulance after developing some chest pains and vomiting. After having an electro cardiogram that revealed nothing alarming, he was sent home a few hours later with the notion that he suffered a virus and the advice to see his doctor in case of a recurring ulcer that he suffered a few years before.

I learnt about the event the following morning stopping at their place like I usually did every day before going to work at the nearby shopping centre.

That afternoon Maman asked Popy and I to spend the night with them as she was concerned about Papa. We did, even though Popy thought that we were over-reacting.

The following afternoon when I visited him after work, I noticed that his speech was slurred but did not worry too much for after all his doctor had called before and after checking his blood pressure etc., thought it best to book him for a stomach xray the following week.

That same day, Papa talked to Gilles about doing the usual procedure at the bank to allow Maman to have access to his accounts in case he could not do so himself. Gilles took care of this straight away, working as a bank teller.

The next day, on the morning of Thursday 7th January, Papa suffered a massive heart attack.

Just prior to the attack, my mother-in-law, Violette and I had been sitting on his bed talking to both my parents, and Papa was telling us how he had some weird dreams during the night and could remember parts of it, including nuns and priests and a chalice that was overflowing with money. A few minutes later as we were about to leave for work, it happened!

Maman panicked and Violette took over. In view of the situation, after trying to reach the doctor unsuccessfully, I rushed to the neighbours across the road to ask them to call for a priest, while Violette used our phone to get medical help. Poor Maman was a mess and my younger sister, Rose-Marie, fifteen at the time, was by her side.

I stayed with Papa, unconscious.

The priest arrived before a doctor. While he administered the last rites of the church, Papa had already passed away which the doctor confirmed later.

Page 177

He asked me for the next of kin and I led him to Maman, to whom he said bluntly, 'He's gone'.

Ivan was at Bendigo (in the army), hours away.

When he got to our place and saw all the cars parked in front of our place, he knew before being told.

We were all in shock. It happened so suddenly!

Papa was buried the next day after we had all gathered at the funeral parlour the previous evening for prayers.

We had tremendous support from family and friends.

As a last tribute from his children, we covered his coffin with his favourite flowers that he tendered himself — pansies.

Papa was laid to rest at the Springvale cemetery in the lawn section. His epitaph reads: 'Il a vecu pour les autres' — 'He lived for others'.

Papa was only a few months short of his 60th birthday. He had never had an operation in his life, exercised daily, never smoked, only drank alcohol occasionally and looked ten years younger. He enjoyed his food though! But his time had come, and I thank God that he did not suffer.

It took me a long time to come to terms with his passing. I really grew up then!

Happy grandparents, Mum and Dad, with Veronique Mallac, Michael Fayd'herbe and Pauline Maujean.

CHAPTER 17

Beginnings ...

Micheline and Jean-Claude, with their one year old daughter, Pauline, moved in with Maman and Rose-Marie. Jean-Claude had just come out of the army and worked in Burwood, an adjoining suburb.

My sister, Rose-Marie, was doing her last year of school. They were good company that helped Maman in her period of mourning. Ivan would spend every weekend with them while being posted in Bendigo.

Papa's death brought many changes in Maman's life. At 46, she was not very independent. Until then she had never even written up a cheque and could not drive.

Micheline and Jean-Claude lived with her for that first year until Miriam, their second daughter, was born on 15th November.

Marie-France gave birth to a son, Gilles, three months after Papa's passing.

That same year, we moved into our brand new home, built by Jennings Constructions at 4 Rosewood Court, Mulgrave, next door to Marie-France and Gilles.

The first house we bought at 4 Rosewood Court, Mulgrave, Victoria.
We lived here for 2 years and 9 months.

My brother, Spr Ivan Nozaïc, Royal Australian Survey Corps, Bendigo, Victoria

I got to look after Gilles junior while his mum was in hospital for the birth of her second child, Denis. Doing so satisfied my motherly instincts. Unfortunately he used to cry a lot, missing his mum, much to my chagrin.

The following year saw us going to Cairns on holidays. It was a spot chosen by my father-in-law and Ivan with the prospect of enjoyable fishing in its tropical waters. Jean-Claude, being such a keen fisherman could not resist the temptation of joining us, so Mum offered to look after their two daughters while they were away.

So it was that we spent ten days in Port Douglas after towing the boat 'Mephisto' all the way, a boat that Popy owned in partnership with his dad.

Violette, Micheline and I enjoyed our days sunbathing, swimming and reading, while the men spent every day fishing. We had not heard of marine stingers then and were blissfully unaware of their threat in that month of October.

Beginnings

We camped in Port Douglas, a sleepy little town in those days, at Brown's Family Caravan Park. Our tents were pitched within walking distance from the beach. It was paradise!

The highlight of our holiday was dining and dancing at its only restaurant on the wharf, decorated with fish nets and sea shells, with a view of the sea both in front and below you through the floor boards.

This town only had one main shop, a combined grocery, hardware, haberdashery store where you could even buy bait for fishing.

Every Saturday evening we attended mass celebrated by a priest from the Mossman parish in an old lopsided little church along the road leading to the hill. Nowadays this old church has been moved to beachfront land and serves all religious denominations. It is known as 'Our Lady of the Sea'.

The men's fishing forecast was accurate. We enjoyed fish in abundance that more than amply satisfied our needs at breakfast, lunch and dinner. We even salted some fish fillets that we used to let dry in the sun, spread on top of a little kiosk's roof of galvanised iron close to the beach. (It is still standing today).

As a result of such profitable fishing expeditions, we became generous and supplied the owner and its patrons who in turn became very choosy when offered such a variety of fish for free.

I think we only went to Cairns once during this holiday, on a shopping errand for souvenirs. We were so impressed from this holiday that we vowed to return north.

The climate was so much like Mauritius!

In those days you were allowed to drive on the beach, very convenient when having a barbecue, as it saved much walking for my father-in-law, Philippe, with his artificial leg.

We went back on holidays a second time while I was expecting my son, Patrick. Monique and John Harris also joined us and Monique was some six months pregnant with Scott. They made the trip from Brisbane where they lived at the time.

Each time we left the north with the decision to come back and settle in Cairns. But as it turned out, we'd get back to Victoria and get settled into our routine again.

The first couples to actually make the move up north were Jean-Claude and Micheline, joined by Marielle and Yves (Fayd'herbe) who had never been to Cairns. They left their jobs and all to start anew.

For the first months they shared a beachfront house at Clifton Beach.

Yves first gained employment at North Queensland Engineers and Agents and Jean-Claude at a Malvern Star store in town.

We made another trip up north and visited them. We were delighted when one evening they served us a 'bouillon of tec-tecs' (pippie soup) that we had not tasted since leaving Mauritius.

I was five months pregnant and my doctor had given me the all clear to travel.

For three and a half years I had felt quite miserable when every month my hope of a pregnancy was dashed.

After numerous consultations with specialists, who could find nothing physically wrong to prevent such an event, I almost resigned myself to the fact that I would never be a mother.

Popy and I even discussed the prospect of adoption that he was against. I can really feel for couples who go through the trauma of infertility.

Feeling depressed, I consulted a new doctor to the medical centre of Chadstone where I worked full time. He advised me to quit work for a while, which I did, and would you believe after settling down to a more relaxed way of life in which I gave myself to my artistic inclinations as I would draw portraits during the day, it happened.

It was some four months after giving up work that I suffered some morning sickness. I thought it was too soon to be sure, and I almost convinced myself that it was due to some virus for fear of being disappointed again.

Popy urged me to seek medical attention, on which I was told that it could still be too early for a pregnancy to show positive but to have it anyway.

That evening we attended the presentation of the musical show 'Jesus Christ Superstar'. All through the performance my mind was racing with anticipation of the next day's test result.

As I did not have a telephone at my place, and could not drive, Popy drove me to Mum's place in Chadstone where I was to call the doctor for the awaited results.

My Mum's visiting cousin, Arlette from New Caledonia, was there and they were both eagerly watching my expressions for an answer as I talked to my GP on the telephone. My heart was pounding!

When he congratulated me I felt myself on cloud nine. I immediately called Popy at work with the good news and he promised to call in at lunch time.

I walked on air as I made my way to the shopping centre where I first called on my co-workers at Myers. They were all happy on hearing my news as they had shared my trials and tribulations. My next stop was at the bottle shop where I bought some cheap champagne, a bubbly wine, for the four of us to celebrate at lunch time.

The whole family was ecstatic and they all got out their knitting needles and crochet hooks, myself included.

Beginnings

There was not a happier expectant mother than myself. I blossomed!

When I attended all the performances of the Russian Bolshoi Ballet, accompanied by my father-in-law (his wife and Popy hated the stuff!), I was attuned with my baby, I believe. Hence Patrick's love of music.

Popy and I wished for a boy as a first child and secretly I thought it would be an added bonus if he had blue eyes and blond hair, even though there was a slim chance that it would turn out so, both Popy and myself having dark eyes and hair.

I kept working at Myers on busy days. In fact I worked the day before his birth and Popy and I celebrated at the special party for Cyril's 21st birthday that evening. After all, the date set by the doctor was for some twelve days later. Even so, I had the feeling that it would not be long before I gave birth.

The Nozaic family in 1973: Back row from left – Micheline and Jean-Claude Maujean, Yves Fayd'herbe, Gilles Mackie, Jean-Raymond Mallac, Phillipe Maujean and Ivan Nozaïc. Middle row from left – Marielle Fayd'herbe, Caroline Fayd'herbe, myself, Mum holding Sophie Mallac, Corrine Mallac and Syvianne Mallac. Front row from left – Rose-Marie Nozaïc, Marie-France Mackie holding Denis Mackie, Gilles Mackie, Pauline Maujean, Myriam Maujean, Veronique Mallac and Michael Fayd'herbe.

Page 183

Sure enough, that next morning after having made Popy a cup of coffee before work, it all started.

The contractions were only two minutes apart. Popy called my sister next door, and Marie-France tells me that I was quite a sight while I practised my deep and shallow breathing learnt from ante-natal classes I had previously attended.

My poor husband did not waste any time taking me to the hospital while the contractions were now only one minute apart.

The nurse told him with a wink not to worry, as it was my first, the baby would probably take a while to be born.

There I was, dying to lie down on the bed and this nurse is filling in all the medical history. So she was quite shocked after Popy had left and she finally asked me to get myself comfortable when she realised there was no time to be wasted, as the birth of my child was imminent.

As it turned out, my beautiful, blond haired, blued eyed baby son was born before the doctor could make it to the hospital. It was on the morning of Wednesday 16th January at 27 minutes past 8 o'clock.

My son Patrick's christening in Melbourne, 1974. Godparents Sylvianne Mallac and Cyril Maujean.

Beginnings

I only went through two hours of labour. All I could think was 'Is that all?'. After all, I imagined such torture as presented on TV and from all the gory details supplied by long suffering female members of the family.

Imagine Popy's surprise when he got to work, frantically trying to unlock the door to his shop while hearing the insistent ring of the telephone, to be finally told that he was the brand new Dad of a son.

I felt so happy and proud when I finally (some eight hours later) held my son in my arms. He looked so beautiful all wrapped up in an aqua bunny rug (Indian style).

Beforehand I had started to worry as soon after the birth he was almost whisked away to the nursery, and when I kept asking the nurses for my baby they all answered that he would be brought to me soon. Even though Popy and Maman assured me that he was perfect and healthy, I began to wonder if perhaps something was wrong.

My fears were proven to be fruitless. He was perfect! The image of health, with his rosy cheeks.

My only regret during those days that I stayed in hospital was that I did not feel as if he belonged to me. The nurses would only bring him to me to be fed, so I could not wait to go back home which happened during a heat wave when the temperature had soared to 100 degrees (Fahrenheit).

A gathering of the grandchildren shortly before leaving for Queensland – from left – Cyril and Chantal Maujean with son Michael, Violette and Philippe Maujean, Phillipe and myself with Patrick and Monique and John Harris with son Scott.

Even though she had two sons of her own, my sister Marie-France proved to be a great help in preparing that first formula of S26.

Unfortunately I could not breast-feed my baby, (having done so the first few days), as he had actually lost weight and was advised to wean him.

Patrick's birth weight was 6 lbs 3 oz.

Patrick was baptised on the 10th February, 1974. We chose my brother-in-law, Cyril, as his godfather and my sister, Sylvianne, as godmother.

Meanwhile, my sister Marielle had given birth to her third child, a daughter, Sandra on the 2nd January in Cairns.

Patrick was the second grandchild to my in-laws, Philippe and Violette after Scott Harris, Monique and John's son.

My little son was only three weeks old when we were invited by Marcel and Peggy (Maujean) to spend some time with them in Rosebud, on the Mornington Peninsula, at a beachside house that belonged to friends of theirs.

We accepted and Popy used to travel the long distance to work every day, something that proved to be worthwhile for him as he so much enjoyed some very productive fishing parties with Marcel every afternoon. They caught some 15 to 20 lbs snapper.

Meanwhile, Peggy and I would enjoy some relaxing days with Jean-Marc and Natasha, her toddler children. We used to go for morning strolls after breakfast and while the children were asleep in the afternoon the two of us used to collect a variety of dried flowers and plants in the adjoining bush and make a bouquet arrangement.

Eric, Geraldine and Catherine Audibert in Brisbane.

CHAPTER 18

A New Start . . .
Moving to Sunny Queensland

Finally we decided to make the move up north. Then was the time to do so while Patrick was small enough. It would have been much harder later on as Popy could not obtain a transfer from his work, so as it was, we were starting fresh.

We sold our house fairly quickly and got $28,000 for it, not bad when you think of it as it had almost doubled in value during the last two and a half years.

It was a sad situation leaving our house as it had harboured such good memories, plus the fact of leaving my sister, Marie-France, next door.

The worst was leaving Maman behind as I was her fourth child to go away since Papa's passing.

My sister, Sylvianne and her husband, Jean-Raymond (Mallac) were also leaving Victoria for Cairns with their three daughters, Veronique, Corinne and Sophie. Our two cars travelled closely on the way.

Our decision prompted Popy's parents to follow us and in the process, their brother and sister, Roger and Paule Maujean, decided to also move north. They did so some two months later, accompanied by Yolande Berenger — Tante Yol.

That year, 1974, was an exodus that saw Marcel and Peggy and family as well as Paul and Jackie Maujean with their baby girl, Sabrina, settling in Cairns.

My brother, Ivan was in the army and posted at Bendigo at the time. He would spend his weekends in Chadstone and was a great comfort to Maman as well as my younger sister, Rose-Marie, who was close to her eighteenth birthday. My sister Marie-France, and husband Gilles, with their two sons, Gilles and Denis, also were very supportive of my mother in those difficult times.

We towed the boat Mephisto all the way to Cairns, close to 2000 miles away. Our two families of Maujean and Mallac, rented a house together at first. It was in Mason Street, Stratford. (It has since been demolished and a set of units erected at the site).

Our first impression was that of being back in Mauritius, the climate and vegetation being similar compared to Melbourne. It was bliss. We felt so free and light after discarding all the woollen gear of jumpers and boots. (It was August, winter time).

Cairns at the time was a small country town, unknown to most Australians to the exception of game fishing fanatics who visited its shore during the marlin season every year.

There was only one set of traffic lights, located on Mulgrave Road.

Suburbs like Woree, Mooroobool and Brinsmead did not exist in those days.

My two sisters, Marielle and Micheline, lived next door to each other, in Pease Street at Edge Hill.

Three weeks after our arrival, one of Sylvianne's daughters developed chicken pox. Needless to say, all the other children caught it as well, including Patrick who was only nine months old at the time.

The timber house we rented had two huge mango trees in its backyard. We were awoken at night by the sound of their fruit falling on the tin roof while bats were having a banquet.

We loved it in Cairns but we had to get physically acclimatised. The four of us adults had trouble keeping our eyes open as we sat in front of the television as early as 8.30 pm. In those days there were only two stations, NQTV and the ABC. We also suffered bouts of upset stomach due to the water.

Almost every Saturday afternoon would see us at the beach, usually Clifton, where the women would sunbake and gossip, still keeping an eye on all our children occupied at building sand castles while our husbands would enjoy some fishing in the adjacent creek (unaware of crocodiles!).

Jean-Raymond used to bring his kyack and a good time was enjoyed by all. Sometimes the older children would join in when we collected tec-tecs (pippies) on the beach along the water line. We were quite a crowd that included our two families plus those of my two other sisters and that of Marcel and Paul.

Almost every Sunday, unless it was blowing a gale, our men went on fishing expeditions on the reef.

They would leave as early as 4.30 am and come back at around 3.30 pm. As a result our fridges and freezers were always full of fish fillet.

The Mallacs soon found a house to buy in Vandeleur Street, Earlville.

Moving to Sunny Queensland

At Clifton Beach – back row, left to right – Caroline and Michael Fayd'herbe, Jean-Marc and Natasha Maujean, Myriam and Pauline Maujean. Front row from left – Corinne and Veronique Mallac.

Popy and I stayed in Stratford as we had not yet found one to our liking. (At this stage we wanted a Queenslander with an established garden).

Violette and Philippe, my in-laws, lived with us on their arrival. They did so for about a month until they bought their present house in Oak Street, Holloways Beach.

When we could not find a house suitable for us, our only option was to have a house built, and after paying only $4000 for our block of land of 32 perches, a Moroccan, Gerard Amoyal, built the one where we have lived since.

It turned out to be a long process, some nine months before its completion, as new building regulations were set after cyclone Tracy had destroyed Darwin the previous Christmas. As a result, we lived with my in-laws for some eight months and moved into our new house just three weeks prior to the birth of my second child, Roselyne.

During that time I finally obtained my driving licence after Popy one afternoon out of the blue told me that he had booked my first driving lesson with an instructor for the following Monday.

Even though it proved to be a nerve-wrecking experience, I'm glad he gave me that push, otherwise I would have kept putting it off. I agree it is a must nowadays but I am the sort who, let's put it this way, I would love to have a chauffeur!

My godchild, Dominic Maujean, was born in February, 1975. That's when it was confirmed that I was expecting another baby.

I felt quite let down when those around me, including my GP, did not congratulate me. I was over the moon! Patrick had turned one in January.

Our daughter, Roselyne, was born on a Tuesday morning close to 8.30 on 21st October, 1975.

As it had been for Patrick, I suffered a very short labour of only two hours.

That event took place at the Cairns Base Hospital and again, my doctor did not make it in time to deliver the baby.

As to avoid disappointment I had more or less convinced myself that it would be a second boy. (My sisters-in-law, Monique and Chantal, had given birth to Christian and Christopher just recently).

I was so proud of my bouncing dark haired baby girl. As much as Patrick was fair, she looked the opposite with an olive complexion. (The same applies for personalities).

I felt so good that I could climb a mountain. Popy came to visit me after leaving my little son in the care of Tante Yolande and gave me a gold plated cigarette lighter to mark the occasion.

What I enjoyed this time as compared to Patrick's birth was that I could have my baby with me as much as I wanted, except at night time.

During my stay in hospital a drama took place in Holloways Beach when a small aeroplane with 13 people on board including the crew, crashed on the land adjacent to the main road.

My son Patrick nursing his little sister, Roselyne.

Moving to Sunny Queensland

This event had just taken place when Popy was on his way home on his motorbike after visiting me in hospital.

He was detoured on the highway and had to go through Freshwater to leave access to emergency vehicles of police and ambulance.

The aeroplane was coming to Cairns from Mt Isa after a business trip. There was a severe thunderstorm in Cairns and the aeroplane was doing an instrument landing with practically no visibility when at a fairly low altitude one of its wings clipped a tall tree that plunged the plane into the mud.

Prior to hearing the noise of the crash, my father-in-law had commented to his wife about its engine sound which he considered to be abnormal as if in difficulty.

There were no survivors of course. The site was cordoned off for days and coming back from hospital, I could see debris scattered over a large area.

In those days, apart from the two supermarkets of Coles and Woolworths in town, there were no suburban shopping centres, except for a cluster of shops in Brinsmead where Popy worked at the Northern Builders Hardware shop.

It was where Micheline and I used to do our weekly grocery shopping. We were spoilt then when a trolley boy used to push our trolley to the car and unload it into the boot.

View of Oak Street, Holloways Beach in 1978.

Page 191

Talk about service! We would do so until a couple of years later when Raintrees was built. It took us a while to finally progress to Westcourt Shopping Centre built a few years later.

When Roselyne was about two years old, which makes it around 1977, we suffered the worst flood in Cairns history.

It all started around New-Years eve celebrated at Micheline and Jean-Claude's place in Yorkeys Knob when I remember us driving home in torrential rains caused by a low pressure system in the Coral Sea. It rained for weeks as one system after another formed off the coast. At first only low lying areas got flooded but it finally got worse.

One morning after some torrential rain that lasted all night, Popy told me that he was still going to work. Well, he did not make it very far. He only drove halfway onto Oleander Street, the main road of Holloways Beach, when it all just looked like a sea in front of him. He could see just the roof of a four-wheel drive near the first turn-off.

He rushed to his parents place in Oak Street to find that the water had reached the letter box.

A king tide had worsened the situation when Thomatis Creek and the Barron River swelled up.

Luckily, Philippe and Violette had been woken up during the night by their friends and neighbours, the Martins (Mauritian family), who were aware of the rising water.

The top of a 4WD vehicle can just be seen in the centre of the photo taken in Oleander Street, Holloways Beach.

They managed to save their furniture by shifting them onto beds and bench tops. They raised Philippe's car onto bricks. The only thing that was ruined was the carpet.

We were cut off from Cairns for days. Our water supply was cut off when some pipes broke and could not be fixed until the water receded. What a nuisance!

The local kindergarten served as refuge for many families. Food at the local shop was rationed, priorities given to young families and the elderly.

My in-laws and the Martin family stayed with us for a few days. Neighbours helped with mattresses and blankets.

We used to take the kids across the road from us where the owners had bore water to wash them under the sprinklers. As for us adults, we would do it by having a natural shower every night, standing under the torrential rains, not a very pleasant experience, I can assure you.

Popy would fill the WC cistern with water collected from the crevaces surrounding our palm trees in the garden.

We were lucky that our street was not flooded, being on higher ground.

The lake near my in-laws had caused much of the flooding as it broke its bank from the excess water coming from Thomatis Creek. The Barron River flooded the whole area of the Cook Highway from Machans Beach to Smithfield. (The existing highway was not built then, not until 1980 in fact).

It was only a one lane main road that went through to Stratford with an old wooden bridge over the Barron.

Two years later we suffered another flood. Fearing the worse, members of the State Emergency Service called on residents who owned a boat to ask for use of them for evacuation if need be.

Popy had just started work for Kenny Industries, and not wanting to be absent so soon, went to work by boat, a punt owned by Roger Martin.

Wearing a raincoat and carrying their socks and shoes in a plastic bag, the two of them were quite a sight when they launched the punt on the sea near the local shop. As it turned out, they were stranded in town for a couple of days as the sea was too rough to venture out. I was on my own with my two kids and was petrified!

Luckily nothing major happened except for once when my brother-in-law, Jean-Claude, asked me to drive him close to the Thomatis Creek bridge as he would set out on foot from there to go home to Micheline and their four kids. Luckily the motor did not conk out or anything, and you should have seen Jean-Claude walking across the bridge, holding both arms up carying plastic bags containing his footwear.

During this period, Chantal and Cyril (Popy's brother), were holidaying in Cairns as well as my mother, who was herself staying with Micheline.

One day my brother Ivan, Cyril and Popy, a bit bored, decided to go and visit the family in Yorkeys Knob. They set off in a punt from Holloways and paddled along through the cane fields when at one stage the boat nearly tipped over a few times due to a strong current. Luckily they did not come to any harm though one of them hit his head on the mangroves.

There were helicopters coming back and forth from Cairns who would fly people to and fro at a special cost. In Holloways, it would land on a vacant block close to the main road.

On the subject of flooding, we had quite an experience once travelling from Brisbane to Cairns after a holiday when the road was flooded near Rockhampton, and with Aunty Daisy (on holidays from Mauritius) with us and Patrick and Roselyne, a toddler and baby, we were stranded for a few days. Imagine the five of us in a car for 1 and a half days until the police directed us to Bajool, a small town a few kilometres inland.

Once, out of desperation, I washed Roselyne's nappies in the muddy water close to the car and lay them on the bonnet to let the rain finish the rinsing.

It was around lunch time when we could not drive any further, being confronted by a vast sea in front of us. We joined the queue in a long line of stranded vehicles.

In the previous town we had unsuccessfully tried to buy some bread to be told that it was not the day for bread delivery. All I had in the car was half a bottle of cordial.

By this time we were hungry and thirsty, but we only gave some to the children. At around 5 pm, Popy was told that there was a pub a few kilometres off the main highway, so decided to attempt to go there to get some food. We had previously asked a truck driver with a cargo of fruits to sell us some, but he had refused.

You should have seen us, for Popy had to drive through the flooded road. At some stage I had to slowly lead him on while checking the road below for pot holes and what have you.

When you think of it, it was madness. But we could not let the children starve. We finally made it, so Daisy and I stayed in the car and Popy disappeared inside for about half an hour, to return with three cold pies and drinks of some sort.

A person quite drunk had offered accommodation at his farm which we refused of course.

After sharing the pies amongst us (when you are hungry, you'll eat anything!), it was back to the side of the road for a long night where we tried to get comfortable and manage some disrupted sleep.

We collected water by placing a bowl under the quarter window of the car.

Moving to Sunny Queensland

The next morning went slowly, listening to the car radio until a good samaritan, a Chinese man who had come by boat from Rockhampton, brought us a loaf of bread, a litre of milk, some tissues and a magazine. We could not thank him enough!

Later on, as I mentioned earlier, the police came and informed us that we could stay in a school hall in Bajool, with a convenience store next door where we could buy some food.

What a relief it was! I had started to worry about the children, wondering how long we could stay stranded.

We came to this community hall that used to be a school. It had a stage and all. Made of timber with an outside latrine, it was crowded with about fifty people of all ages. The noise! It echoed!

We managed to find ourselves a spot in a corner, where Popy laid out our mattress from the station wagon. We had assured ourselves a place to spend the night.

After buying enough tin food to last us a while, Popy enquired if it was possible to get to Rockhampton by train, car and all. We abandoned the idea as it would have cost a small fortune, so decided to make the best out of the situation.

Roselyne's 3rd birthday party in 1978 – clockwise from left – Patrick Maujean, Sandra Fayd'herbe, Myriam Maujean, Violette Maujean, Caroline Fayd'herbe, Micheline Maujean, Roselyne, myself, Pauline Maujean, Marielle Fayd'herbe, Dominic and Daniel Maujean.

Back at the hall, we were told by some kind soul that there was a large iron tub at the back (in the kitchen) where we could have our turn at having a wash if we wanted. Out of desperation we decided to go for it. So, accompanied by Daisy, it was first a long process to fill it up with water, using a jug. After sprinkling some Dettol antiseptic in the tub first, we washed the children and had them dressed for the night. It was quite funny, come our turn when one of us would lean against the door to stop some unwanted guests to spoil our privacy. Ordeal or not, it felt good afterwards.

We finally settled for the night, the five of us lying sideways on the mattress. A few moments later, someone turned off the light. We thought 'That's it, we'll be able to sleep at last!'. How wrong! Shortly after, we were disturbed by some party trying to find their space in the dark. The noise went on for a while until, finally, exhausted, sleep claimed us.

When we ventured off to the highway the next morning to see if we could go across, our hopes were dashed as the situation remained unchanged.

Later on we were approached by a couple living on a farm nearby who were nice enough to invite us to their place for lunch. We spent some pleasant two hours with them and after thanking our hosts for their generous hospitality it was back to the highway.

When a man driving a four-wheel drive offered to tow us across for a charge, Popy accepted.

I felt my heart pounding as we set out, the three adults in the front seat and the children lying on the mattress in the back.

It did not help seeing a car floating about, only its dome showing.

About halfway through, the rope snapped! I thought "Oh my God! That's it! I can't swim and won't be able to save the children!'. Honestly, if it was not for Daisy to distract me, I would have passed out!

Popy never removed his foot off the accelerator and signalled the guy ahead to keep going. Luckily the motor kept going. As we progressed further, water started to get into the car and I panicked again when the level reached just above our ankles.

We made it though. What a relief when we reached dry land and Popy immediately opened all the car doors and being on a slope, the water gushed out.

Poor Daisy. By then she was quite resigned to the fact that the brand new pair of shoes and accessories she had bought in Brisbane for the special occasion of her son's wedding would be ruined, as it was packed at the bottom of the car. But it was a miracle for the mud and water did not get to them.

As the highway out of Rockhampton on the northern side to Mackay was also flooded, we were again stranded for two more days. We could not afford a motel, and all caravan parks were fully booked.

Our only option was to park in a rest area next to a little kiosk with amenities close by. We managed having a shower in a nearby service station.
Nappies and personal garments were washed under the tap and hung to dry under the shelter of the kiosk where Popy had stretched a line for us.
We finally made it back north following a truck. We should have heeded Monique's advice to wait a while in Brisbane before setting back.

In those early days, Roger Maujean had bought a service station, situated at the corner of Florence and Minnie streets in Cairns. Philippe, his brother, worked with him. When the site was claimed by the Kamsler family for extension of their Trade-winds motel, Roger's only option was to close the business.

Meanwhile, Violette and Nicole Martin managed a little food kiosk at Wallamurra Medical Centre as partners in this venture. After running it for a few years, they sold the business.

Later on, Roger and Philippe bought a corner store, Earlville Superette. It lasted for some two years after which Roger gained employment in an office and Philippe and Violette started a cleaning business that saved them enough money to travel to Mauritius some five years later.

Jean-Raymond Mallac was working for the ANZ Bank after obtaining a transfer from Melbourne.

Yves Fayd'herbe worked for a boat building company.

Jean-Claude first worked for Malvern Star before moving to IAC, a finance company. When he left the first one, Yves took his job.

Paul Maujean was in real estate and his brother Marcel worked as a debt collector for Waltons in town.

Later on Yves moved to Chandlers.

Jean-Raymond and family moved to Townsville when he was transferred by the bank.

Marcel and Jean-Claude opened Cairns Economy Autos which they eventually sold and opened a factory for boat building named Cairns Custom Craft. They kept that business for years until it went into receivership some three years ago. Jean-Claude is presently working for Ron Guppie of Cairns Economy Autos. Marcel is into another business called Marcel's Boat Designs.

Dressed up in period costume are Patrick Maujean, twins Fiona and Michelle O'Bryan and Anne O'Bryan.

CHAPTER 19

The Seventies and Eighties!

We had the O'Bryan family living two doors away from us. Don and Margaret had a young family like ours, three daughters consisting of Anne, a few months older than Patrick, and identical twins, Michelle and Fiona.

Our children have grown up together, and they still live here today. We have shared driving our children to kindergarten and school.

Every year we have been part of their St Patrick's Day celebrations as they are both of Irish origin.

Anne acted as a little mother to Patrick when he started school at Mother of Good Counsel on Sheridan Street.

I also became a friend to Marja, of Dutch origin, then married to Michael Balmforth, living across the road from the O'Bryans. She had two sons, Michael and Nigel. The two of us would have a game of Yahtsee while our children had their afternoon nap.

Patrick and Michael started kindergarten together and two years later, Roselyne and Nigel.

It used to be a time when I was solely a housewife and enjoyed it. On some mornings I would take the children to the beach.

It was also a time when tourists from Victoria and New South Wales had 'discovered' Cairns. You could say that it was also the start of the tourist industry here.

Those people from down south, the 'southerners' as we called them, having discovered our numerous deserted beaches, had no qualms in removing their clothing for sunbaking.

I witnessed a funny situation once when a gentleman in his birthday suit, ironically wearing a cap for protection against the sun, was strolling along the waters edge when suddenly a German shepherd chased him and feeling the threat to his manhood had no option but to dive in the water for cover. I thought 'Serves you right!'

From Island to Continent   *Marie-Josée Maujean*

We used to enjoy some camping weekends on the islands off the coast. We usually went to Fitzroy before it became a tourist resort, some outings where the whole family would be present as Jean-Claude and Yves owned a boat. My in-laws would also join us then, and a good time would be had by all. The cousins have always been pretty close and looked forward to the camp fire at night.

When our families from down south would come to Cairns on holidays, we always managed a few days on the Frankland Islands. We would enjoy fresh oysters off the rocks and practically had the whole island to ourselves.

On one particular stay, when the two Maujean and Harris families were fishing off the beach one night, someone caught something 'big' and called for help to bring it in. It ended up with a tug of war, all of us fighting what was at the other end of the line, a stingray as we later found out.

We had a lot of gear to ferry on these camps, as there was no running water on the island. We had to bring gallons of it.

What I enjoyed the most was the relaxation, and no cooking! The men would take charge of it.

We once went camping on Hope Island with some Australian friends of ours, Roger and Pam Brown, with four children of their own.

As the island is close to Cooktown, it took us a while to get there, in fact some four hours as the sea was quite rough that day.

In view of the situation we stayed fairly close to the coast all the way up.

Camping at Frankland Islands.

It was a beautiful place, all to ourselves for the weekend. Unfortunately that first night was quite eventful when we endured a spectacular thunderstorm.

The four of us adults had anticipated sleeping under the stars while the children were in a tent. As the storm raged we had to join the children, all ten of us cramped in.

When the sea swelled from its effect and we could see our boat bopping on top of the waves, the men's only option was to swim to it to bring the boat closer to the coast otherwise it would have broken its anchorage.

Until this process was accomplished, Pam and I suffered some anxious moments as our imaginations went riot with ideas of sharks close to shore at night.

As it turned out, after our husbands came back safely to us, we still could not get any sleep. Everything was soaking wet as the tent leaked.

As is always the case after a storm, followed a beautiful serene morning when we all gathered birds eggs for breakfast.

We have enjoyed numerous camping trips through the years in various sites by the sea, on river banks, in the bush and by the side of Lake Tinaroo.

Our son, Patrick, and his cousins Dominic and Daniel, followed in their father's footsteps and became keen fishermen, receiving numerous trophies as junior anglers in the fishing club of which the Maujean and Fayd'herbe families were members.

My son Patrick with the home-made boat and trailer towed by his pushbike.

Pat even enjoyed fishing in creeks, especially one close to his cousin Michael's place in Earlville.

When he was around 12 years old, Popy bought him a small boat made of wood with oars, that he would pull on a makeshift trailer with bicycle wheels attached to his own bike. Popy repainted it a bright yellow and named it 'The Little Devil'.

Patrick made great use of it at weekends, fishing in creeks or close to the shore of Holloways.

I enjoy fishing, but unfortunately I do not make a good sailor, for even the gentle rocking of the boat is enough to make me seasick. I joined Popy a couple of times in his early expeditions, but had to stop for this reason.

A few times our husbands have left us on Michaelmas Cay while fishing. It was a time before the tourist boom, when we could sunbake at leisure and swim in the beautiful crystal clear water.

My sister-in-law, Monique, and I were quite horrified last year when early one morning our husbands left us for a couple of hours there while they went for a bit of fishing. We were on our own for half an hour, lying on the beach, birds flying above use, with a peaceful view of the sea when pandemonium broke.

It started with some motor engine noise breaking the silence as a vessel load of tourists were brought to our shores.

Fishing the Daintree River in North Queensland are Philippe Maujean with his grandson Patrick and son Philippe Jnr.

The Seventies and Eighties!

In a matter of minutes it was an invasion of diving instructors in their scuba gear, deckhands erecting large umbrellas everywhere while more charter boats arrived. In no time, the whole sand cay was occupied and the water full of swimmers attired with goggles and flippers.

I'm afraid if this keeps happening, pretty soon there won't be any birds left on that cay.

We have recently started to enjoy camping and outings to the islands again, as Popy has bought a new boat, 'Mistress Three' (can't say that I am keen about the name!), after selling 'Mephisto' a few years back when the maintenance and fuel were causing a strain on our budget.

Both Patrick and Roselyne can water-ski as well as Popy, so we sometimes have outings to Fitzroy Island where they can enjoy the sport.

At present Patrick owns a surf board and does a bit of surfing off the coast with his cousin, Nicholas, now living in Cairns.

The Mackie boys – from left – Denis, Nicholas and Gilles in Springwood, Brisbane.

Sisters, Violette and Paule Maujean, Yolande Berenger and Jeanne D'unienville.

My mother and Arthur Hogan visiting the families at Holloways Beach, Cairns.

CHAPTER 20

An Insight into Cairns History

I was quite fascinated when reading the book 'Trinity Phoenix — A History of Cairns' by Dorothy Jones, to find some connection with Mauritius from its early chapters.

Dorothy Jones was chosen by the people of Cairns to write their centennial history in 1976.

I will be forever grateful to our cousin Paul Maujean for giving me this particular book that I had found very hard to obtain when published sixteen years ago. By chance, Paul discovered a copy when organising an old lady's auction and gave it to me knowing how much I wished for one.

As Cairns has been home to us for some twenty years, I find it fitting to write about its history without making it too boring, I hope.

The area of Cairns was first named Trinity Bay by Captain James Cook on Trinity Sunday, 1770.

On 29th April, 1770 after his first landfall on what is now Australia, Captain Cook sailed northward on the Endeavour, having also on board a Mr Banks and his private party, including an artist, Parkinson, both passionate of natural history.

It is interesting to note that in his journal, Captain Cook used ship's time, meaning from noon to noon instead of the civilian midnight to midnight.

As a result he was not only a day behind by date, but always 12 hours previous in time.

The Endeavour was in tropical waters by early June and along his way Captain Cook named the islands of Halifax, Dunk and the group of islands that he named the Franklands to honour two eighteenth century sailors, Sir Thomas Frankland (Bart.) one of the Lords of the Admiralty from 1733-42 and his nephew, Admiral Sir Thomas Frankland, who passed away in 1784.

Fitzroy Island was named after the Duke of Grafton whose family name was Fitzroy.

Page 205

Green Island obtained its name when from his anchorage Captain Cook saw "a low, green, woody island bearing 35 degrees east. By 11 am on Cook's Trinity Sunday, they passed outside a small low island well awash with a high tide, to the west was another island, chartered but not named. As the shore between Cape Grafton and the northern most land in sight formed a large but not very deep bay, Cook named it Trinity Bay after the day on which it was discovered - Trinity Sunday, 10th June, 1770".

Cape Tribulation got its name when he noted in his diary 'Here began all our troubles'.

The Endeavour struck hard on a coral outcrop north of Cape Tribulation. The ship was then lighted by throwing overboard 6 brass cannons, ballast and stores. The little ship remained on the reef until using the anchors taken out in the long boats, combined with a high tide, she was refloated.

The coral had cut a gaping hole in her oaken hull, which was stuffed with canvas and wool.

In 1815, after the Battle of Waterloo took place resulting in the destruction of Napoleon and the French land forces, England remained supreme on the sea. The British Admiralty turned to marine survey work in Australia as one area likely to prove a prolific field for the collection of specimens of strange flora and fauna awaiting discovery to the Old World.

Phillip Parker King, the son of the colony's governor, Phillip Gidley King, 1800-1805, was appointed to the marine survey work in 1817. He was granted from Governor Macquarie, a cutter, newly arrived from India, the 84 ton 'Mermaid', length 56 ft, beam 18'6", which laden drew 9 feet.

In reporting the circumstances of King's voyage, the name Australia was used for the first time in official correspondence by Governor Macquarie.

In the course of his duty, King made three cruises with the Mermaid and one with the Bathurst. As botanical collector was Allan Cunningham, famous in the history of Queensland exploration.

After sailing around Australia several times, King charted and corrected, marked dangerous shoals and rocks and attached names of Old World dignitaries to this new land for the benefit of succeeding seafarers.

Only Captain Cook had preceded King on survey work in northern waters. On 22nd June, 1819 he passed the land between Double Point and the Franklands at night and saw nothing to impress him when he examined the place closely, apart from a towering range which he named 'Bellenden Ker' after John Bellenden Ker Esq., one of the first private orchid growers, at the request of Allan Cunningham.

I find it interesting to quote a passage in the book:

"The Franklands were passed about 1 pm and by 4 pm, the Mermaid was anchored in a bay on the western side of Fitzroy, in complete shelter from the wind blowing up a fresh gale from the south-east.

The weather had become so bad, the Mermaid remained at anchor all the following day, using the time to fill water casks from a hollow at the back of the beach.

British tars looked to their shell collections and dived for coral. Well worn black's tracks were seen heading to all parts of the island from the beach. While evidence was seen of their obvious occupation for periodic feasts, none seemed to be inhabiting the place at the time of the Mermaid's stay.

Cunningham went off botanizing and found a species of nutmeg, three of palm, two of olive and some orchids. No quadrupeds at all were seen and a few birds. This no doubt explained the visits of Aboriginals whose hunting methods paid no lip service to conservation.".

"24th June, King weighed anchor and steering around Cape Grafton, hauled in towards the centre of Trinity Bay. To the west of Cape Grafton, King noticed an opening on the beach which judging by the irregular form of the hills behind it, could, he thought, be the mouth of a rivulet. This he noted on his chart. By noon of the same day, they passed to the eastward of three small islands and charted them as Low Isles.

At 2.30 pm he anchored under Snapper Island and was disappointed to find the anchorage not only more exposed than anticipated, but lacking a supply of fresh water. All around were to be seen ashes from cooking fires and piles of empty shells, but no Aboriginals".

"With a fresh breeze from the southeast, the Mermaid next morning steered around Cape Tribulation. The seas rose to become so heavy that the boat towed astern, filled and capsized to be dashed to pieces in moments. To shelter, they hauled into the opening of a rivulet which Bedwell examined. King named it the Bloomfield." — *Trinity Phoenix.*

This maritime survey by King in the 1820s was all that was known of Queensland beyond Moreton Bay, a penal colony then.

In the 1840s, as there was need for pastoral areas to accommodate impatient squatters (persons acquiring land belonging to governments by settling on it), pushing their flocks further afield from New South Wales and the idea to consolidate trade routes with the East and the ties between the British colonies and strongholds in Asia and Australia had begun, there was need for a port of entry on the northern coastline.

As a result, Ludwig Leichhardt started land exploration in 1844. It lasted two years and covered from the south to the very top of the continent.

By 1849 a settlement was established at Port Curtis named for Mr Gladstone.

In 1845 the British Admiralty had replaced the surveying ship, Fly, with the Rattlesnake, an old donkey frigate with 28 guns. She was commissioned at Portsmouth on 24th September, 1846 by Captain Owen Stanley with a complement of 180 officers and men.

Also on the Rattlesnake were John MacGillivary who wrote the official narrative of the voyage, and young Thomas Huxley, one of Charles Darwin's supporters on the theories of evolution and to become one of the world's greatest biologists.

Owen Stanley's main commission was the survey of the inner passages from Dunk Island to Torres Strait by an unbroken series of triangulation.

It covered an area varying in width from five to fifteen miles with a coastline of upwards 600 miles.

"While off Cape Tribulation, a hill in the background so strongly reminded the men of the Peter Botte in Mauritius that Stanley named it Mount Peter Botte.'— Trinity Phoenix. Incidently, the name here is spelt Peter Botte compared to Pieter Both (Dutch name).

Many ships made their way north before the trades, Fitzroy Island was the place they stopped as there was a snug anchorage and both water and wood could be obtained on their way round through the straits to India and the East.

It was due to private enterprise that the north of Australia was settled by squatters pushed further north.

In 1859, the government of the new colony of Queensland began business with applications for inherited leases.

The Kennedy district was opened for selection and in 1861 G. E. Dalrymple was sent as first Land Commissioner to form a port at Port Denison (now Bowen).

In 1864 Cardwell, and a few months later, Townsville, were founded by private endeavour.

It was not until 1872 that some beacons were erected in the Far North. The first one was on a reef, 25 miles south of Cooktown.

As these ports were opened, fishermen in search of beche de mer (sea slugs) to trade with the Chinese, progressively moved to the northern reefs.

It was a very profitable business as the beche de mer was considered an aphrodisiac by them. A beche de mer station was then erected on Green Island followed by one on Fitzroy and the Franklands.

When Cardwell was designated as a separate police district around 1864, the area for patrol reached as far as Trinity Bay under Lieutenant Murry and Sub-Lieutenant Arthur Johnstone who was to contribute much to the history of Trinity Bay.

In 1868, he became manager of the first northern sugar plantation at Bellenden Ker Plains north of Cardwell.

The history of the north is rife with stories of murders and cannibalism between natives. One of those is about Daniel Kelly, William Rose and William White, who left Townsville on 4th March, 1873 on board the cutter 'Goodwill' to re-occupy and work a beche de mer station on Green Island with four Aboriginals and two women recruited at Palm Island.

They reached Green Island on 8th March.

Everything went smoothly for a while until the Aboriginals resented the fact that they were not allowed to sleep on board as compared to the women.

On the 12th April, as Kelly waited for his two mates while sitting in his dinghy to take them back to the cutter for the night, he saw Rose badly wounded staggering to their hut chased by one of the divers brandishing an axe. White, who tried to help his mate, was also attacked and killed while trying to reach the dinghy.

Daniel Kelly escaped by heading for Oyster Cay where he knew Philip Garland of the ketch 'Telegraph' to be.

Later on their arrival to Green Island they were to be confronted with the sight of White's and Kelly's mutilated bodies, heads and limbs cleft open and almost severed.

They were buried on the island although there is no trace of their graves left nowadays.

According to Yorkey (George Lawson), an early beche de mer fisherman who later returned to Green Island as caretaker, the island was haunted by ghosts that he had seen. To his accord some Aboriginal women were also murdered there and he told of his encounter with the spirit of a black woman drawing water from a well located in the centre of the island who when approached would disappear.

A later expedition to explore the northeast coast with George Dalrymple in charge, left Cardwell on 29th September, 1873.

On his way he discovered Trinity Inlet and was impressed by the harbour facilities and felt that wharves and roads could be built without difficulty in the 'magnificent shipping capabilities of this perfectly land-locked harbour ever require to be drawn upon for the use of an auriferous back country or coast sugar lands.'

He named this new port, Trinity Harbour.

He is considered as the founder of North Queensland. Dalrymple also named the Walsh's Pyramid after his friend, the Hon. W. M. Walsh, Speaker of the Legislative Assembly.

The three prominent mountains of the main coast range were named after his friends, Brinsley Guise Sheridan - Police Magistrate at Cardwell, F. W. Williams - commissioner of Crown Lands, and Edwin Whitfield - a Cardwell merchant to whom the expedition was obliged for many courtesies.

Later on, Robert Johnstone and Townsend returned to Trinity Bay to help in establishing a settlement.

Dalrymple passed away in England on 22nd January 1876.

In reading Trinity Phoenix, I was also amazed to learn that in an expedition organised by Daniel Hart who later claimed to be the first man on the Mossman River, were two natives from Mauritius.

In 1874, Daniel Hart sailed in a whale boat from Cardwell to explore the land further north looking for cedar, sugar and minerals. In such expedition they came upon some Aboriginals with a canoe made of cedar who led them to the northern end of the Mossman River where they found some fine stands.

They organised another party from Cooktown and Hart had two parties of men felling cedar, one on the Daintree and one near Mossman.

After about a month both groups became sick with fever and had to head north to take the sick to hospital in Cooktown.

All the men of Hart's party recovered while two of the Mossman group died.

After suffering two bouts of sickness that forced him to go to Cooktown, Hart had to give up his interest for a while to the care of two men, Cleve and Henriques.

After recuperating, he organised a party with a man named Page. (It is presumed that he was Clayton H. Page who was later granted a timber license in Cairns). George Pritchell, 'German Harry' (Captain Soren/Christensen) reputed to be one of the most dangerous men in reef waters, once his temper was aroused, 'Old Alick' and two Mauritian natives. This group bought a boat, three months provisions and with great difficulty cut a cargo of cedar on the Mossman.

On their return to Cooktown they engaged the brig 'Ariel' to take their cedar to Sydney. By negotiating with the Bank of New South Wales they only realised eleven pounds sterling each, on terms of 'sold to deliver' to Sydney after paying expenses.

As they became dissatisfied with the matter, they resolved to break up and sell the boat and tools.

After forming another party which eventually pulled out after some unfortunate business transaction, Hart remained alone on the Mossman, well armed to protect himself and with some vegetable seeds that he hoped would provide him with a bare existence.

After Hart, Captain Phillips and O'Grady also worked on the rivers.

The natives which Hart had found to be friendly at first did not end up this way. After spearing two of O'Grady's men on 28th July, 1876, they attacked the crew of the schooner 'Violet' after it was wrecked at the mouth of the river and they had just managed to get to a cedar camp.

As a result of the attack, two whites were wounded with tomahawks, one black was shot and another taken to Cooktown with the wounded and survivors.

An Insight into Cairns History

It was found that this one was of a party of eleven who had absconded from a pearling schooner at Cape York to make way overland to the Daintree. The others had died or been eaten on the way.

There are gory stories of explorers coming upon half eaten bodies left around a camp fire.

When the Freshney brothers of Melbourne sent a cedar speculator and two hired men up the river, it was considered by Hart to be a start to the monopolising of the rivers by Melbourne capitalists. In those days newspapers had a shipping list where often the complement of a ship was assessed by mentioning so many passengers and so many capitalists.

As he had a nice clearing of his choice on the bank of the river, and a fair growth of population, Hart applied for the title to his land to the Cooktown Land Agent who refused this grant because the district could not be defined.

When hearing about a settlement on Trinity Bay, Hart decided to go there and sold his produce of maze to the first person he saw on arrival, for one sterling pound a bag. It was to Inspector Clohesy.

Eventually it was gold that drew more people to the north and Cooktown was the first seaport to gain notoriety for such a reason.

I will quote some passages from the book 'Queen of the North' by Glenville Pike to give you an idea of what it was like in those heady days.

Cooktown was the third busiest seaport in Queensland and was, for more than fifty years, the state's most northerly municipality.

"Just as golden Charters Towers was said to be 'the world', so was Cooktown 'the queen of the north'".

"For 103 years the serene Endeavour River remained as Cook had found it, the untrammelled home of the Kokobothan people."

But for the gold greed of Europeans and Asians, no civilised habitation may ever have arisen to disturb this lonely river mouth.

It was to "become the gateway to El Dorado, the landing place for thousands of white men and women, and Chinese by the shipload."

The hectic period of the Palmer rush saw the influx of almost every adventurous spirit from Victoria, New South Wales and New Zealand.

"Even California heard the call and in Kwangtung, Macao and Hong Kong, news of abundant gold in the land of the 'white devils' only a couple of weeks sail to the south, made rich merchants and Mandarins send ships crammed with coolies to get gold for them and to act as human pack trains on the track from the port to the goldfields.".

"Hundreds of Chinese were killed, cooked and eaten by the cannibal spearmen who waited in ambush at Hell's Gate and other places."

White men and women died too on the 120 miles long Palmer track." The cause was not only due to Aboriginals, but from starvation and fever.

Page 211

"Men died from hunger with thousands of ounces of gold in their possession, their hard earned wealth useless when caught between flooded rivers in the wet season of 1874." – *Queen of the North*.

The main street of Cooktown, Charlotte Street was the beginning of the Palmer road. For two miles it was once lined with substantial wood and iron buildings, most of the hotels two-storeyed. By late 1874 there were 94. In the month of April alone, 65 licenses were issued.

At the peak of the 'roaring days' there were 24 restaurants, twelve large general stores, and scores of small shops. Five bakers, six butchers, four tent makers, seven blacksmiths, four wheelwrights, three saddlers, three chemists, four doctors, three banks and two newspapers.

For a short time there was even a Chinese newspaper and a Chinese shipyard. "Chinese merchants invested heavily in the land and businesses, believing Cooktown would become the 'Canton of the south'". – *Queen of the North*

The only talk amongst wild-eyed prospectors with bags of gold dust to spend was always of more gold.

"All this faded away as the gold of the Palmer, said to have yielded more than fifty tons of alluvial, became exhausted and other goldfields such as the Hodgkinson and other seaports such as Port Douglas and Cairns attracted trade and population." – *Queen of the North*

I have visited Cooktown twice and felt the history of the place. I fell in love with the place and it was quite an experience standing on Grassy Hill to look at the scenery surrounding me and thinking 'Captain Cook had the same view in front of him so many years ago'.

It was quite interesting visiting the cemetery and Julie, a friend of mine, Roselyne and I inspected every grave and some of the epitaphs would really draw at the heart's strings.

I loved the old convent turned into a museum with old photographs of past students and nuns as well as the special room dedicated to the Chinese people of those early days.

It was an odd feeling when looking at the view of the coast and sea on the horizon to think that it had remained unchanged. It was exactly what those people of the past had gazed on from the top of that balcony so many years ago!

My daughter Roselyne who was not too keen at visiting the place at first, thinking it would be boring, loved every minute of it as well.

Cairns was first known as 'Thornton', the name given by Guise Sheridan, Cardwell's Police Magistrate who was instructed by the Queensland Government to go to Trinity Bay to report on the facilities for a harbour and a possible town site.

Sheridan spent a fortnight in the area after which he reported that he found the harbour to be 'a magnificent sheet of water four or five miles long and about 300 yards wide with 9 feet at low water on the bar with a rise and fall of 13 ft at spring tides. Inside, the depth was from 4 fathoms at low water and was sufficiently sheltered to accommodate a whole fleet.

As far as he could judge there was well grassed country around it but what lay behind was unknown to him. He selected a town site near the mouth of the inlet and named it Thornton.

It was initially William Bairstow Ingham on the little stern wheel paddle steamer 'Louisa', who reached Trinity Bay in 1876 and was soon joined there by another party on board the 16 horse power, 62 ton 'Porpoise' who were James Burns, Robert Phillip, Andrew Ball, Charles O'Brien, William Aplin, two sawyers and two newspaper correspondents from the Brisbane 'Courier' and the Townsville 'Herald'.

Ingham guided them to the anchorage in the inlet. In those days it was important that an inland track be made to the Hodgkinson and as the government was offering a reward for its finding, many were interested.

One of them was Bill Smith, who was born in England between 1822 and 1828 and came to Australia in 1850.

As a beche de mere fisher, Smith witnessed the Florence Agnes massacre of 1873 at Green Island. Later on he became a miner and purchased the Diggers Arms Hotel in Cooktown. At some stage he became a packer to the Hodgkinson.

It is said that at Cooktown, Smith hired a cutter and formed a party consisting of John Mackay, Joseph Brown, John Stevens, John Manly, Charles Lipton and two blacks from Frazer Island, and set for Trinity Bay.

It is not clear whether the cutter was sailed or taken as deck cargo on the 'Lord Ashley'. The party went up the inlet and set up camp at that clear patch of land Smith always called the landing, later called Smith's Landing. This landing is thought to have taken place on 1st September, 1876.

The early beginnings of Cairns are very hard to define. Bill Smith did find a track to the Hodgkinson.

This range track began near Kamerunga, climbed up the spur through which the number 9 railway tunnel was dug, followed the top of the range westwards to drop over to the upper waters of Stoney Creek which it crossed a short distance above the falls. From there it ran almost due west to Grove Creek, thus avoiding the middle crossing of the Barron River near Kuranda. It is not known if Smith did receive a reward from the government.

Down Smith's track came the new port's first settlers. Not a very impressive lot who camped at Smith's Landing. Some sent for their families and settled permanently.

It took many years for the number of them to be of any significant importance as surrounded by mangroves it was not a very pleasant spot in those days and no governmental colonisation took place as such.

Some names of importance in those early days were: David Spence, a second officer of customs at Townsville who came to Cairns to prepare the ground for the official opening of Trinity Bay as a port of entry and clearance on 1st November, 1876.

Land Commissioner Sharkey, whose task was to select and lay out various town sites.

Spence stayed in Cairns for some years while Sharkey did not last long.

J. Gillespie remained a while in Cairns as he was listed in the Blue Book, 1st February, 1879 as Master of the lightship at Clermont Island.

Another name is that of John Mylchreest from Maryborough who came to Cairns as a widower with his two daughters, Christine and Elizabeth. He was master of the schooner 'Mona'.

In point of time the first establishments were three calico and bough structures on the beachfront run by Limerick Nell, Mother Brady and the cassowary, a Mrs Thaler who ran a coaching house on Cobb & Co's route which became renowned for excellent meals.

The first person to set foot on the later site of Cairns was the Yorkshireman, Edwin Crossland, a blacksmith by trade who was to have a long career as a contractor, principally on government buildings and wharves.

The first baker in the area was a man named Willis.

Sharkey changed the name of the town from Thornton to Cairns. He began his initial trial survey lines on 16th October, calling on volunteers to help clear the mangroves along the beach.

Boat building was the main activity with the first of the fleet launched in mid-October.

Cairns at the time consisted of an accumulation of calico dwellings running west in almost one long street. The exception to calico was Solomon's iron store near the landing.

A few points of interest: Cairns children first attended a private school conducted by Hugh Harrison. They paid one shilling each per week. The first teacher was Mr Albercombie. There were neither desks nor chairs, blackboard nor slate. It was in a building located on the Esplanade bought by the government from a Mr James Pyne.

As this school was a thousand miles from the government education office, it took some time for communication, something which must have been quite frustrating for the teacher who was eventually told that the reason for the delay of supplies was due to pillage and subsequent damages to any merchandise sent to the north.

Paul Ducas of Charters Towers visited Cairns in 1877 and celebrated the first mass in the court house.

An Insight into Cairns History

The first doctor was Dr Myers who ironically hobbled about on one leg.

Regular sabbath services were conducted in a bonded warehouse known as the Old Bond by Robert Taylor Hartley. It was also the place for Sunday school run by a Mrs Latreille.

The first service conducted by a resident was held in March, 1884 by the Reverend G. R. F. Nobbs.

Augustinians Fathers T. Tanganelli, Luigi Fabris and Cherubino de Romanis visited from Cooktown and Port Douglas in 1878.

The first hospital was opened on the Esplanade between Shields and Aplin streets. A 50 ft by 20 ft building that consisted of many rooms, with special quarters for its first medical officer, Dr Byrn.

The town of Smithfield was established about two months after Cairns. Miners from the Thornborough would come down to it.

This new town was Cairns downfall. All of a sudden it was deserted. The Bank of New South Wales closed its doors in October 1878, not to re-open until November 1885.

Smithfield was originally a popular packer's camp and was situated on the northern bank of the Barron River. It was a preferred site to Cairns port because of its well-grassed, flat surrounding country to pasture and rest animals.

Before long, such entrepreneurs from Cairns as C. Sparre and W. B. Ingham introduced small, flat-bottomed boats to go up and down the river carrying goods back and forth from Cairns to the camp. Two of the better known lighters were the 'Fitzroy' and the 'Louisa'.

This use of the river route saved packers from having to make their way through the difficult remaining eight miles of swamp and scrub from the river to the inlet.

Very quickly Smithfield got its own police station and three constables. Many hotels were set up including the Bee-Hive owned by Bill Smith. Edwin Crossland ran a blacksmith. Henry Tuffley was the hairdresser. There were the usual butcher, saddler and baker shops. James Arbouin and John Newell managed a branch of the Jack & Newell stores.

The notorious lady of the night, Palmer Kitty from Cooktown, moved to Smithfield to cater for the basic needs of the miners and packers.

Robert Craig was one of the first businessmen to settle in Smithfield as an agent for the business firm of Aplin, Clifton and Co.

Craig erected one of two wharves built in Smithfield and also the halfway house situated halfway along the Barron River (just upstream from Stratford) where goods were offloaded so the lightened boats could continue up to Smithfield with passengers.

Smithfield could even boast about its own race track.

In 1877 the town was almost submerged during the wet season and in 1878 it suffered the effects of a cyclone to boot.

In 1879, the death knell of the town had sounded for it suffered a tremendous flood during the wet season that completed its destruction already begun by time and termites. It is said that Smithfield died for the same reason as it was born — the preference of the packers for the best dray road available.

Referring to an article that appeared in the Cairns Post edition of 11th October, 1991, taken from a collection of historical episodes published by the Historical Society of Cairns — 'Establishment of Trinity Bay':

'The road from Smithfield to Thornborough had never been good since loaded drays had to be double-banked to get over the steep range. So when Christie Palmerston and Layton discovered a better route from the Hodgkinson to the coast at Salisbury (later known as Port Douglas) in June 1877, the decline of Smithfield and Cairns was rapid.

Just as businessmen had deserted Cairns for Smithfield in November 1876, now they abandoned both towns for the new promise of success at Salisbury.

By 1881 the township was deserted with only some of the decaying houses still standing.'

Bill Smith met a tragic end in Smithfield when as a pub owner of the Bee-Hive he became short of funds when due to too much of the demon drink, his business faltered. It got to the stage where Robert Jackson Craig refused to continue his supply of liquor until his accounts were settled.

On Boxing day 1877, Smith invited Craig to his hotel to discuss the account settlement. The visit seemed to have gone smoothly until Craig walked across the street to his store when Smith shot him in the back.

When Doctor Myers summoned urgently from Cairns arrived, it was too late. Craig was dead as well as Bill Smith, who had shot himself in the chest after.

The whole district was shocked. They felt so much for Craig who was only 34 years old and much respected, leaving behind a wife and children who were holidaying in the south at the time.

All of Cairns and Smithfield went into mourning as every house and business was closed on the day of Craig's funeral.

Craig was buried in Cairns, possibly in the Eplanade's cemetery. Smith was buried near the Thornborough road, beside the Smithfield joining track.

Later on Cairns flourished with the start of the sugar industry. Frenchman Creek, along the highway out of Cairns, was named after a De Nas Tourris family who used to own a property in the vicinity of Russell Heads.

That same family, who were originally from France, had stayed in Mauritius prior to settling in North Queensland.

Chapter 21

Extracts from my Journal

July 1990.
Since I started writing five months ago, a new avenue has opened up for me.
Not only do I find it fascinating and a great personal satisfaction, but I have gained a lot from it already. Not only will my typing keep arthritis at bay for a little bit longer (I've learned to type, self taught from my daughter Roselyne's exercises from school, a very frustrating experience as I'm learning on an old typewriter, not even electric, mind you!), but it has given that forty onward brain of mine a kick start that hopefully to your benefit will take you to interesting pastures.
I now find that should I go back to Mauritius. I will enjoy my stay even more than if we had gone back let's say, a year ago.
I have learnt so much about that island of mine I will know exactly what places I'll want to visit. It will certainly be a very satisfying experience both physically and emotionally. If anything else, I feel I would be a perfect guide to Popy and my children.
Of course Mauritius has progressed with the times. You must realise that our way of life over there dates back to my childhood. For such a small island so far away, it was still on par with other countries in world affairs. I want to go back there now as an adult and visit my family, some of whom I haven't seen since I left Mauritius so many years ago.

13th September, 1990.
On the world side, things are not looking too bright at the moment. It all started when Iraq invaded Kuwait on 4th August. There is the threat of war breaking out in the Middle East. Sadam Hussein, the Iraqi leader, has been compared to Hitler!

America has some troops posted in Saudi Arabia and has organised a naval blockade to try and intimidate Hussein. Australia, Britain and France have joined forces by sending ships to sustain the blockade. God knows how it will all end. Hussein is feared as he used chemical gas on Iran two years ago.

As a result of the crisis, the price of oil of course is going up and up. In Cairns at the moment, petrol costs 71.9 cents per litre.

This Gulf crisis is coming at a time when the world had just started witnessing some incredible changes for the better by the tearing down of the Berlin Wall (Iron Curtain) that separated Germany into two states, the east and the west for the last 40 years. We are also seeing the tumbling of most communist governments. Russia, under the leadership of Mikail Gorbachiev has changed for the better, freedom of religion and overall a democratic government is taking place. Gorbachiev is even supporting George Bush in the Gulf crisis.

There are still some hundreds of Europeans, Americans and Australians being held hostage in Kuwait. Luckily Sadam Hussein has released the women and children.

My sister Sylvianne and her family are holidaying in Cairns at the moment. Next Sunday they will come and spend a week with us. My son Patrick has started a part-time job in Woolworths and Roselyne is starting at Donut King in Smithfield, working Thursday evenings and Saturdays.

I am going to be a great aunt next December as my niece, Caroline (Marielle's daughter) is expecting a baby. So my mum will be a great-grandmother at 66 and Grand-Mère a great-great-grandmother.

I had my hair cut short today. I suppose it is a milestone in the sense that I am getting older, no more long hair. I will be 42 next November. I feel that I need glasses too. I have trouble reading the newspaper. The strange thing is that I do not feel older. I still do my 20 minutes of aerobic exercises every day.

We own a boat now, a 19 foot half-cabin cruiser called 'Mistress 3'. I think that this name will have to go!

Wednesday, 4th April, 1991.

It has been many months since I last wrote. If I remember correctly it hasn't been since last October, the 25th anniversary of our arrival in Australia.

I've been quite busy and so many things have happened that I have not had much time to give this book of mine much attention.

We were expecting the family of Cyril and Chantal (my in-laws) to visit from Brisbane. My sister Marie-France and her son Nicholas also spent some time with us.

Well, here we are into a new year! I do hope that it's end will be happier than the beginning.

Extracts from my Journal

Christmas 1990 will be long remembered because of cyclone 'Joy'. Even though it caused some minor damage and brought us a lot of rain, it disrupted our Christmas by lack of electricity and water. We can consider ourselves lucky since it did not cross the coast near Cairns, as it was showing signs of doing for a couple of days.

'Joy' was classed as a severe tropical cyclone of the same calibre as 'Tracy' that devastated Darwin in 1974. On hearing the news in Brisbane and Melbourne, Mum and my sisters were terribly worried for us and rang to wish us courage in our forthcoming ordeal.

At one stage at night, when the gusts of wind were picking up strength, the falling of a branch off a tree crashing on our roof startled us by its noise. Popy and John said 'The roof is going!'. Roselyne and her cousin Belinda started screaming. We all sprung out of our chairs, while the men went out to investigate. I must admit that I am very much frightened of cyclones having lived through one in Mauritius in 1960.

'Joy' luckily moved away from us and a few days later after considerably weakening, crossed the coast near Mackay and caused some severe floods near Rockhampton.

We still managed to enjoy our Christmas lunch at Monique and John's place. I am sure that Cyril and Chantal won't forget that holiday in a hurry.

We had a big new years eve party at our place. Our cousin Leon (Zoum) from Brisbane spent a few days with us. The party lasted until 3 o'clock the next afternoon, as numerous people spent the night not wanting to drive after drinking alcohol. As Popy celebrated a bit too much, I had some difficulty in waking him up!

A few days after saw us going camping to Frankland islands. Three other families came with our own. Poor Popy had to make two trips back and forth. Plus Cyril had brought his newly acquired punt, bought from his Dad.

We spent a whole day setting up the tents. The weather had not been the best, luckily it only rained at night. Even though some of us whinged, saying it was not worth the hassle, I thoroughly enjoyed my stay there. Our friends, Julie and Lawrence Skowe came with us. We even climbed on top of a small hill across the island. (Great achievement for me as I am not an adventurous person!).

A ray of sunshine has been the birth of my grandnephew, Cairo, Caroline's son on 3rd January. Mother and son are doing well.

As we will be going to Brisbane in May for my niece Sophie's wedding, we will have a photo taken of the five generations - Grandma, Mum, Marielle, Caroline and Cairo.

We've just had a family portrait of the Maujeans done. My in-laws took the opportunity of their son, Cyril's stay here with his family.

Page 219

From Island to Continent *Marie-Josée Maujean*

Five generations – great-granddaughter Caroline, great-great-grandson Cairo, granddaughter Marielle, daughter Myriam and matriarch Zelie Arnulphy.

Those photographs were taken on the day that war broke out in the Persian Gulf on 15th January (also Cyril's birthday), after America had given Sadham Hussein an ultimatum to pull out of Kuwait by this date, which he failed to do. As a result, George Bush gave the command for operation Desert Storm to begin.

That war lasted six weeks. It was the first time that the American military included females sent to the war zone. Due to improved technology, we saw a complete coverage of the first three days on television.
Luckily, Sadham Hussein had not used chemical warfare as it was first feared. In fact they hardly resisted. America's ploy has been hailed a success.

Unfortunately while cease fire between the Middle East and the West is in effect, there is civil war in Iraq. Thousands of rebels are reported to have been executed by Sadham's army.

The price of petrol has gone up to 80 cents a litre in Cairns, after having recently gone down to 62 cents a litre.

I am very sad to report that Uncle Roger (Maujean) passed away on 9th March. Fortunately it was a peaceful death. Uncle Roger was moved to a nursing home six weeks before when he had suffered another light stroke, which made it impossible for his wife Paule to give him all the car needed at home, being more handicapped by the stroke

Extracts from my Journal

Philippe and Violette Maujean with their offspring. Back row from left – Cyril, myself and Popy. Middle row – Belinda, Christopher, Patrick, Roselyne, Michael, John and Christian. Front row – Michael, Chantal, Philippe and Violette, Monique and Scott.

Roger was 71 years old, the same age that his father passed away.

Even though it was a release for him, his death has left a void in the family. Roger was such a cheerful person that used to enjoy life.

My father-in-law, Philippe was deeply affected as the two brothers were so close.

Violette and Philippe left for Mauritius yesterday. They will spend two months there with Philippe's two sisters, Aliette and Daisy.

Roselyne turned fifteen last October. We had a special family party for the occasion. She wore a special white dress and numerous photos of her were taken with the family.

Roselyne's independent streak is coming to the fore with vigour. I swear she enjoys the shock to my system like the time she turned up one day, her hair dyed jet black at her friends place.

Patrick has started at TAFE College this year, doing a pre-vocational course. Unfortunately he could not get an apprenticeship as the job market is at its lowest, in fact Australia is in a recession. Hopefully with this course, it should be easier for him next year.

From Island to Continent   *Marie-Josée Maujean*

Roselyne's 15th birthday with all her cousins

Pat obtained his driving license last March. He drives a Gemini that Popy bought for him at a good price.

Micheline's daughter, Miriam, is in Brisbane at university studying for hotel management.

My nephew Michael (Fayd'herbe), is going to Melbourne in a couple of weeks to live and work there for a while after completing a four year art course at TAFE College in Townsville.

Scott Harris (another nephew) has started work at the Commonwealth Bank. He wants to become a pilot. Scott finished school last year with excellent academic results.

My Godchild, Dominic, is doing the same course as Pat at TAFE.

My Mum and Arthur are having trouble selling their house in Victoria. They can't wait for it to happen as they want to move to Brisbane.

Saturday, 8th June, 1991.

Philippe and Violette came back from Mauritius yesterday. We have planned to go there, Popy and I, at the end of next year.

It should be so interesting to see the place again as an adult.

We went to Brisbane last month for Sophie's wedding to Troy Austin. We spent a week there. The wedding was a success. I've got a video of it made by Cyril. It was good seeing people that we hadn't seen for years.

I found Grand-Mère looking very frail this time. She will turn 96 next August. The photo of the five generations turned out good.

Extracts from my Journal

There was also one of Maman with her six daughters. Unfortunately my brother, Ivan, could not come.

While in Brisbane I was lucky to win a Mother's Day prize at the chemist shop in the Hyperdome shopping complex next to Cyril and Chantal's place. It was a basket containing several Max-Factor cosmetics that I won after filling in a form on the morning of the wedding before having my hair done for the occasion.

We nearly missed the wedding ceremony as we got lost on the way to the church. Chantal, Marie-France and I were driven by François Mackie, while our husbands had gone earlier for photos and videos. At one stage it was ten to three, the time it would start and we were still a fair way away after looking at the map. I had visions of us lost somewhere and missing the whole thing! Luckily we were only five minutes late, and walked in the church just in time to see the couple exchanging their marriage vows.

Sophie looked beautiful. We had great fun at the reception and danced a lot.

A week after, my Godchild Veronique spent a week with us in Cairns, during which time I got to appreciate her as an adult. We had lived apart since she left Cairns with her family, only a child.

Gabriel Lionnet, Aliette Mayer, Daisy Lionnet, Phillipe and Violette Maujean in Mauritius.

I must tell you of my accomplishment when I walked 15 kilometres, accompanied by my friend Julie, from Smithfield shopping centre to the Palm Cove Travel Lodge during a promotion for Care For Kids to raise money towards the expansion of the Royal Brisbane's Children Hospital. Organised by Woolworths, the firm I work for, it took us two hours and fifteen minutes to reach our destination. Quite a challenge. My son Patrick also took part. Being younger, he managed to jog most of the time.

Wednesday, 23rd October, 1991.
A sad event has taken place. Sophie gave birth to a still-born baby boy, Joshua Austin, on 7th October. The whole family is devastated by this.
The first part of my book is being put through the word processor by Dennis. It was a strange feeling when I read the first chapter in print.

Wednesday, 29th July, 1992.
The end of 1991 was as bad as the start. Last November saw my father-in-law, Philippe, become gravely ill after a routine gall bladder operation when he suffered a ruptured ulcer and was in intensive care for some weeks.
We went through some very anxious moments as it was touch and go for a while. His son, Cyril, had to come up followed by his wife, Chantal. Luckily Philippe recovered after spending nearly three months in hospital.
My sister, Marie-France, is living in Cairns now and has a new love in her life, Neville Harris, John's brother. The two of them met at our place on Christmas Day.
Our son, Patrick, finally started an apprenticeship last June with Shortland Oil Services in Cairns. At the moment he is working in Bamaga. It is the first time that he has gone away for so long, some three weeks.
We have bought another house. It is in our street at number 8. A high-set bought in partnership with Monique and John. We have just finished painting the inside before Micheline and Jean-Claude move in next weekend.
Roselyne will be staying with them while we are in Mauritius.
I have started dreaming about our trip to Mauritius. It is so exciting. My only regret is that Pat and Rose won't be coming with us. We will spend five weeks there, leaving Cairns on Friday 21st August at 5.30 pm. We bought a brand new suitcase and are ready to go.

Wednesday, 5th August, 1992.
I make this entry into my diary feeling very sad. Grand-Mère's cremation took place this morning at 9.30 am in Brisbane. She passed away suddenly on Monday evening while watching a TV show, sipping a little glass of port after dinner.

What a peaceful way to go! Even though we knew it would happen soon due to her age, it was still a shock.

Grand-Mère had always been around like a solid tree. Grand-Mère felt that the end was near, but was hoping to reach her 96th birthday on 30th August and had started to crochet a suit, mind you, for the occasion. She had finished the skirt and was half way through the vest.

The grand lady will live through our memory.

Thursday, 20th August, 1992.
This is it! The big day is tomorrow. We are going to Mauritius.

The last few weeks have been hectic. What with Popy away and only Roselyne to keep me company, I've been very busy indeed, getting ready for our trip with all the washing and ironing and working on my book as I wanted to finish it and have my mind all clear to take in all the new impressions and feelings in Mauritius.

I got quite a shock one Sunday when Popy rang and told me he had an accident that morning on the way from Bamaga to Weipa, which is a rough road with lots of sharp corners.

It happened when taking such a bend and the oncoming car was almost in the middle of the road. The other guy tried to swerve but the road being mainly sand, his car swerved and Popy hit him on his side.

Popy assured me that he was unhurt, not even a scratch, with the only unfortunate fact that the accident taking place in the middle of nowhere and the four wheel drive damaged to the point where it could not be driven. They relied on some good samaritan to give them a lift and they stayed at a ranger's station where they were very well looked after.

They stayed there for two days until a truck was despatched in Cairns to fetch them.

As a result, his boss Noel from Brisbane and himself, were a sorry sight when they got back at 11.30 pm the next Tuesday night.

Pat also had a lucky escape the following day when a sheet of iron that blew away during a strong gust of wind just missed his head. God is certainly looking after them!

I am so happy as Patrick will be back in an hour or so after being away for nearly four weeks. He has talked to us on the phone every week and has missed the family a lot.

My cousin Suzelle (Nozaïc), rang me from Brisbane last week. She is now married to my first cousin Leon Arnulphy (Zoum). That big event took place last June, on the 11th to be precise.

I finished work on Tuesday to have a few more days getting organised before our departure. My suitcase is packed and Popy's is partly done.

The house is immaculate! The indoor plants have been placed outside under the trees and now I am just waiting for Patrick's clothes, a big load of them to be washed and pressed, ready to be taken to his grandparents tomorrow.

Last night the whole family (mine) had dinner at the restaurant Fawlty Tom on the occasion of my sister, Marie-France, celebrating her birthday. She turned the big 40.

It was a surprise for her as she was told by Neville that only the two of them would be having a private celebration.

She was quite touched by it when we all turned up to help her celebrate. All her family was there, including her three sons.

Leon and Suzelle Arnulphy (nee Nozaïc) on their wedding day.

Extracts from my Journal

Paule and Roger Maujean with their five children.

Patrick, myself, Roslyne and Philippe going to a formal dance.

A romantic sunset for myself and Philippe on Hamilton Island.

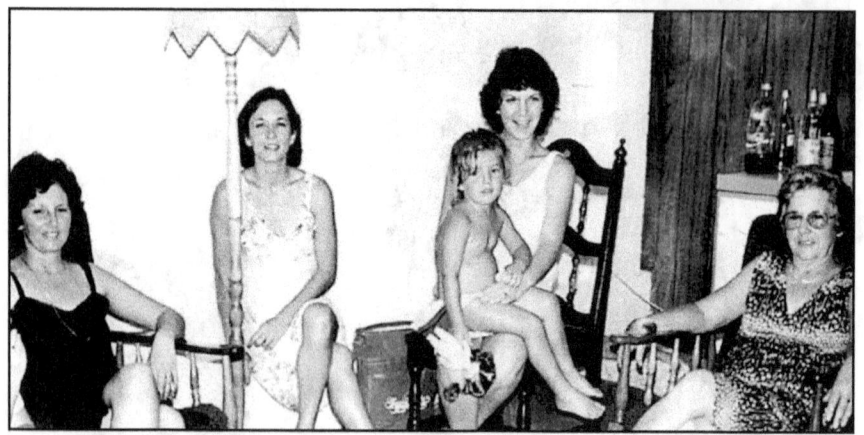

Danielle Mallac, Mariane Simpson, Christine Bechard with daughter Claudine and their mother Lise Mamet.

CHAPTER 22

Back to Mauritius...
The Trip of a Lifetime

Saturday, 22nd August, 1992.
We've just woken up at the Perth Airways Hotel overlooking the Swan River. We arrived last night after a seven hour flight from Cairns.

Patrick drove us to the airport with Roselyne just back from school. My in-laws and brother Ivan also came to wish us well.

Our time of departure was delayed from 5.30 to 6.10. Roselyne wished she was accompanying us and we were both overcome by tears when we said goodbye.

We landed three times on our way. First at Alice Springs, a fairly modern airport where we spent about 15 minutes in the terminal before boarding again. It was quite cold on the tarmac, only 12 degrees celcius.

Our next stop was at Ayres Rock where we did not see any dingo but were greeted by swarms of moths attracted by the airport's lights. A quick cigarette was enjoyed by me as smoking is not allowed on board.

Before landing at Perth as was first scheduled, the plane had to divert to Kalgoolie, an auriferous town, to refuel as there was a strike in progress at Perth since yesterday.

As a result it is unsure whether we will be able to depart for Mauritius this afternoon. Popy has tried to contact the airline company, but to no avail so far.

As we have to vacate the premises by 10.30 am, we will try to contact my cousin, Alain Pastor, who we haven't seen for some twenty years.

I am quite impatient to leave as I feel so excited and eager to reach our destination.

It is now 4 pm and are on our way to Mauritius, sitting quite comfortably on board Air Mauritius. It won't be a direct flight as we are flying to Adelaide airport for refuelling.

For this reason, we will now land in Mauritius at 2 am local time.

After breakfast this morning, Popy and I walked to the city centre and found Perth a beautiful and clean place where I would not mind returning for a few days.

I was a sight wearing high heel shoes and trailing behind my husband. Luckily we caught a taxi back. The city has beautiful old buildings that add character to the place.

What a small world. Our cabbie lived in Cairns a few years ago!

As soon as we got to the International airport, we were surrounded by the French language at the Air Mauritius counter. It felt as if we were already in another country.

It was quite funny at first and now after hearing it for the past three hours we are starting to feel immersed, so to speak, in the ambiance.

Popy and I had quite a laugh listening to some native Sega on the head phones.

Thank goodness I can smoke on board, especially now that the flight is extended.

I feel sorry for the poor relatives who will be meeting us at the airport. It certainly won't be the same now. Imagine, in the middle of the night!

We only had five hours sleep last night. We are bound to feel exhausted on our arrival.

Monday, 24th August, 1992 (Mauritius).

We've finally been able to have a decent night's sleep and I've just woken up with a major headache. I don't know whether to blame it on Gaby's delicious home made port or to the onset of a cold. (I hope not the latter. Not now! It wouldn't be fair!).

Air Mauritius landed at Sir Seewasagar Ramgoolam's international airport at exactly 2.30 am. Another slight delay due to the strong headwinds encountered by the pilot in the Indian Ocean.

I was quite surprised at the change of name of the airport. It used to be called Plaisance.

As the aeroplane was gradually making its descent and we could see the lights of the island below, I felt quite moved. It was the place of my birth, and will always hold a special place in my heart.

I asked Popy how he felt and his answer was a simple 'Nothing'. I put it to his macho front. He won't admit to his emotions.

After a fairly brief exit through immigration and customs, we found our way outside. Popy pushed the mountain of luggage on the trolley and we were greeted by our cousins Gilles and Caroline Lionnet. The last time we had seen Gilles he was about 12 years old.

Back to Mauritius ... The Trip of a Lifetime

It was a very amicable trip to Monchoisy when even though it was dark outside, we could see a few familiar places on the way. After about one hour when we reached our destination, we were quite surprised at the sight of some very large hotels and resorts in Monchoisy.

Poor Tante Daisy had tried to wait for our arrival but sleep had claimed her a short time before.

We were taken to a beachfront bungalow looking very rustic and tastefully decorated with a spiral staircase leading to the bedroom upstairs.

After enjoying a coffee with Gilles and Caroline, it was time for a much needed sleep before meeting the rest of the family the next day.

We were told that Popy's cousin, Clifford Mayer and his family, had come to spend the weekend with us.

Would you believe? I hardly slept! Too much excitement I suppose!

At about 6.30 I could not stay in bed any longer. I had to have a look outside and walked to the door opening onto a balcony overlooking the beach. I can't describe how it felt looking at a calm sea with a few charter boats moored near a jetty. A pirogue was slowly moving out to sea for a day's fishing. It looked so peaceful.

We soon got to meet the whole family. It was so good to hug Gaby and Daisy, their son Noel living with them and to meet Clifford, his wife Sylvie and their two daughters and 13 months old son.

We all sat together for breakfast and found all of them so 'sympa'. It was a heart-warming welcome.

On that first day we met a lot of people of all ages who came visiting and even managed a game of cards called 'belotte'.

We enjoyed a delicious spicy fried rice for lunch and mouth-watering flan, a specialty of Daisy.

It was nice to see Odile, a relative on my father's side, who had come to visit us. Now a widow with four grown-up children, Odile formed part of our teenage friends. I spent a lot of time showing all the photos of the family brought from Australia to all of them.

I will now stop my chit-chatting as I am eager for the day that awaits us.

Tuesday, 25th August, 1992.

It looks like a beautiful day ahead for the wind has died down and the sea looks like a mirror.

Yesterday will stay engraved in my memory as I've visited some places that had stayed dear to me.

After visiting my Godmother who lives two doors away and catching up on the latest about her family (she came to Australia a few years ago as four of her sons are settled in Melbourne and Cairns), Marc, one of Gaby and Daisy's sons took us for a drive to see the island.

It was so exciting! We travelled through Grand-Baie (large bay), a coastal town that I hardly recognised as it is bustling with tourists and has hotels built all along the coast line.

On the way to Port Louis we detoured to Beau-Plan, the sugar estate where Popy used to live. The place looked almost unchanged except that it seemed to have shrunk, as we remembered it about twice its size. Popy commented how he remembered the employee's houses as being much further from the factory and the road as being much steeper.

On one occasion driving through a village, we saw an Indian with his ox pulling a cart of sugar cane. I was surprised as I thought that it was not done anymore.

Those Indian females wearing their saris looked so colourful and added an exotic touch to the scenery. I had forgotten those 'faubourgs' (back streets of a village), with their narrow roads bordered by tabagies selling from cigarettes to spicy fried cakes called badgha and chilli cakes in their box-like containers, the boutiques where they even sell alcohol.

I thought of my children who would have found it all so colourful. Roselyne would have surely wanted a sari. I can even see her wearing one!

It was quite an experience to feel part of the bustling life surrounding us when our senses were revived so to speak with that special smell dating back to our childhood.

As we drove along it felt good to see all those familiar mountains in the background like the Pieter Both, La Montagne Des Signaux (Signal Mountain, more like a hill, where ships got signals during the war).

In Port Louis we could see La Citadelle (an old fort) and Marie-Reine de la Paix standing tall amongst the scenery (statue of Mary dominating the town).

We went past churches like L'Imaculee where it was quite funny to see a sign against smoking — 'Ne Fumez Pas!' (Quit Smoking!) — and the old cathedral of Saint Louis.

As we went past the Champ de Mars Hypodrome I was again surprised of how much smaller it now looked to me.

We travelled on the new highway (L'auto route) to Rose Hill town where I used to live as a child. There again, all the familiar places looked much smaller, like the Route Royale (main road) for instance.

I was delighted to see Notre Dame de Lourdes, the church where we attended mass every Sunday for years and where family events of wedding and baptism took place, the bus stop we walked to every school day morning, the local Chinese shop at its corner, still standing. It brought back all those childhood memories.

Especially the one of that morning when being around twelve years old I felt quite miserable on hearing the news on radio that Caryl Chessman would be executed in America that day, after twelve years of appealing against the death sentence and even taking up his own defence.

Marc took us to the house where Grand-Mère used to live. The house looked very old and much smaller than I remembered. The house on their property where we used to live while my parents were away in Europe had been demolished, replaced by one built of concrete, but the huge lychee tree under which we used to play at being St Bernadette and the Virgin Mary was still standing tall. The road leading to the property that looked so wide and steep to us children, I felt I could hop across yesterday.

On the Rue Vandermeersh where my other grandma's house used to be, did not look the same, but I could recognise the local shop where we used to stop after school to buy those milk lollies. I could not locate the house but did pass an alley where our nanny used to take us for our afternoon strolls. I walked through that old tunnel with only its walls standing nowadays where we used to go through on our way to church and the cinema plaza all those years ago. The adjacent railway lines had been removed and garden beds planted in their place.

I saw the Corp de Garde mountain in the distance with new eyes, and could now see how it was given its name in the first place as at one side it looks like the body of a soldier lying down with his arms folded on his chest.

I can't wait to visit the town of Quatre Bornes now.

We visited a new place called Le Domaine des Pailles, which is a setting of old Mauritius with carriages and colonial buildings surrounded by a deer park and an equestrian area where Sabrina, Marc's fiance works as an equestrian teacher.

Our relatives are spoiling us and it feels great!

I must write to Patrick and Roselyne today and tell them about it all.

We went to a local shop yesterday and I could not believe the service! Actually, it was quite funny at first when going to different aisles looking for coffee, milk and bread, all the usual necessities, as I was followed by two Indian girls who stayed close to me. My first impression was they want to make sure nothing is stolen or the like. When picking up an item from the shelf, I realised that it was done with good intentions, as they wanted to carry it for me. They were very helpful and carried everything to the counter where they packed it all after being verbally abused by their father for not using a cardboard box in the first place. I wanted to laugh at the Creole expressions of the Dad. Popy bought 12 stubbies of beer there and the whole thing worked out quite cheap.

We stopped at a boulangerie (bakery) on the side of the road and paid less than 50 Australian cents for six bread rolls.

Friday, 28th August, 1992.

It is becoming a habit! First thing every morning I am drawn to the window to contemplate the sea. Today promises to be warm and sunny. It is already a week since we left Cairns. I can't wait to receive some news from Patrick and Roselyne.

The family is so warm and doing their utmost to make our stay memorable.

Daisy is excelling herself in the kitchen with the help of her domestic, Mariette and for lunch every day we are enjoying her delicious cuisine Creole that includes fricasses and chutneys.

Gaby's specialty is a passionfruit punch concocted with a fair amount of rum. Delicious, but watch out!

Noel, their eldest son who lives with them, is genuinely happy to see us and has some fond memories of Australia. He visited with his Mum in the early seventies.

Marc and his fiance, Sabrina, live close by and we see them every day. He has driven us to various places like I mentioned earlier. He only came back to Mauritius some months ago after living in Corsica for many years.

The youngest son, Gilles, and his wife Caroline, have two children. Loic, an eleven year old son who is a fanatic of boats and fishing and their six year old daughter, Anais, who has taken a liking to Popy and I and follow us everywhere. She reminds me of Roselyne as a child, even in personality.

Gaby took us to an Indian temple close by. It consists of a main building surrounded by seven chapels. It is consecrated to the God Shiva and its seven divinities. Popy has filmed it on video and it is quite interesting to listen to the young Indian guide who took us on a tour of the place. Before entering each building, we had to remove our shoes as a sign of respect to the gods. This temple was built in 1897 and its architecture is beautiful.

The island is now doing very well economically. Everywhere you go, even in small villages, there is a video club, for all the natives own a TV and video, affordable as most of them work in factories now that so many industries have been established. We were told that there is no unemployment on the island.

It is so amusing to hear the Creole expressions. I am told that even the uneducated natives can now speak French, English and Italian as well as their native tongue. All this due to the influx of tourists.

I was lying on the beach yesterday and soaking up the sun when a young Creole man came to me carrying numerous baskets containing necklaces, earrings and beautiful copper ornaments for sale. It's his job like so many of them to walk the beaches and approach tourists to sell his merchandise. I believe they can become close to being a nuisance sometimes.

This particular one first quoted me 100 rupees for a necklace but changed his tune to 60 on finding out that I was Mauritian born.

As I was buying eight of them, I consulted Daisy on the value to which she advised me to offer 400 rupees for the lot to which he proposed 450. That I thought was fair enough after all.

At present one Australian dollar is equivalent to about 10 Mauritian rupees. The notes have changed now of course and represent Indian dignitaries as the government is now a republic.

It was quite strange to see a friend of ours prior to leaving Mauritius on television as Paul (Paulo, we used to call him) Berenger is now a famous politician of Mauritius as Minister for Foreign Affairs. He is also a distant relative of ours as his father was a first cousin to Violette, my mother-in-law. Paulo used to go out with my sister Marielle.

Popy, Noel and myself enjoyed a pleasant afternoon going out to sea in the pirogue built by Marc a few months ago. We held a line for a while but had to bring them back in as there were too many windsurfers about. We could see various resorts along the coast including Club Med with its beautiful white sand.

As soon as we got back, Gilles and Caroline took us to a new resort, Le Maritime, beautifully set on the deserted beach of Balaclava. It is of the same standard as Ramada in Cairns. We enjoyed a drink there after which they took us for a drive to Le Goulet, an estuary near Baie Du Tombeau.

We stopped in front of a beautiful church built by slaves such a long time ago called Notre Dame De La Salette.

On the way back we stopped at Grand-Baie and enjoyed some spicy Indian savouries made of chokos and egg plant. We have also had some gateaux piments (chilly cake) and samoosas.

Today we will be eating some dahl puree, a very fine pastry made with yellow peas flour served with some hot and spicy chutneys.

We haven't seen the other side of Popy's family, the Mayer's, yet due to some health problems in the family. We'll go and see them later. I rang my Nozaïc aunts and will visit them as soon as we hire a car.

Gilles has organised an outing for next Sunday to cruise to Balaclava on the occasion of our 23rd wedding anniversary on a large charter boat belonging to the firm he works for. As there will be some 25 of us on board, it should be fun!

We met some relatives of ours yesterday, Aude (Maujean), married to Bernard Valette, a very friendly couple. We also met Philippe Merven whose mother is Josée Maujean. (I did not know that there was some relative bearing my name).

Wednesday, 2nd September, 1992.
It is a quarter past twelve local time and far away in Australia a quarter past six in the evening.

I can't help thinking of my children, wondering what are they doing at this time. We are having a fabulous holiday.

Our wedding anniversary was memorable. We spent the whole day cruising along the coast in a 53 ft yacht sipping a glass of wine and soaking up the sun on the top deck before enjoying a delicious lunch while listening to some Mauritian segas that brought back loads of memories. I wished that Pat and Ros could celebrate with us.

I was very interested after we left Gran Baie when we passed close to the whale rock that unfortunately was completely submerged that day and whose spot was defined by a buoy.

To refresh your memory it was mentioned in an earlier chapter concerning the sinking of the Caprera near the Coin De Mire (Gunner's Coin). I could observe that indeed it did happen very close to the coast.

That evening, back at our relative's place in Mon Choisy, we were surprised when presented with a large cake, decorated with the number 23 as candles. Daisy had ordered it for that special occasion and Gaby contributed by uncorking a couple of bottles of French champagne.

On Monday it was shopping day, driven there (Gran Baie) with Odile and her teenage daughter, Alexandra. I bought lots of clothes for Pat and Ros.

After lunch, Gilles took us for a drive along the east coast through Roche Noire where I used to spend some time during school holidays at my Nozaïc cousins bungalow.

Next was Poste Lafayette that also held some childhood memories as we passed my aunt Jacqueline's campement.

We went as far as Belle Mare that evening and it was interesting as I had never been to some of those beaches that looked so inviting with their white powdery sand contrasting to the special aqua colour of the sea.

Yesterday was very special as it was spent with my cousin, Joëlle (Nozaïc) and her friend Ian, who took us to his house for lunch at the Mount sugar estate after visiting the dam, La Nicoliere.

Ian took us to a chassé (place where deer hunting takes place) and I found it so interesting as I had never been to one. As I love nature it was quite enjoyable to see herds of deer at such a close range.

The flaura was outstanding, with such varieties of palms mixed among some proud eucalyptus.

We came upon the hut where the deer are fed in a trough filled with molasses. It added a special charm with its thatched roof as well as the log cabin, a special place where hunters meet to share the produce of the kill.

Joëlle took us for the much anticipated visit of Quatre Bornes in the afternoon. I was quite excited at the prospect of seeing her family again after so many years.

Back to Mauritius ... The Trip of a Lifetime

As we approached the street where we used to live prior to leaving the island, my heart was beating quite fast. The house in Avenue Cossigny with its bamboo hedge at the front was still there and looked much smaller than I remembered. The garage has been converted into another room and the whole street did not really look familiar as some houses have been demolished and flats erected at the site.

The reunion with the Nozaïc family of Tante Geneviève and her daughters was quite emotional for me especially when Françoise and I hugged and kissed each other.

Françoise is an artist and there were numerous of her recent paintings displayed in her lounge room, beautiful ones featuring historical landmarks and old colonial houses.

Unfortunately we did not get to see my uncle Roland that day as he was home enjoying his afternoon nap while Tante Geneviève was visiting her daughters.

Tuesday, 8th September, 1992.
We have just entered our third week and enjoying every minute of it.
We have hired a yellow mini car, and every day we are going out to the towns and through coastal roads.

One thing I know for sure, I can't see myself driving here! It is fine on the highway that goes from the north to the south of the island with exits at various towns, but believe me it is quite an experience driving through villages and towns. Not only are the roads in poor condition, there is no traffic order and every road rule is forgotten by cyclists, pedestrians, motorcyclists and bus drivers, especially as they have no qualm in overtaking other buses.

I nearly suffered numerous heart attacks one afternoon when going through Port Louis, the capital, at peak hour.

I kept braking as I sat next to Popy, closing my eyes each time we came to a near miss. In the end I just covered my face with my hands and prayed to the good Lord to please spare me for a while!

I must admit that I have now started to relax a little.

So far we have seen most of the family except for the ones on my maternal side.

We spent last weekend at Popy's Aunt Aliette and her husband, Hervé Mayer, and got to meet the rest of her children. I found all of them friendly and warm.

We spent a very enjoyable evening at a barbecue and cabaret organised by the Mon Desert Alma sugar estate.

The cabaret show was performed by the estate's employees and their families. Believe me, there were some great talents!

Page 237

We were especially impressed by Carol Lemport, a young woman who sang with such ease and sentiment, songs of Edith Piat when she excelled herself. I am sure it is only a matter of time before she makes a career of it. She should go far!

Yesterday was spent in Port Louis visiting the Citadel, the old fort used nowadays for musical shows. The view from there as it is located on a hill is magnificent. We could see the town and harbour below.

We visited the church of Sainte Croix and the vault of Père Laval.

I felt privileged to be there at this time of his anniversary. It was quite moving to see people of different religious beliefs pay their respect at his grave, praying so fervently and reaching for the stone of his grave to touch, believing that this simple gesture will fill them with graces.

Some people would take petals off the numerous bunches of flowers laid on top of the glass encasing his effigy to take to their sick, hopeful of a miracle.

Since this morning people from every corner of the island have started to walk to Sainte Croix in pilgrimage, as tomorrow will mark the anniversary of this priest's death when a special mass will be concelebrated by the Mauritian Cardinal, Monsignor Jean Margeot and an Indian Monsignor visiting the island for that special event. It will be televised, so I'll make sure that I don't miss it.

Next we visited Marie Reine De La Paix where again it felt special.

Gaby informed me that his monument was erected to Mary by the clergy after World War II, in thanksgiving to Our Lady for protecting the island in such dangerous times. It is the place where Pope John Paul 2nd celebrated mass on his visit during the eighties.

In Port Louis we walked to Government House where we saw the statues of Queen Victoria, Sir William Newton, the first British Governor to the island and Captain Willoughby, a British Captain famous for the Grand Port battle.

It was also pleasing to see the statue of Mahé De Labourdonnais standing proud across the road, dominating the harbour.

It was exciting mixing with the crowd and be part of the colourful scene while the nostrils were filled with the spicy smells of gateaux piments and dal puree sold off the sidewalk at numerous street corners.

We approached the bazaar where it looked so exotic to see the crowd consisting of Chinese, Indians, Muslims and Europeans all gathered at various stalls selling t-shirts, musical cassettes, colourful baskets made of rafia while numerous pigeons could be seen on the pavement looking for a feed as if they too wanted to be part of the excitement.

Meat was sold in different buildings. There were special ones with signs on the outside stating their specialty of beef, goat, mutton and pork.

When we entered the one selling beef, it was interesting to see a muslim amongst the salesmen uttering his hourly prayer, unaware of the crowd. It is their belief that after an animal has been killed it must be bled first while saying the special prayer called alhal to purify the flesh before consumption.

Today we went for a drive to Poudre D'or (Gold Dust) and came across a monument on the coast erected by the Historical Society of Mauritius in memory of the ship Le Saint Géran (mentioned in an earlier chapter) that sank off the coast during a cyclone. As this ship was connected with the legend of Paul and Virginie, it is called the Monument of Paul and Virginie.

After learning so much about the history of the island I am seeing those places with new eyes, so to speak, and it adds a special feeling to the experience.

Letters are slow to arrive from Australia. Today was special when I received one from my mother-in-law, Violette. I can't wait to hear from my children.

Last week Popy and I visited places that are dear to us. We've been to see the schools we used to attend and they haven't changed much. We could not get to Trou Aux Cerfs (the crater of an extinct volcano) as it was raining and would not be able to enjoy the view that is worth seeing on a sunny day.

The town of Quatre Bornes where I used to live has changed the most. Somehow it did not look familiar with all the tall buildings that have been constructed since.

Invitations to dinner have started to arrive. We spent some time with my Aunt Claude Nozaïc in Rose Hill. She has not changed much. She was quite interested at hearing about the rest of the family and delighted in seeing all the photos I had brought with me.

Thursday, 17th September, 1992.
We are now at Pointe D'esny, a beach situated on the southern side of the island where we have been blessed with splendid weather.

Today we are enjoying a relaxing day after numerous lunch and dinner parties.

It is a warm feeling experiencing all the attentions being lavished upon us by family and friends.

Our cousin, Rivaltz, has in his possession a collection of books relating to the history of Mauritius from various writers. I was delighted in discovering a couple of them were works of my great uncle, Clement Charoux, thus disclosing his talent after reading his contes disparates (novels).

Aliette, our aunt, took us to the naval museum of Mahebourg where we signed our name in the visitors book. I found the place very interesting and took notes. We were grateful to the guide in allowing us to film inside.

Popy has been terrific in complying with my numerous requests to photograph and film sites of interest.

I felt quite emotional at seeing my two uncles, Roland Nozaïc and Cyril Arnulphy after so many years. With Uncle Roland it was a bit like seeing my own father again and Cyril reminded me of my grandfather (not that he looks that old!). It is hard to describe the feeling when you are reunited with someone from your past. That bond never dies!

Living close by is Tonton Pierre (Masson) whom we visited. His wife, my Aunt Madeleine (whom the family reckons I take after) passed away some ten years ago. We got to meet his new wife, a charming lady, mother of one of my ex-teachers who is now the Principal of the Quatre Bornes Catholic Convent.

Tuesday, 22nd September, 1992.

We are now back at Mon Choisy, to our bungalow overlooking the sea. What a terrific week we've just had! I can't describe the warm welcome we've experienced by family and friends except to say that our wish is their command!

We've been spoilt in all areas from being taken to see so and so, visiting places of interest, being served mouth watering dishes of Mauritian cooking including venison (deer meat) to hearing a special song, having this memory immortalised on a cassette presented to us.

To top it off, Gaby, Daisy and Noel with their warm hospitality.
Clifford and Sylvie Mayer had a barbecue at Sauve Terre sugar estate during the week and invited my Arnulphy relatives, Cyril and Sonia as well as my first cousin Caroline (nee Bouchet), daughter of Aunt Marcienne (now deceased), now married to Jean-François Lenferna.

Caroline had just turned one when we left Mauritius, so I met her for the first time. We had seen Cyril and Sonia when they came to Australia some ten years ago.

We spent a very nice evening together and felt as if we had never been parted.

Beforehand, we had been to L'Ilot Brochus where I fell in love with the place. You can see raging seas breaking on the rocks below while standing on a natural bridge of rocks above a cave through which the waves form a boiling mass of white foam, its spray enveloping the surrounds. Magnificent! It was magic at sunset. This place will stay engraved in my memory.

I had the pleasure in seeing Alain Pastor, a second brother to me who had come back to Mauritius to live after spending many years in South Africa where he met his wife Lyn and also living in Australia (Perth). Alain had left Mauritius in 1963.

That reunion was quite unique. Alain and Lyn are living at his brother's place, Maxo, before they get settled. That weekend the two families had come to Maxo's house at Pointe D'Esny.

Sylvie took us to their house and left. Popy and I walked into the house to be greeted by Maxo, unaware of our identity. A puzzled look on his face as his visitors certainly knew him.

I then said 'I am one of your cousins, Myriam's daughter'. His face lit up, but he still did not know which one. By this time, Alain had come out and I could not keep them in suspense any longer. After all, I was so young when I left. We all hugged each other. They were all so pleased and would not let us go. We enjoyed some time over drinks getting to know their wives and catching up on all the time passed.

We saw them again that day at the beach club where they shouted us more drinks. Popy managed to film them on video for the rest of the family to see.

I have been blessed!

I even got to see another first cousin, Arianne Buonino (nee Baudouin) living in France who came to Mauritius to spend only ten days with her Mum (Claude Nozaïc). It was a surprise visit.

I had last seen Arianne in 1968 when she came to Australia to live, but ended up staying just a few months after her parents and my grandmother could not stand the climate.

After so many years we found it easy to talk to each other. There is no doubt about it, family ties are very strong!

We left each other with the hope of seeing one another again as she wishes to visit Australia with her family. (She has two young daughters).

I have visited the cemetery of St Julien where my Nozaïc ancestors are buried.

We finally made it there with Joëlle, as Popy and I had not been able to get there after going to the wrong one amidst a cane field where I must have been a sight walking amongst the graves where weeds had overgrown the place, in search of some inscription that would identify some relative's name, in vain!

So I was grateful to Joëlle for offering to take us there. We first went to the Pamplemousses cemetery where again I had not been able to locate my grandfather, Eugène Arnulphy's grave previously.

We made it there this time after talking to Father Murphy, a priest of Irish descent living at the presbytery. (One of the oldest houses in the district built before 1756, belonging to a Colon who later sold it to the East India Company to be used as a church before the actual one of Saint François was built in 1756).

Father Murphy even took us for a tour of the place. Apparently the house itself is unchanged except for the surroundings.

My grandfather's remains were placed in a family vault belonging to the Rougier and Raffray families. Today it is being looked after by my Uncle Cyril, his only son, living in Mauritius. All inscriptions are gone except for my grandfather's name. My grandmother's ashes will be put in there as she wished.

It was a day when after I paid my respect to my ancestors and enjoyed a delicious Chinese meal for lunch at Chez Emanuelle in the District of Flacq, Joëlle drove us to Saint Julien where my Nozaïc relatives are buried.

The cemetery is across the road from an old stone church dating back to 1764 that we visited. It was a strange feeling thinking that at some stage this place marked a special event in their lives at instances of baptism, weddings and burials. We were impressed by the beautiful glass-stained windows and a beautifully carved spiral staircase.

The family vault was not hard to find. Generations had been put to rest there. We discovered another two graves bearing the Nozaïc surname, a short distance away.

It was the most peaceful place, fairly close to the sea that could be viewed on the horizon.

One of the graves where two young children had been laid to rest with their grandfather read:

ICI REPOSED (Here Lies) François Etienne Nozaïc
Né a Vannes De Bretagne
Le 17 Juin 1768
Décedé Le 2 November 1823

Louis Evenor Nozaïc
Né En Cette Ile Le 24 Aout 1822
Décedé Le 27 Juillet 1823

Etienne Simon Nozaïc
Né En Cette Ile Le 26 September 1826
Décedé Le 18 Mars 1827

Passant sous cette simple Pierre
Un aieul est couché près de ses deux enfants.
Et semble en ecoulant l'ivresse la plus chère
Les entourer encore de ses soins caressans
Qu'elle douce et touchante image,
Ici malgre les glaces du trépas,

Le penchant le plus pur, la flamme
La plus sage, parait à l'innocence
Ouvrir encore les bras.

I will try to give you a translation:

Buried under this simple stone
A grandparent rests with his two children
And seems through this blissful state
To still hold them in his loving arms.

What a sweet and touching picture
Now, beyond the realm of death
It seems that the purest of sentiments,
That flame of wisdom is passed on
Lovingly to those cherished ones.

    We spent the weekend with Joëlle who had organised a special lunch with the family for Sunday.
    Her parents and sisters plus Tante Claude and cousin Jacqueline were invited.
    After so many years, Jacqueline hadn't changed much in appearance. She still had her long hair. We exchanged photos and it seemed like old times while we joked and reminisced.
    We enjoyed a delicious meal of curry served with dalh purees and faratahs, with a choice of delicious chutneys complemented with a few bottles of red wine.
    We could not leave without having a family photo taken which we did before saying goodbye with the hope of seeing each other in the near future as one of the family, Suzelle, lives in Australia.

Friday, 2nd October, 1992.
A week has gone by since our return.
    I could not find the time to write in that last week of our stay in Mauritius as we were too busy enjoying the time with family as our day of departure approached.
    Rivaltz took us to the movies one night and we saw the film 'L'Amant' (The Lover), a French film that we enjoyed very much.
    After all those years living in an English speaking country our French seemed to come back to us quite naturally, especially in Popy's case where he was so conscious of his French. He spoke it like a charm, not even mixing in an English word as he normally does here.

With my Nozaïc family in Mauritius. Back from left – Chrisiane and Pascale Nozaïc, Ian Bestel and Joelle Nozaïc. Sitting – Roland Nozaïc, Jacqueline Descroizilles, Genevieve Nozaïc, myself, Claude Nozaïc and in front Francoise Nozaïc.

We spent a whole week with the Mayer family. They had made a plan of how each day would be spent that they showed us for our approval, and we all laughed about it.

We visited the market, went to places of interest like the monument erected to the memory of French and British soldiers having taken part in the naval battle of Grand Port.

While there, I was pleasantly surprised when Rivaltz pointed out an island to us, famous for being the place where special birds are seen as the island is under environmental protection, called Le Mouchoir Rouge, the place where my parents spent their honeymoon.

During that week we went to the village of St Hubert where my Mum used to live until her marriage. We could see the chimney of the now defunct sugar factory.

Aliette took us to the naval museum known a long time ago as Rivière La Chaux, residence of the De Robillard family, who lent it to the state to be used as a hospital during that famous naval battle.

As I learnt more that day concerning this event I will pass on my knowledge to you. For instance, that the naval battle was first won by the French when, even though British artillery did hit their vessels, they would not sink as it was so shallow inside the reef that their keel rested on the sea bed, thus enabling them to target the enemy, causing the British to lose that battle.

It is known as the Battle of L'Ile De La Passe. We later on visited that island and you can still see some forts standing.

Three months after, at the end of November 1810, Britain sent an important concentration of troops to Ile De France.

They first went to Rodrigues, an island off the coast of Mauritius, until all the forces had arrived. It included 10,000 British soldiers on some sixty vessels that landed near Cap Malheureux on 29th November, 1810.

Under the command of General Albercombie, those troops walked inland towards Port Louis, the capital. Other troops were also transported to Petite Rivière, later on.

As the army of French General Decaen comprised only of 4000 soldiers, after five days of fighting their only option was to surrender, on 3rd December, 1810.

At the time, Napoleon could not send more troops to the island because the campaigns against Russia were taking place.

Uncle Gaby was very helpful in providing me with some details concerning those events.

He had an ancestor, Doctor Henri Lionnet who was on board the vessel Le Victor who was later stationed at the hospital of Rivière La Chaux to take care of the wounded. I wonder if he got to treat Willoughby?

Some points of interest concerning the history of Mauritius:

1. 1697 - Arrival of pirates.
2. 1736 - Colonisation of Port Louis.
3. 17th August, 1744 - Shipwreck of Le St Géran.
4. 1767 - Start of botanical gardens of Pamplemousses known as Les Jardins De Mon Plaisir.
5. 7th November, 1768 - Arrival of the ship 'La Boudeuse' taking part in the expedition of Bougainvile.
6. 12th November, 1783 - Arrival of the Bailli of Suffren (East India Company).

7. 23rd-26th August, 1810 - Naval battle of Grand Port.
8. 29th November, 1810 - Landing of British troops.
9. 1835 - Start of Indian immigration at Albion Dock.
10. 24th May, 1864 - First railway line.
11. 1867 - Beau Rivage, one of 233 sugar factories operating.
12. 10th November, 1933 - First air link between Reunion Island and Mauritius.

A poem of my Great Uncle - Clement Charoux

Repas Créole

Nous pecherons pour vous complaire
Dans les roches de la rivière
Ecrevisse a notre manière
Le camaron.

Nous abattrons dans la ravine
Sans respect de sa fière mine
Pour son coeur a la chaire si fine
Le chou-palmiste.

Nous servirons en bonne aubaine
Dans un grand bol de porcelaine
Du riz de chine ou bien de l'inde
Aux grains laiteux.

Agrémentant cette blancheur
Sous le parfum et la couleur
Nous dispenserons sa saveur
Poule au carri.

Complément de notre ripaille
Flanquant le cari de volaille
Les pommes d'amour en rougaille
Seront en fleurs.

Pour corser de facon experte
Le piquant de l'agape offerte
Nous hacherons la mangue verte
En chatini.

La gamme des feux du tropique
Exprimera sa politique
Par ces representants toniques
Piments, achards.

Constitueront notre réserve
Pour que chaque jour on les serve
Modérateurs de notre verve
Bouillons de brèdes.

Atte, bibasse, bigarade
Letchis à pulps delectable
Le verger sera sur la table
Exquis dessert.

Rhums de chez nous et vins de
France Cafés de chaude succulence
Complèteront avec science
Notre régal.

Chere, laissant votre auréole,
Par le prochain 'zinc' qui décolle
Venez ce soir à la créole
Diner aux iles.

(Clement Charoux - Chronique du pays créole the Mauritius Printing and Stationery Coy. Ltd. 1953).

Our Aunt Daisy Lionnet has written many poems relating to people, things that are dear to her and special events. I felt privileged that she let me read her 'book' of them. Here are a couple.
The first one is about the boat 'Le Cygne', owned by Gaby Lionnet and Philippe and Roger Maujean.

Le Cygne

Tu portes bien ton nom le cygne!
Ton air si fier, ta belle allure
Fait qu'on envie ta jolie ligne
Et les plaisirs que tu procures.

Par tous les temps, bons ou mauvais
Par mer très calme ou agitée
Qui donc pourrait craindre jamais
Nous sommes en toute securité.

Combien d'entre nous te devons
Le couronnement de tout pecheur
Heureux lorsque nous retournons
De se dire c'est mon empereur!

Joyeux du club nous recevons
La coupe enfin toute desirée
C'est à toi que nous la devons
Car de toi viens tout nos succés.

An ode to the sea by Daisy Lionnet.

Homage a la mer

Majestueuse mer dont l'immence etendue
Depasse l'horizon et charme notre vue
J'aime a venir rever pres de tes flots d'azur
Et gouter sur tes bords le bonheur le plus pur.

J'aime ta fraiche brise et ta vague mourante
Tes plages, tes recifs, ta douce mer grisante
Le flot qui se retire et revient tour a tour
Sur le tas de rochet, se briser nuit et jour.

Et lorsque sous la rage des terribles tempètes
Tes vagues se brisent, grondent comme des bètes
Muette d'epouvante, j'ecoute en frissonant
De tous ces bruits affreux, l'echo retentissant!

Malheur au pauvre pécheur qui n'est pas prés du port
Dans tes vagues profondes l'attend l'horrible mort
Je préfère te voir souriante et tranquille
Bercant le vieux pécheur dans sa barque fragile.

Sous tes charmes trompeurs cachant ta cruauté
Ne presente aux yeux que ta seule beauté
Oh mer en ton repos que tu me Parais belle

Avec tes douces vagues, ta splendeur eternelle
Et le soleil lui meme avec ses rayons d'or
Se penche, te caresse puis doucement s'endort.

We left Mauritius on the rainy morning of Friday, 25th September.
Gaby and Daisy preferred to say their goodbyes at home, Noel also was going to miss us. At the airport we were greeted by Aliette and her sons Rivaltz and Clifford. I felt quite sad that morning and Aliette to say that the rain was appropriate. We were leaving. One thing we knew for sure, we would come back!

We filmed five hours of video cassettes of our holiday. That's modern technology for you. Those memories will live on.

One day sitting on the beach at Mon Choisy, I felt the urge to express my feelings on paper. This is the poem I wrote - it's in French because I can express myself better in that language.

Retour a l'ile Maurice

Petite ile Maurice, berceau de mon enfance
Aujourd'hui tu m'accueuilles, grace à la providence
Apres tant d'années passés, presque une eternité
Il est bon de revenir vers tes plages enchantees.

Mon premier regard au reveil, sur la mer s'est posée
Son calme, sa beautée m'ont drolement impressioné
ta plage au soleil m'invitait
Tandis que ton souffle leger m'a calinement caressé.

Parents et amis, qu'il est bon de se revoir
Ca chauffe le coeur et j'ai peine à y croire
Que je suis ici sur mon ile natale
Que j'ai quitté tres jeune pour les Terres Australe.

Cocotiers et filaos m'ont chanté la bienvenue
Sur le sable moelleux, j'ai marché les pieds nus
La nuit a etalé son manteau etoilé
Tandis que la mer doucement me bercait
Tu semblais dire comme une mère l'aurait fait
Viens mon enfant, c'est tout oublié.

Aujourd'hui c'est la fête, il faut jouir du présent
Car c'est lui qui demain sera le bon vieux temp

De ces jours de merveille, par la famille entourée
Dans le cadre de ton île, en mon coeur incruste
Ce reve accompli, dont je rêvais
Durera l'eternité!

The meaning of it all!

A Comeback to Mauritius

Small island of Mauritius, cradle of my youth
Thanks to providence, today you welcome me
After so many years, almost an eternity
It feels good to be back to your enchanted shores.

My first glance, on the sea has rested
It's calm, it's beauty, really moved me
Your sunny beach was so inviting
While I felt the caress of your gentle breeze.

Family and friends, it's good to be reunited
It warms my heart and I can hardly believe
That I am here, on my native island
That I left as a youth, so many years ago.

Coconut palms and filaos have sung their welcome
On the soft sand, I have walked bare feet
The night has spread it's star lit cloak
While the sound of the sea has gently rocked me.

You seemed to say, as a mother would have done
Come to my arms, child, it's all forgotten
Today is special, one must enjoy the present
For tomorrow it will become one of the good old days.

All those marvelous days surrounded by family
Spent on the island I used to dream about
This dream now accomplished, engraved in my heart
Will last for eternity.

Mauritius

Back to Mauritius ... The Trip of a Lifetime

O small island, jewel of the sea
I'll remember how you welcomed me
With your sunny shores fringed by your palms
Engraved in my soul like a soothing balm.

Your breath I could feel by a gentle breeze
That caressed my face and played with my hair
Then stirred the leaves of palms and filaos
That burst into song which my heart echoes!

I saw all your familiar mountains
Felt your tears as it turned to rain
Above the ocean you displayed a colourful sunset
The sight of which I'll never forget.

After so many years, that I lived away
It's good to be back on this holiday
The warmth, the welcome is so marvellous
Thanks to you people of dear Mauritius.

It has taken me three years and five months to complete this book. After all, I've had a lot of work and living to do during that time. Life has not always treated us kindly, but one thing I've learnt, family ties keep you strong! Never forget that, no matter what. What really counts, is family.

I have paused for a while and looked back into the lives of all those people that formed our ancestry. I have come across some who weren't perfect, after all that's what humanity is all about. I've learnt that compassion and faith are two ingredients that keep us going on our journey.

Today is special. My daughter, Roselyne, is having her formal in her last year of school. Her partner is Denis de Speville.

On this Saturday, 24th July, 1993 I'm glad I've finished the book and hope you find it worth reading.

I have done my best. I will forever be grateful to Dennis, for after all, if it was not for his hard work it would not have been presented to you.

God Bless.

Marie-Josée Maujean

From Island to Continent   *Marie-Josée Maujean*

Australia

She's a land of contrast, of desert and forests
With golden beaches and high mountain crests
Who can be charming and sometimes relentless
Through floods and drought, she's sometimes merciless
Come cyclones and bushfires, she'll put you to the test.

She can surprise us depending on her mood
With clear blue sky and no time to brood
Hold our breath when she decides to set
Her most spectacular display of a radiant sunset.

I love Australia, that sunburnt country
Home it is today to our family
From Mauritius we came, a new generation
To settle on her land filled with anticipation.

She was then like a newly found diamond
Of which through the years our hearts grew fond
Of her facets, through the sun, shining
Like it's Southern Cross in the sky some evening.

We learnt to appreciate its new history
Of brave Diggers who fought for their country
The song of Waltzing Matilda, its corroborees
We've even felt for the young Ned Kelly.

Through the years we've toiled and done our share
We've travelled through this land on our time to spare
She's treated us kindly, this grand lady
Foreign we are not to its beauty!

She's a land of rich opportunity
To each of us lies the responsibility
To set an example, to give of our best
To this land, in which the future of our young, rests.

Marie-Josée Maujean.

NOZAÏC GENEALOGY

Descendants of Louis Nozaïc and Marie Jeanne Trauden

Louis Nozaïc
b. 1731 (Britanny) — d. 1792 (Isle de France)
Arrived in the colony in 1773
m.
Marie Jeanne Trauden

1. François Etienne Nozaïc

François Etienne Nozaïc
b. 17-6-1768 — d. 1822
Arrived in the colony in 1773
m. 16-1-1789
Marie-Anne Bulle
b. 1775 — d. 1802

1. Edouard François Etienne Nozaïc
2. Louis Nozaïc
   b. 1790 — d. 1792
3. Marie-Louise Nozaïc
   m. Nicholas Brouard
4. François Nozaïc
   b. 1795 — d. 1797
5. Jeanne Louise Nozaïc
   b. 1802
   m. Guillaume Honoré Brouard

Edouard François Etienne Nozaïc
b. 1797 — d. 1840
m. 18-4-1820
Suzanne Aglae Peltier
b. 23-6-1799 — d. 1844

1. Edouard François Alphonse Nozaïc
   b. 1821
2. Louis Evenor Nozaïc
   b. 1822 — d. 1823
3. Etienne Simon Selmour Nozaïc
   b. 1826 — d. 1827

Edouard François Alphonse Nozaïc
b. 1821
m. 20-4-1840
Marie Louise Angeline Perrin

1. Edouard Felix Nozaïc
2. Augustine Nozaïc
   m. Gustave Bussy de St Romain

Edouard Felix Nozaïc
b. 1848 — d. 1904
m. 19-6-1876
Marie Suzanne Jollivet
b. 1854

1. Joseph Alphonse Armand Françis Nozaïc
2. Felix Nozaïc
3. Raoul Nozaïc
4. Odette Nozaïc
5. Giselle Nozaïc
6. Andrée Nozaïc
7. Eva Nozaïc
8. Marthe Nozaïc
9. Edith Nozaïc

Joseph Alphonse Armand Françis Nozaïc
b. 1886 — d. 1953
m. 9-10-1909
Marie Julie Charoux
b. 1889

1. Jules Felix Joseph France Nozaïc
2. Madeleine Nozaïc
3. Noël Nozaïc
4. Rose-May Nozaïc
5. Roland Nozaïc
6. Thérèse Nozaïc
7. Claude Nozaïc

Jules Felix Joseph France Nozaïc
(My father)
b. 1911 — d. 1971
m. 11-1-1943
Marie Zelie Myriam Arnulphy
b. 9-5-1924

1. Paul France Ivan Nozaïc
2. Marielle Nozaïc
3. Micheline Nozaïc
4. Marie-José Nozaïc
5. Sylvianne Nozaïc
6. Marie-France Nozaïc
7. Rose-Marie Nozaïc

Paul France Ivan Nozaïc
b. 16-12-1943
m. 16-12-1979
Françoise Geneviève Hoarau
b. 19-1-1952

1. François Ivan Nozaïc
2. Joëlle Nozaïc
3. Laïta Nozaïc

François Ivan Nozaïc
b. 25-2-1982 (Australia)

See Chapter 6 for mention of other family members.

NOZAÏC GENEALOGY

Descendants of Edouard Felix Nozaïc (b. 25-10-1842 – d. 17-9-1904) and Marie Suzanne Jollivet (b. 1854)
Married 19-6-1876

1 Joseph Alphonse Armand Francis Nozaïc
  (My grandfather)
  b. 27-2-1886 – d. 22-11-1953
  m. 9-10-1909
  Marie Julie Charoux
  b. 1889 – d. 1975

  1. France Nozaïc
  2. Madeleine Nozaïc
  3. Noël Nozaïc
  4. Rose-May Nozaïc
  5. Roland Nozaïc
  6. Thérèse Nozaïc
  7. Claude Nozaïc

2. Felix Nozaïc
  Migrated to South Africa
  m.
  Isabelle de Fontenay

3. Raoul Nozaïc
  Migrated to South Africa
  m.
  Alice D'Hotman de Villiers

4. Odette Nozaïc
  m.
  Clément Charoux (Mauritius)

  1. Clément Charoux
    m.
    Irène Feuilrhade
  2. Guy Charoux
    m.
    Thérèse Lagesse
  3. Suzanne Charoux
    m.
    Clément Mamet
  4. Marie-Claire Charoux
    m.
    Frederick Mayer
  5. Hughes Charoux
    m.
    Christiane Rivalland

      1. Mario Mamet
      2. Roxanne Mamet
      3. Suzon Mamet
      1. Brigitte Mayer

5. Giselle Nozaïc
  m.
  Carl Marié D'Unienville

  1. Henri Marié D'Unienville
    m.
    Jeanne Berenger
    b. 28-5-1914 – d. 27-2-1990

    1. Jean-Henri D'Unienville
      b. 9-1-1954
      m.
      Diane Brokenshaw (Divorced)
      1. Jean-Luc D'Unienville
        b. 11-8-1979
      2. Nicole D'Unienville
        b. 14-2-1981
      3. Leandra D'Unienville
        b. 20-3-1983
    2. Francine Marié D'Unienville
      b. 28-6-1955 (South Africa)

6. Andrée Nozaïc
  m.
  Fernand Trebuchet

  1. Edmonde Trébuchet
    m
    André Gauld
    1. Odile Gauld
      m. 1964
      Erique D'Hotman de Villiers
      m.
      Noël Desveaux de Marigny

        1. Didier D'Hotman de Villiers
          Married in South Africa
          1. Xavier D'Hotman de Villiers
            b. 1997
        2. Audrey D'Hotman de Villiers
        3. Alexandra D'Hotman de Villiers
          m. 1995
          Olivier Maujean
            1. Laetitia Maujean
              b. 1997
        4. Elizabeth D'Hotman de Villiers

NOZAÏC GENEALOGY

Descendants of Edouard Felix Nozaïc and Marie Suzanne Jollivet (Continued)

7. Eva Nozaïc
  m.
  Maxime Deschamps

                        1. Irene Deschamps

8. Marthe Nozaïc
  m.
  Eugène Deschamps

9. Edith Nozaïc

NOZAÏC GENEALOGY

**Descendants of Joseph Alphonse Armand Francis Nozaïc (b. 27-2-1886 – d. 22-11-1954)
and Marie Julie Charoux (b. 1889)
(Married 9-10-1909)**

1. France Nozaïc
   b. 14-4-1911
   Migrated to Australia 6-10-1965
   m. 11-1-1943
   Myriam Arnulphy
   b. 9-5-1924

   1. Ivan Nozaïc
   2. Marielle Nozaïc
   3. Micheline Nozaïc
   4. Marie-Josee Nozaïc
   5. Sylvianne Nozaïc
   6. Marie-France Nozaïc
   7. Rose-Marie Nozaïc

2. Madeleine Nozaïc
   b. 1913
   m.
   Pierre Masson

3. Noël Nozaïc
   b. 1915
   Migrated to South Africa
   m. 1940
   Lily Mackie (Divorced)
   m.
   Marie Desplace

   1. Jean Nozaïc
      b. 1946 – d. 1965
   2. Noelle Nozaïc
   3. Mario Nozaïc
      m.
      Janine Mackie
   4. Guy Nozaïc

4. Rose-May Nozaïc
   b. 1917
   Migrated to South Africa
   m. 1942
   Henry Masson (Divorced)

   1. Aubrey Masson
      b. 1943
   2. Jacqueline Masson
      b. 1945
      m. 1970
      Paul Descroizilles (Divorced)
   3. Alain Masson
      b. 1946

      1. Isabelle Descroizilles
         b. 1972 (Mauritius)

5. Roland Nozaïc (Mauritius)
   b. 1921
   m. 1945
   Geneviève Suzor
   b. 1923

   1. Christiane Nozaïc
      b. 7-11-1944
   2. Joëlle Nozaïc
      b. 22-12-1946
   3. Françoise Nozaïc
      b. 25-10-1949
   4. Pascale Nozaïc
      b. 1951
   5. Suzelle Nozaïc
      b. 1957
      m. 12-6-1992 (Australia)
      Léon Arnulphy
      b. 18-2-1953

6. Thérèse Nozaïc
   b. 1923
   m. 1942
   Roger Doger de Speville
   b. 1916 — d. 1997

   1. Roger Doger de Speville
      b. 1943
      m.
      Christine Bianchi
   2. Roselyne Doger de Speville
      b. 31-12-1945
      m. 1964
      Patrick Tyack

   3. Sylvain Doger de Speville
      b. 12-3-1946
      Migrated to Australia in 1970
      m. 24-11-1969
      Georgina Maurel (Divorced)
      b. 24-3-1951
      m.
      Elisha Ward

   1. Randolphe Doger de Speville
      b. 1975 (Mauritius)
   2. Alban Doger de Speville
      b. 1979 (Mauritius)
   1. Natalie Tyack
   2. Sandra Tyack
   3. Christine Tyack
   4. Angélique Tyack
   5. Joanha Tyack
   1. Denis Henri Doger de Speville
      b. 2-1-1971
      Roselyne Maujean (de facto)
      b. 21-10-1975
      1. Krysten Doger De Speville
         b. 30-4-1994
   2. Josephine Doger de Speville
      b. 21-9-1976
      Paul Jorgensen (de facto)
      1. Marc Jorgensen
         b. 2-3-1995

Page 256

NOZAÏC GENEALOGY

Descendants of Joseph Alphonse Armand Francis Nozaïc and Marie Julie Charoux (Continued)

	4. Daniel Doger de Speville b. 1948 m. 13-12-1973 (Australia) Charlotte Maurel b. 23-1-1949	
	5. Marianne Doger de Speville b. 27-1-1950 Now living Reunion Island m. 1967 Robert Le Maire	1. Philippe Le Maire b. 1969 2. Virginie Le Maire b. 1971 3. Emanuela Le Maire
	6. Dominic Doger de Speville b. 1951 m. Wendy Hector (Australia)	1. Sabina Doger de Speville 2. Thomas Doger de Speville
	7. Patrice Doger de Speville b. 1952 Migrated to Australia m. Martine Maujean	1. David Doger de Speville 2. Claudia Doger de Speville
	8. Jean-Michel Doger de Speville b. 27-2-1957 m. Jenny Espinosa b. 6-4-1967	1. Ayrton Doger de Speville b. 18-1-1993
7. Claude Nozaïc b. 1925 m. 1959 René Baudouin	1. Arianne Baudouin b. 4-6-1960 Now living in France m. 2-1-1987 Eric Buonino	1. Morgane Buonino b. 2-2-1990 2. Maïle Buonino b. 5-5-1992

Page 257

NOZAÏC GENEALOGY

Descendants of France Nozaïc and Myriam Arnulphy (Married 11-1-1943)

1. Paul France Ivan Nozaïc
   b. 16-12-1943
   m. 18-12-1979
   Françoise Genevieve Hoarau
   b. 19-1-1952

   1. François Nozaïc
      b. 25-2-1982
   2. Joëlle Nozaïc
      b. 16-2-1983
   3. Laita Nozaïc
      b. 24-2-1986

2. Marielle Nozaïc
   b. 4-3-1945
   m. 16-12-1967
   Yves Fayd'herbe de Maudave
   b. 5-6-1944

   1. Michael Fayd'herbe de Maudave
      b. 25-11-1969
      Heather Tait (de facto)

      1. Jeremy Fayd'herbe de Maudave
         b. 23-8-1995
      2. David Fayd'herbe de Maudave
         b. 22-12-1997

   2. Caroline Fayd'herbe de Maudave
      b. 15-12-1971
      Richard O'Shane (de facto)

      1. Cairo Fayd'herbe de Maudave
         b. 2-1-1991
      2. Jordan Fayd'herbe de Maudave
         b. 20-3-1995
      3. Alexandria Fayd'herbe de Maudavee
         b. 19-9-1996

   3. Sandra Fayd'herbe de Maudave
      b. 2-1-1974
      Stephen Rogers (de facto)

      1. Grace Rogers
         b. 28-11-1994
      2. Liberty Rogers
         b. 27-10-1995
      3. William Rogers
         b. 28-2-1997

3. Micheline Nozaïc
   b. 22-12-1946
   m. 5-7-1969
   Jean-Claude Maujean
   b. 10-12-1947

   1. Pauline Maujean
      b. 14-1-1970 – d. 22-7-1986
   2. Miriam Maujean
      b. 12-11-1972
   3. Dominic Maujean
      b. 7-2-1975
   4. Daniel Maujean
      b. 11-5-1976

4. Marie-Josee Nozaïc
   b. 5-11-1948
   m. 30-8-1969
   Louis Philippe Maujean
   b. 26-11-1948

   1. Patrick Robert Maujean
      b. 16-1-1974
   2. Roselyne Maujean
      b. 21-10-1975
      Denis Doger de Speville (de facto)
      b. 2-1-1971

      1. Krysten Doger de Speville
         b. 30-4-1994

5. Sylvianne Nozaïc
   b. 13-5-1951
   m. 31-8-1968
   Jean-Raymond Mallac
   b. 4-5-1945

   1. Veronique Mallac
      b. 13-1-1970
      m. 21-10-1995
      Garry Rhule

      1. James Rhule
         b. 17-3-1997

   2. Corinne Mallac
      b. 17-1-1972
      m. 23-4-1997
      Alexander Barkway
      b. 22-7-1971
   3. Sophie Mallac
      b. 14-6-1973
      m. 4-5-1991
      Troy Austin
      b. 9-9-1972

      1. Joshua Austin
         b. Stillborn 1992
      2. Kayla Austin
         b. 31-7-1993
      3. Luke Austin
         b. 6-3-1997

6. Marie-France Nozaïc
   b. 19-8-1952
   m. 15-8-1970
   Gilles Mackie (Divorced)

   1. Gilles Mackie
      b. 1-4-1971
   2. Denis Mackie
      b. 5-5-1973
   3. Nicholas Mackie
      b. 23-7-1976

   m. 2-5-1998
   Murray Roberts

Page 258

NOZAÏC GENEALOGY

Descendants of France Nozaïc and Myriam Arnulphy (Continued)

7. Rose-Marie Nozaïc
   b. 12-3-1954
   m. 27-3-1976
   François Audibert
   b. 4-10-1953

      1. Geraldine Audibert
         b. 13-5-1979
      2. Eric Audibert
         b. 14-3-1981
      3. Catherine Audibert
         b. 22-8-1984

MAUJEAN GENEALOGY
(Roger's branch)

Descendants of Nicolas Maujean and Catherine Peltier

Nicolas Maujean
b. circa 1723 Metz — d. 1759
m. 6-7-1751 St Etienne, Metz
Catherine Peltier
b. circa 1729

1. Nicolas Maujean

Nicolas Maujean
b. 1756 Metz — d. 1820 Isle de France
Arrived in the colony in 1784
m. 17-6-1777 St Eucaire parish, Metz
Anne Pelte

1. Nicolas Maujean

Nicolas Maujean
b. 29-11-1793 Isle de France — d. 9-8-1877
m. 4-2-1824
Marie Geneviève Coralie Treize
b. 24-10-1796

1. Louis Alphonse Amédée Maujean

Louis Alphonse Amédée Maujean
b. 8-4-1832 — d. 18-2-1882
m. 6-6-1853
Henriette Ringuet
b. 18-8-1827

1. Louis Amédée Maujean

Louis Amédée Maujean
b. 9-1-1861
m. 30-7-1888
Alice Marie Marot
b. 1872

1. Raoul Maujean
   m. Thèrése de Robillard
2. Maxime Maujean
   m. Alice d'Hotman de Villiers
3. Louis Marcel Maujean
   m. Miriam d'Hotman de Villiers
4. Miriam Maujean
   m. Philippe d'Hotman de Villiers
5. Lucien Maujean
   m. Madeleine d'Abbadie
6. Inèse Maujean
   m. Lucien Brouard
7. Suzanne Maujean
   m. Henri Bouchet
8. Thérèse Maujean
   m. Henri Bolton
9. Irène Maujean
   m. Philippe de Robillard
10. Amédèe Maujean
    m. Simonne de Robillard

Louis Marcel Maujean
b. 15-9-1891 — 20-7-1962
m. 24-2-1917
Marie Françoise Josephine D'hotman de Villiers
b. 18-4-1897 — d. 1951

1. Louis Marcel Maujean
   b. 1918 — d. 1928
2. Louis Roger Maujean
   b. 17-10-1919 — d. 9-3-1991
3. Louis Pierre Maujean
   b. 10-1-1921 — d. 9-4-1991
4. Daisy Maujean
   b. 28-2-1922
5. Louis Philippe Maujean
   b. 3-7-1924
6. Aliette Maujean
   b. 14-8-1932

Louis Roger Maujean
b. 17-10-1919 — d. 9-3-1991
m. 5-2-1943
Paule Berenger
b. 27-8-1921

1. Louis Roger Maujean
   b. 9-11-1943
2. Louis Yves Maujean
   b. 23-10-1944 — d. 9-11-1948
3. Jean-Claude Maujean
   b. 10-12-1947
4. Paul Maujean
   b. 10-8-1950

Page 260

MAUJEAN GENEALOGY
(Roger's branch)

Descendants of Nicolas Maujean and Catherine Peltier (Continued)

        5. Chantal Maujean
           b. 28-3-1953
        6. Marie Christine Maujean
           b. 16-1-1955

Louis Roger Maujean   1. Jean-Marc Maujean
  b. 9-11-1943   b. 1-11-1970 in South Africa
  m. 1965 in South Africa   2. Natasha Maujean
  Peggy Westergreen (Divorced)   b. 30-10-1971 in Australia
  b. 14-5-1945   3. Marcel Maujean
  m. 2-5-1992   b. 17-1-1981 in Australia
  Julie-Ann Mee
  b. 28-12-1959

Jean-Marc Maujean   1. Luke Maujean
  b. 1-11-1970 in South Africa   b. 17-2-1989 in Australia
                                  Son of Karen Jervis

Page 261

MAUJEAN GENEALOGY
(Philippe's branch)

Descendants of Nicolas Maujean and Catherine Peltier

Nicolas Maujean
b. circa 1723 Metz — d. 1759
m. 6-7-1751 St Etienne, Metz
Catherine Peltier
b. circa 1729

1. Nicolas Maujean

Nicolas Maujean
b. 1756 Metz — d. 1820 Isle de France
Arrived in the colony in 1784
m. 17-6-1777 St Eucaire parish, Metz
Anne Pelte

1. Nicolas Maujean

Nicolas Maujean
b. 29-11-1793 Isle de France — d. 9-8-1877
m. 4-2-1824
Marie Geneviève Coralie Treize
b. 24-10-1796

1. Louis Alphonse Amédée Maujean

Louis Alphonse Amédée Maujean
b. 8-4-1832 — d. 18-2-1882
m. 6-6-1853
Henriette Ringuet
b. 18-8-1827

1. Louis Amédée Maujean

Louis Amédée Maujean
b. 9-1-1861
m. 30-7-1888
Alice Marie Marot
b. 1872

1. Raoul Maujean
   m. Thèrése de Robillard
2. Maxime Maujean
   m. Alice d'Hotman de Villiers
3. Louis Marcel Maujean
   m. Miriam d'Hotman de Villiers
4. Miriam Maujean
   m. Philippe d'Hotman de Villiers
5. Lucien Maujean
   m. Madeleine d'Abbadie
6. Inèse Maujean
   m. Lucien Brouard
7. Suzanne Maujean
   m. Henri Bouchet
8. Thérèse Maujean
   m. Henri Bolton
9. Irène Maujean
   m. Philippe de Robillard
10. Amédèe Maujean
    m. Simonne de Robillard

Louis Marcel Maujean
b. 15-9-1891 — 20-7-1962
m. 24-2-1917
Marie Françoise Josephine D'hotman de Villiers
b. 18-4-1897 — d. 1951

1. Louis Marcel Maujean
   b. 1918 — d. 1928
2. Louis Roger Maujean
   b. 17-10-1919 — d. 9-3-1991
3. Louis Pierre Maujean
   b. 10-1-1921 — d. 9-4-1991
4. Daisy Maujean
   b. 28-2-1922
5. Louis Philippe Maujean
   b. 3-7-1924
6. Aliette Maujean
   b. 14-8-1932

Louis Phillipe Maujean
b. 3-7-1924
Migrated to Australia in 1965
m. 10-11-1947
Violette Berenger
b. 3-7-1925

1. Louis Phillipe Maujean
   b. 22-11-1948
2. Monique Maujean
   b. 28-1-1950
3. Cyril Maujean
   b. 15-1-1953

MAUJEAN GENEALOGY
(Philippe's branch)

Descendants of Nicolas Maujean and Catherine Peltier (Continued)

Louis Phillipe Maujean
  b. 22-11-1948
  m. 30-8-1969
  Marie-Josèe Nozaïc
  b. 5-11-1948

Patrick Maujean
  b. 16-1-1974 in Australia

1. Patrick Maujean
  b. 16-1-1974 in Australia
2. Roselyne Maujean
  b. 21-10-1975 in Australia

1. Krysten Doger de Speville
  b. 30-4-1994
  Daughter of Denis Doger de Speville

Page 263

MAUJEAN GENEALOGY

**Descendants of Louis Marcel Maujean (1891-1962) and
Marie Françoise Josephine Miriam D'Hotman de Villiers (1896-1951)
Married 24-2-1917**

1. Marcel Maujean
   b. 1918– d. 1928

2. Roger Marcel Maujean
   b. 17-10-1919 – d. 9-3-1991
   m. 5-2-1943
   Paule Berenger
   b. 27-8-1921

   1. Roger Marcel Maujean
      b. 9-11-1943
      m. 1965
      Peggy Westergreen (Divorced)
      b. 14-5-1945

      m. 2-5-1992
      Julianne Mee
      b. 28-12-1959

      1. Jean-Marc Maujean
         b. 1-11-1970
      2. Natasha Maujean
         b. 30-10-1971
      3. Marcel Maujean
         b. 17-1-1981

   2. Yves Maujean
      b. 23-10-1944 – d. 9-11-1948
   3. Jean-Claude Maujean
      b. 10-12-1947
      m. 5-7-1969
      Micheline Nozaïc
      b. 21-12-46

      1. Pauline Maujean
         b. 14-1-1970 – d. 22-7-1986
      2. Miriam Maujean
         b. 12-11-1971
      3. Dominic Maujean
         b. 7-2-1975
      4. Daniel Maujean
         b. 11-5-1976

   4. Paul Maujean
      b. 10-8-1950
      m. 9-9-1972
      Jacqueline Mamet (Divorced)
      b. 28-8-1953
      m. 23-3-1985
      Diane Teale
      b. 27-5-1955

      1. Sabrina Maujean
         b. 3-1-1974
      2. Katrina Maujean
         b. 14-10-1976

   5. Chantal Maujean
      b. 28-3-1953
      m. 15-1-1972
      Neville Harris (Divorced)
      b. 3-1-1949
      m. 18-7-1992
      Michael Spaulding
      b. 10-7-1942

      1. Simon Harris
         b. 3-5-1973
      2. Paul Harris
         b. 26-8-1975

   6. Marie Christine Maujean
      b. 16-1-1955
      m. 21-9-1975
      Jacques Mamet (Divorced)
      b. 28-8-1953
      m. 22-10-1983
      Glenn Cowans
      b. 9-10-1948 – d. 8-9-1987
      Dennis Hillen (de facto)
      b. 15-8-1949

      1. Shannon Cowans
         b. 12-10-81

3. Pierre Maujean
   b. 10-1-1921 – d. 9-4-1991
   Migrated to South Africa
   m.
   Thérèse d'Abbadie

   1. Martine Maujean
   2. Jocelyne Maujean
   3. Jean-Pierre Maujean

4. Daisy Maujean
   b. 28-2-1922
   m. 6-6-1944
   Gabriel Lionnet
   b. 23-7-1916 – d. 4-2-1995

   1. Noël Lionnet
      b. 23-12-1947
   2. Marc Lionnet
      b. 3-12-1949
      m. 13-11-1973
      Dany Albertini (Separated)
      Sabrina Marcelli (de facto)

      1. Marie Angélique Lionnet
         b. 20-7-1995 in Mauritius

   3. Gilles Lionnet
      b. 23-9-1952
      m. 23-10-1979
      Caroline Monplé

      1. Loïc Lionnet
         b. 7-3-1981
      2. Anaïs Lionnet
         b. 8-7-1987

MAUJEAN GENEALOGY

Descendants of Louis Marcel Maujean and Marie Françoise Josephine Miriam D'Hotman de Villiers
(Continued)

5. Louis Philippe Maujean
   b. 2-7-1924
   m. 10-11-1947
   Marie Jeanne Violette Berenger
   b. 3-7-1925

   1. Louis Philippe Maujean
      b. 26-11-1948
      m. 30-8-1969
      Marie-Josee Nozaïc
      b. 5-11-1948

      1. Patrick Robert Maujean
         b. 16-1-1974
      2. Roselyne Maujean
         b. 21-10-1975

   2. Monique Maujean
      b. 28-1-1950
      m. 9-5-1970
      John Charles Harris
      b. 3-10-1947

      1. Scott Harris
         b. 7-12-1973
      2. Kristian Harris
         b. 3-9-1975
      3. Michael Harris
         b. 9-1-1977

   3. Cyril Maujean
      b. 15-1-1953
      m. 30-12-1972
      Marie Chantal Mackie
      b. 28-3-1954

      1. Michael Maujean
         b. 25-5-1974
      2. Christopher Maujean
         b. 27-5-1975
      3. Belinda Jane Maujean
         b. 1-6-1976

6. Aliette Maujean
   b. 14-8-1932
   m. 16-12-1952
   Herve Mayer
   b. 19-11-1930

   1. Rivaltz Mayer
      b. 15-5-1953
   2. Clifford Mayer
      b. 30-4-1956
      m. 29-6-1978
      Sylvie Regnard
      b. 25-6-1958

      1. Diane Mayer
         b. 20-2-1981
      2. Natasha Mayer
         b. 8-11-1983
      3. Kevin Mayer
         b. 9-8-1991

   3. Marie-Anne Mayer
      b. 8-5-1954
      m. 17-10-1980
      Alain Lamusse
      b. 31-??-1956

      1. Stéphane Lamusse
         b. 15-8-1981
      2. Fabrice Lamusse
         b. 9-7-1984
      3. Christophe Lamusse
         b. 19-2-1991

MAUJEAN GENEALOGY

Descendants of Louis Roger Maujean and Paule Berenger

1. Louis Roger Maujean
b. 9-11-1943
m. 1965
Peggy Westergreen (Divorced)
b. 14-5-1945

   m. 2-5-1992
Julianne Mee
b. 28-12-1959

   1. Jean-Marc Maujean
b. 1-11-1970
   2. Natasha Maujean
b. 30-10-1971
   3. Marcel Maujean
b. 17-1-1981

   1. Luke Maujean
b. 17-2-1989
Son of Karen Jervis

2. Yves Maujean
b. 23-10-1944 – d. 9-11-1948

3. Jean-Claude Maujean
b. 10-12-1947
m. 5-7-1969
Micheline Nozaïc
b. 21-12-46

   1. Pauline Maujean
b. 14-1-1970 – d. 22-7-1986
   2. Miriam Maujean
b. 12-11-1971
   3. Dominic Maujean
b. 7-2-1975
   4. Daniel Maujean
b. 11-5-1976

4. Paul Maujean
b. 10-8-1950
m. 9-9-1972
Jacqueline Mamet (Divorced)
b. 28-8-1953
m. 23-3-1985
Diane Teale
b. 27-5-1955

   1. Sabrina Maujean
b. 3-1-1974
   2. Katrina Maujean
b. 14-10-1976

5. Chantal Maujean
b. 28-3-1953
m. 15-1-1972
Neville Harris (Divorced)
b. 3-1-1949
m. 18-7-1992
Michael Spaulding
b. 10-7-1942

   1. Simon Harris
b. 3-5-1973
   2. Paul Harris
b. 26-8-1975

6. Marie Christine Maujean
b. 16-1-1955
m. 21-9-1975
Jacques Mamet (Divorced)
b. 28-8-1953
m. 22-10-1983
Glenn Cowans
b. 9-10-1948 – d. 8-9-1987
Dennis Hillen (de facto)
b. 15-8-1949

   1. Shannon Cowans
b. 12-10-81

MAUJEAN GENEALOGY

Descendants of Louis Phillipe Maujean and Marie Jeanne Violette Berenger

1. Louis Philippe Maujean
   b. 26-11-1948
   m. 30-8-1969
   Marie-Josee Nozaïc
   b. 5-11-1948

2. Monique Maujean
   b. 28-1-1950
   m. 9-5-1970
   John Charles Harris
   b. 3-10-1947

3. Cyril Maujean
   b. 15-1-1953
   m. 30-12-1972
   Marie Chantal Mackie
   b. 28-3-1954

1. Patrick Robert Maujean
   b. 16-1-1974
2. Roselyne Maujean
   b. 21-10-1975

1. Scott Harris
   b. 7-12-1973
2. Kristian Harris
   b. 3-9-1975
3. Michael Harris
   b. 9-1-1977

1. Michael Maujean
   b. 25-5-1974
2. Christopher Maujean
   b. 27-5-1975
3. Belinda Jane Maujean
   b. 1-6-1976

1. Kristen Emilie Doger de Speville
   b. 30-4-1994
   Daughter of Denis Doger de Speville

ARNULPHY GENEALOGY

Descendants of Joseph Claude Arnulphy (b. in Marseille, France) and Marie Geneviève Granier
(Married in France)

1. Louis Delphine Arnulphy
   b. 22-10-1773 — d. 25-8-1832
   m. 5-11-1801
   Rosalie Gestat de Carembé
   b. 1880 Isle de France
   m. 5-7-1809
   Louise Gestat de Carembé

2. Louis Amédée Arnulphy
   b. 30-8-1817
   m.
   Jeanne Angélique Coralie Doumergue

3. Léon Arunulphy
   b. circa 1845 — d. 1893
   m.
   Augusta Toussaint

   m. Marie-Clémence Rougier
   b. 1848

1. Lise Clara Arnulphy
   b. 20-12-1804

1. Alfred Arnulphy
   m.
   Jeanne Leonie Doumergue
2. Louis Amédée Arnulphy
   b. 30-8-1817

1. Léon Arunulphy
   b. circa 1845 — d. 1893

1. Cecile Arnulphy
   m. Jean-Baptiste Adam
2. Leonie Arnulphy
   m. William Griffiths

1. Eugène Arnulphy
   b. 14-11-1891 — d. 4-3-1966
   m. 1918
   Marie Zélie Monnier
   b. 30-8-1896 — d. July 1992

1. André Griffiths
2. Maxime Griffiths
3. Hilda Griffiths
4. Mary Griffiths
5. Annie Griffiths

1. Léon Arnulphy
   b. 1919 — d. 1972
   m. Monique Brousse de Laborde
   b. 1-4-1932
2. Roger Arnulphy
   b. 1920 — d. 1997
   m. 1953
   Madeline D'Hotman de Villiers
   m. Mary Griffiths
3. Lise Arnulphy
   b. 24-12-1922
   m. 1944
   Henri Mamet
   b. 1910
4. Myriam Arnulphy
   b. 9-5-1924
   m. 11-1-1943
   France Nozaïc
   b. 14-4-1911 – d. 7-1-1971
   m. 22-10-1987
   Arthur Hogan
5. Annie Arnulphy
   b. 24-5-1927
6. Marcienne Arnulphy
   b. 13-3-1933 – d. 1982
   m. 1960
   Serge Bouchet
7. Jacqueline Arnulphy
   b. 8-9-1934
   m. 1957
   Henry Brousse de Laborde
   b. 5-10-1922
8. Cyril Arnulphy
   b. 1936
   m. 1964
   Sonia Fayd'herbe

ARNULPHY GENEALOGY

Descendants of Eugene Arnulphy and Marie Zelie Monnier
(Married 1918)

1. Léon Arnulphy
 b. 1919
 m.
 Monique Brousse de Laborde
 b. 11-4-1932

    1. A daughter who passed
 away a few days after birth
 2. Léon Arnulphy
 b. 18-2-1953
 m. 12-6-1992
 Suzelle Nozaïc
 b. 1957

2. Roger Arnulphy
 b. 1920 – d. 1995
 Migrated to South Africa
 m. 1953
 Madeline D'Hotman de Villiers
 m.
 Mary Griffiths

    1. Jacques Arnulphy
 m.
 Patricia Rougier Lagane
 2. Louis Arnulphy
 d. 1990

    1. Nicholas Arnulphy
 2. Angelique Arnulphy

3. Lise Arnulphy
 b. 1922
 m. 1944
 Henri Mamet
 b. 1910

    1. Danielle Mamet
 b. 14-9-1946
 m. July 1969
 Robert Mallac
 2. Marc Henri Mamet
 b. 8-9-1949
 3. Marie-Anne Mamet
 b. 1952
 m. 1975
 George Simpson
 b. 1952
 4. Christine Mamet
 b. 1953
 m. 1973
 Gilbert Béchard
 b. 1948

    1. Robert Mallac Junior
 b. 1971
 2. Christopher Mallac
 b. 1972

    1. Ludovic Simpson
 b. 1978
 2. Isabelle Simpson
 b. 1981

    1. Melissa Béchard
 b. 1977
 2. Claudine Béchard
 b. 1978

4. Myriam Arnulphy
 b. 9-5-1924
 m. 11-1-1943
 France Nozaïc
 b. 14-4-1911 – d. 7-1-1971

    1. Paul France Ivan Nozaïc
 b. 16-12-1943
 m. 16-12-1979
 Françoise Genevieve Hoarau
 b. 19-1-1952

 2. Marielle Nozaïc
 b. 4-3-1945
 m. 16-12-1967
 Yves Fayd'herbe de Maudave
 b. 5-6-1944

 3. Micheline Nozaïc
 b. 22-12-1946
 m. 5-7-1969
 Jean-Claude Maujean
 b. 10-12-1947

 4. Marie-Josée Nozaïc
 b. 5-11-1948
 m. 30-8-1969
 Louis Philippe Maujean
 b. 26-11-1948
 5. Sylvianne Nozaïc
 b. 13-5-1951
 m. 31-8-1968
 Jean-Raymond Mallac
 b. 4-5-1945

    1. François Nozaïc
 b. 25-2-1982
 2. Joëlle Nozaïc
 b. 16-2-1983
 3. Laita Nozaïc
 b. 24-2-1986

    1. Michael Fayd'herbe de Maudave
 b. 25-11-1969
 2. Caroline Fayd'herbe de Maudave
 b. 15-12-1971
 3. Sandra Fayd'herbe de Maudave
 b. 2-1-1974

    1. Pauline Maujean
 b. 14-1-1970 – d. 22-7-1986
 2. Miriam Maujean
 b. 12-11-1972
 3. Dominic Maujean
 b. 7-2-1975
 4. Daniel Maujean
 b. 11-5-1976

    1. Patrick Robert Maujean
 b. 16-1-1974
 2. Roselyne Maujean
 b. 21-10-1975

    1. Veronique Mallac
 b. 13-1-1970
 2. Corinne Mallac
 b. 17-1-1972
 3. Sophie Mallac
 b. 14-6-1973
 4. Tristan Mallac
 b. 3-1-1982

ARNULPHY GENEALOGY

Descendants of Eugene Arnulphy and Marie Zelie Monnier (Continued)

                        6. Marie-France Nozaïc   1. Gilles Mackie
                           b. 19-8-1952   b. 1-4-1971
                           m. 15-8-1970   2. Denis Mackie
                           Gilles Mackie (Divorced)   b. 5-5-1973
                                                           3. Nicholas Mackie
                           m. 7-5-1998   b. 23-7-1976
                           Murray Roberts

                        7. Rose-Marie Nozaïc   1. Geraldine Audibert
                           b. 12-3-1954   b. 13-5-1979
                           m. 27-3-1976   2. Eric Audibert
                           François Audibert   b. 14-3-1981
                           b. 4-10-1953   3. Catherine Audibert
                                                                    b. 22-8-1984
  m. 22-10-1987
  Arthur Hogan

5. Annie Arnulphy
    b. 24-5-1927

6. Marcienne Arnulphy   1. Caroline Bouchet   1. Yannick Lenferna
    b. 14-3-1933 — d. 1982   b. 1964   2. Ludovic Lenferna
    m. 1960   m.
    Serge Bouchet   Jean-François Lenferna
                             2. Sophie Bouchet   1. Mathieu Sauzier
                                b. 1966   2. Romain Sauzier
                                m.   3. Julie Sauzier
                                Dominic Sauzier
                           3. Benoît Bouchet
                             b. 1973

7. Jacqueline Arnulphy   1. Martine Brousse Laborde   1. Adrian Rivalland
    b. 8-9-1934   b. 5-6-1958   b. 19-6-1988
    m. 1957   Migrated to Australia   2. Stefan Rivalland
    Henry Brousse de Laborde   m. 1985   b. 9-4-1991
    b. 5-10-1922   Cyril Rivalland   3. Fabrice Rivalland
                                                                    b. 18-11-1993
                        2. Boris Brousse de Laborde   1. Pascale Brousse de Laborde
                           b. 14-9-1959   b. 4-12-1991
                         m. 1991   2. Jacob Brousse de Laborde
                         Régine Marié D'Unienville   b. 13-9-1993

8. Cyril Arnulphy   1. Didier Arnulphy   1. Jonathan de Chateauneuf
    b. 1936   b. 1966   b. 1996
    m. 1964   m. 1992
    Sonia Fayd'herbe de Maudave   Natalie de Chateauneuf
                         2. Patricia Arnulphy   1. Olivier de Chateauneuf
                         b. 1973   b. 1997 (twin)
                         m. 1994   2. Sophie de Chateauneuf
                         Nicolas de Chateauneuf   b. 1997 (twin)

ARNULPHY GENEALOGY

Descendants of Myriam Arnulphy and France Nozaïc (Married 11-1-1943)

1. Paul France Ivan Nozaïc
   b. 16-12-1943
   m. 16-12-1979
   Françoise Genevieve Hoarau
   b. 19-1-1952

   1. François Nozaïc
      b. 25-2-1982
   2. Joëlle Nozaïc
      b. 16-2-1983
   3. Laita Nozaïc
      b. 24-2-1986

2. Marielle Nozaïc
   b. 4-3-1945
   m. 16-12-1967
   Yves Fayd'herbe de Maudave
   b. 5-6-1944

   1. Michael Fayd'herbe de Maudave
      b. 25-11-1969
      Heather Tait (de facto)

      1. Jeremy Fayd'herbe de Maudave
         b. 23-8-1995
      2. David Fayd'herbe de Maudave
         b. 22-12-1997

   2. Caroline Fayd'herbe de Maudave
      b. 15-12-1971
      Richard O'Shane (de facto)

      1. Cairo Fayd'herbe de Maudave
         b. 2-1-1991
      2. Jordan Fayd'herbe de Maudave
         b. 20-3-1995
      3. Alexandria Fayd'herbe de Maudavee
         b. 19-9-1996

   3. Sandra Fayd'herbe de Maudave
      b. 2-1-1974
      Stephen Rogers (de facto)

      1. Grace Rogers
         b. 28-11-1994
      2. Liberty Rogers
         b. 27-10-1995
      3. William Rogers
         b. 28-2-1997

3. Micheline Nozaïc
   b. 22-12-1946
   m. 5-7-1969
   Jean-Claude Maujean
   b. 10-12-1947

   1. Pauline Maujean
      b. 14-1-1970 – d. 22-7-1986
   2. Miriam Maujean
      b. 12-11-1972
   3. Dominic Maujean
      b. 7-2-1975
   4. Daniel Maujean
      b. 11-5-1976

4. Marie-Josee Nozaïc
   b. 5-11-1948
   m. 30-8-1969
   Louis Philippe Maujean
   b. 26-11-1948

   1. Patrick Robert Maujean
      b. 16-1-1974
   2. Roselyne Maujean
      b. 21-10-1975
      Denis Doger de Speville (de facto)
      b. 2-1-1971

      1. Krysten Doger de Speville
         b. 30-4-1994

5. Sylvianne Nozaïc
   b. 13-5-1951
   m. 31-8-1968
   Jean-Raymond Mallac
   b. 4-5-1945

   1. Veronique Mallac
      b. 13-1-1970
      m. 21-10-1995
      Garry Rhule

      1. James Rhule
         b. 17-3-1997

   2. Corinne Mallac
      b. 17-1-1972
      m. 23-4-1997
      Alexander Barkway
      b. 22-7-1971
   3. Sophie Mallac
      b. 14-6-1973
      m. 4-5-1991
      Troy Austin
      b. 9-9-1972

      1. Joshua Austin
         b. Stillborn 1992
      2. Kayla Austin
         b. 31-7-1993
      3. Luke Austin
         b. 6-3-1997

6. Marie-France Nozaïc
   b. 19-8-1952
   m. 15-8-1970
   Gilles Mackie (Divorced)

   m. 2-5-1998
   Murray Roberts

   1. Gilles Mackie
      b. 1-4-1971
   2. Denis Mackie
      b. 5-5-1973
   3. Nicholas Mackie
      b. 23-7-1976

ARNULPHY GENEALOGY

Descendants of Myriam Arnulphy and France Nozaïc (Continued)

7. Rose-Marie Nozaïc
   b. 12-3-1954
   m. 27-3-1976
   François Audibert
   b. 4-10-1953

   1. Geraldine Audibert
      b. 13-5-1979
   2. Eric Audibert
      b. 14-3-1981
   3. Catherine Audibert
      b. 22-8-1984

BERENGER GENEALOGY

Descendants of Jean Honoré Nemour Berenger and Marie Boulle (nee Basset)

1. Jean Honoré Nemour Berenger
   Born in France
   m.
   Marie Boulle

   1. Louise Berenger
   2. Paul Berenger
   3. Gaston Berenger
   4. Jean Honoré Raoul Berenger
      b. 20-5-1882 — d. 13-3-1938
      m. 21-2-1811
      Pauline Canton
      b. 9-8-1883 — d. 30-4-1958
   5. Eliane Berenger
   6. Roger Berenger
   7. Marcel Berenger
   8. Fernande Berenger

2. Jean Honoré Raoul Berenger
   b. 20-5-1882 — d. 13-3-1938
   m. 21-2-1811
   Pauline Canton
   b. 9-8-1883 — d. 30-4-1958

   1. Marcelle Berenger
      b. 15-7-1913
   2. Jeanne Berenger
      b. 28-5-1914 — d. 27-2-1990
   3. Yolande Berenger
      b.1-2-1916 — d. 23-1-1995
   4. John Nemour Berenger
      b. 5-10-1917
      m. 31-1-1953
      Eleanor Reily
      b. 1910 Scotland — d. 19-10-1988
   5. Jessie Berenger
      b. 16-9-1919 — d. 21-1- 1934
   6. Paule Berenger
      b. 27-8-1921
   7. Lily Berenger
      b. 9-1-1924 — d. 8-12-1942
   8. Marie Jeanne Violette Berenger
      b. 3-7-1925

3. John Nemour Berenger
   b. 5-10-1917
   m. 31-1-1953
   Eleanor Reily
   b. 1910 Scotland — d. 19-10-1988

Page 273

BERENGER GENEALOGY

Descendants of Jean Honoré Raoul Berenger (20-5-1882 – 13-3-1938) and Pauline Canton (9-8-1883 – 30-4-1958)
(Married 23-2-1911)

1. Marcelle Berenger
   b. 15-7-1913
   m. 1938
   Auguste Esnouf

    1. Jacques Esnouf
      b. 1939
      m.
      Jane Watson

         1. Anita Esnouf
         2. Dawn Esnouf

      2. Francette Esnouf
      b. 1940
      m.
      Angus Young

         1. Andrew Young
         2. Simon Young
         3. Peter Young

      3. Raoul Esnouf
      b. 1943
      m.
      Linda

         1. Lee Esnouf
         2. Trevor Esnouf

      4. Josee Esnouf
      b. 1945
      m. Ray Carling

         1. Ingrid Carling
         2. Linda Carling

2. Jeanne Berenger
   b. 28-5-1914 — d. 27-2-1990
   m. Henri Marié D'Unienville

      1. Jean-Henri Marié D'Unienville
      b. 9-1-1954
      m.
      Diane Brokenshaw

         1. Jean-Luc Marié D'Unienville
         b. 11-8-1979
         2. Nicole Marié D'Unienville
         b. 13-2-1981
         3. Leandra Marié D'Unienville
         b. 20-3-1983

      2. Francine Marié D'Unienville
      b. 28-6-1955

3. Yolande Berenger
   b.1-2-1916 — d. 23-1-1995

4. John Nemour Berenger
   b. 5-10-1917
   m. 31-1-1953
   Eleanor Reily
   b. 1910 — d. 19-10-1988

5. Jessie Berenger
   b. 16-9-1919 — d. 21-1- 1934

6. Paule Berenger
   b. 27-8-1921
   m. 5-2-1943
   Roger Marcel Maujean
   b. 17-10-1919 — d. 9-3-1991

      1. Louis Roger Maujean
      b. 9-11-1943
      m. 1965
      Peggy Westergreen (Divorced)
      b. 14-5-1945

         1. Jean-Marc Maujean
         b. 1-11-1970
         2. Natasha Maujean
         b. 30-10-1971
         3. Marcel Maujean
         b. 17-1-1981

      m. 2-5-1992
      Julianne Mee
      b. 28-12-1959

      2. Yves Maujean
      b. 23-10-1944 – d. 9-11-1948

      3. Jean-Claude Maujean
      b. 10-12-1947
      m. 5-7-1969
      Micheline Nozaïc
      b. 21-12-46

         1. Pauline Maujean
         b. 14-1-1970 – d. 22-7-1986
         2. Miriam Maujean
         b. 12-11-1971
         3. Dominic Maujean
         b. 7-2-1975
         4. Daniel Maujean
         b. 11-5-1976

      4. Paul Maujean
      b. 10-8-1950
      m. 9-9-1972
      Jacqueline Mamet (Divorced)
      b. 28-8-1953
      m. 23-3-1985
      Diane Teale
      b. 27-5-1955

         1. Sabrina Maujean
         b. 3-1-1974
         2. Katrina Maujean
         b. 14-10-1976

BERENGER GENEALOGY

Descendants of Jean Honoré Raoul Berenger and Pauline Canton (Continued)

        5. Chantal Maujean   1. Simon Harris
           b. 28-3-1953   b. 3-5-1973
           m. 15-1-1972   2. Paul Harris
           Neville Harris (Divorced)   b. 26-8-1975
           b. 3-1-1949
           m. 18-7-1992
           Michael Spaulding
           b. 10-7-1942

        6. Marie Christine Maujean
           b. 16-1-1955
           m. 21-9-1975
           Jacques Mamet (Divorced)
           b. 28-8-1953
           m. 22-10-1983
           Glenn Cowans   1. Shannon Cowans
           b. 9-10-1948 – d. 8-9-1987   b. 12-10-81
           Dennis Hillen (de facto)
           b. 15-8-1949

7. Lily Berenger
   b. 9-1-1924 — d. 8-12-1942

8. Marie Jeanne Violette Berenger   1. Louis Philippe Maujean   1. Patrick Robert Maujean
   b. 3-7-1925   b. 26-11-1948   b. 16-1-1974
   m. 10-11-1947   m. 30-8-1969   2.Roselyne Maujean
   Louis Philippe Maujean   Marie-Josee Nozaïc   b. 21-10-1975
   b. 3-7-1924   b. 5-11-1948   1. Krysten Doger de Speville
                                                                                                 b. 30-4-1994

                                     2. Monique Maujean   1. Scott Harris
                                     b. 28-1-1950   b. 7-12-1973
                                     m. 9-5-1970   2. Kristian Harris
                                   John Charles Harris   b. 3-9-1975
                                   b. 3-10-1947   3. Michael Harris
                                                                                b. 9-1-1977

                                   3. Cyril Maujean   1. Michael Maujean
                                   b. 15-1-1953   b. 25-5-1974
                                   m. 30-12-1972   2. Christopher Maujean
                                   Marie Chantal Mackie   b. 27-5-1975
                                   b. 28-3-1954   3. Belinda Jane Maujean
                                                                              b. 1-6-1976

BIBLIOGRAPHY

Philippe Lenoir, *Ile Maurice Ancienne Isle de France.*

Father Gerald Bowie C.C.SP., V*enerable Father Laval 1803-1864.*

Auguste Toussaint, *Le Domaine de Beau-Plan 1745-1963.*

Mauritian Archives.

Robert Willcox, *Mauritius, Reunion and Seychelles – A Survival Kit.*

Britannica Encyclopoedia.

Dorothy Jones, *Trinity Phoenix – A History of Cairns.*

Glenville Pike, *Queen of the North – A Pictorial History of Cooktown and Cape York Peninsula.*

Jean-Claude Nourault, *Ile Maurice – Mauritius.*

The Mauritius Printing and Stationery Coy, 1953, *Clement Charoux – Chronique du Pays Creole.*

The Historical Society of Cairns, *Establishment of Trinity Bay. (Published in The Cairns Post on 11/10/1991).*